D0146195

Robert E. Linneman, PhD
John L. Stanton, Jr., PhD

Marketing Planning in a Total Quality Environment

Pre-publication
REVIEWS,
COMMENTARIES,
EVALUATIONS . . .

"**L**inneman and Stanton have done it again. This book looks at the marketing planning process from a sound academic base as well as a practical point of view. In this, they have achieved an elusive goal–to satisfy both the critical academic and the hard-nosed business person. Numerous useful and interesting examples of marketing strategies are given in this easy-to-read book. Strategic marketing planners–be they academics or business people–will find much of value in this indispensable, thoughtful, and practical book."

C. F. van Veijeren, DBA, ITP
*Professor of Corporate
and Marketing Strategy,
School of Business Leadership,
University of South Africa*

"**L**inneman and Stanton have written an excellent guide for every marketing manager who wants to build total quality into the marketing plan. They provide ideas and techniques for marketing planning, and they also demonstrate that total quality marketing pays off only if the leadership of the company is TQ-oriented so that TQ mentality can spread downward, and the different functional areas can be involved in cooperation.

As total quality management is a system of dealing with quality at every stage of the production process, collaboration is essential, particularly with the production function. If you are committed to TQ you must offer a product with a unique characteristic, while also remembering that your standard must always be customer perception of quality.

The book is a very practical guide with which you can be your own expert of the highest standard."

Penttl Malaska,
Professor of Management,
and **Karin Holstius,**
Professor of International Marketing,
Turku School of Economics
and Business Administration, Finland

"***M****arketing Planning in a Total Quality Environment* is a well-written, entertaining book that does much to demystify the planning process. I would be confident that, put into the hands of a competent manager, it would immediately transform the quality of the planning activity. It clarifies the processes that are essential to effective planning. The worksheets are easy to follow and are all available in the Appendix for use. I found the section of optimizing competitive advantage particularly robust.

This is a hands-on book–better than most of its rivals–because its dynamic style drives the process forward; the reader is carried along by the authors' enthusiasm."

Michael J. Thomas
Professor of Marketing,
The University of Strathclyde
in Glasgow;
National Chairman
of the Chartered Institute of Marketing

The Haworth Press, Inc.

Marketing Planning in a Total Quality Environment

HAWORTH Marketing Resources
Innovations in Practice & Professional Services
William J. Winston, Senior Editor

New, Recent, and Forthcoming Titles:

Marketing Planning in a Total Quality Environment

Robert E. Linneman, PhD
John L. Stanton, Jr., PhD

The Haworth Press
New York • London

The Haworth Press, Inc., 10 Alice Street, Binghamton, NY 13904-1580

Library of Congress Cataloging-in-Publication Data

Linneman, Robert E., 1928-
    Marketing planning in a total quality environment / Robert E. Linneman, John L. Stanton.
        p.   cm.
    Includes bibliographical references and index.
    ISBN 1-56024-938-2
    1. Marketing–Planning. 2. Total quality management. I. Stanton, John L. II. Title.
HF5415.13.L538 1994
658.8′02–dc20
                                                    94-48363
                                                     CIP

CONTENTS

ABOUT THE AUTHORS

Robert E. Linneman, PhD, is Professor of Marketing at the School of Business Administration at St. Joseph's University in Philadelphia, Pennsylvania. He has been involved in industrial sales as director of marketing for a major corporation and has participated in marketing and planning projects for over 60 companies. Dr. Linneman is the author of the book *A Shirt-Sleeve Approach to Corporate Planning* and of numerous other publications which have appeared in various professional journals, including *The Harvard Business Review, Long-Range Planning, Journal of Marketing*, and *Sloan Management Review*. He was a National Director and Vice President of Professional Development for the American Marketing Association and also a recipient of the Lindback Award for distinguished teaching.

John L. Stanton, Jr., PhD, a consultant, author, practitioner, and teacher of marketing research, currently holds the C. J. McNutt Chair of Food Marketing Research at Saint Joseph's University. As a consultant, his clients include Campbell Soup Company, Proctor & Gamble, Frito-Lay, Miles Laboratories, Kellogg, PepsiCo, and others, and he recently spent eight months in Germany analyzing retail food store strategies for the European Community. A prolific author, Dr. Stanton has written pioneering articles on sample survey methodologies, data analysis techniques, advertising research, brand preference, segmentation, and positioning research which have appeared in a variety of professional journals. His book *Making Niche Marketing Work* has been published in three languages.

Preface

This book is based on the idea that you're a believer in total quality, that you'd like your marketing plans to reflect this belief, and that you're interested in knowing more about preparing and implementing a marketing plan. We assume you have a basic working knowledge of marketing. So we do not define such terms as "marketing," "marketing channels," and "market segments."

A total quality environment demands three essential elements. The first is total quality planning. To some, planning for total quality might seem commonplace. Mundane. After all, isn't this what every firm does? Aren't all the activities of the firm really directed at total quality? As one executive said "... even though we might not call it planning for quality, the result of our business planning is higher quality. What do you think we're doing planning for–*lower* quality?"

But things are not always what they seem. In fact, doing business as usual may be quite different from total quality planning. The traditional business approach is to make the various functional areas as efficient as possible. For example, a shipping department might be evaluated in terms of management's interpretation of efficiency; say, total shipping costs. But that's not total quality planning.

The differences may be subtle, yet they are vast. Subtle in that departmental efficiencies are measured against standards. But vast because if you're committed to total quality, your standards must be customer perception of quality, not management's interpretation of efficiency.

Total quality planning begins with the questions, "Who are our customers?" "What do our customers value?" "What are we offering them?" "Is there a gap between what our customers value and what we have to offer?"

The next step is developing product/service features that respond to targeted customers' needs and developing processes able to produce the features.

The second key element is quality control: evaluating actual product/service performance; comparing actual performance to product/service goals; and acting on the difference.

The third key element in a total quality environment is continuous improvement.

Central to these three key elements is employee involvement and empowerment. And, to make sure that they have the right "tools," employee training. But more on a total quality environment later.

This book is also based on the idea that you, like many other marketing professionals, are faced with one or more of the following situations:

- You're doing a good job but you'd like to do even better.
- You're always putting out fires. You lack time to do the things that need to be done. You want to work smarter, not harder.
- You're always having a hard time coordinating major marketing programs. Sometimes things just "fall between the cracks."
- You're faced with a major discrepancy between where you are and where you'd like to be. You've got a real planning gap. It's going to take creativity and tight control to bridge this gap.
- You realize that you've got to offer your customers more quality if you're going to be competitive in the new marketing environment.
- You'd like to have a professional marketing plan–one that will be well received by management and will also keep you and your staff focused.

You may be a:

- manager of a product/service
- group product/service manager
- marketing manager
- president (or senior vice president) of a smaller company

And you know that marketing planning is very complex. You recognize that you need guidance. After all:

- There are so many factors to consider, such as: present and potential target markets, competitors, channels of distribution, substitute products, government actions, the economy, and your own capabilities. You want guidelines on how, where, and when to focus your energy.

- It's tough to put together different and varied parts of a marketing plan. For example, it's not easy to integrate many product/service market plans into one that is unified and synergistic.

- There are also the plans of other functional areas, such as operations/production, finance, and human resources. How can you make sure that *their* plans mesh with yours to make a unified business plan?

Yes, marketing planning is complicated. That's why so many marketing plans are at best ineffectual. Others completely fail. You want a plan that works.

You're looking for ideas and techniques–those that have been used successfully by operational people. You want step-by-step procedures, rules of thumb, and formats to follow. You want a way to present information so that it makes sense. Furthermore, you want a marketing plan that won't sit on the shelf. You want one that will guide you throughout the entire year.

If this describes what you're looking for, then this book is for you. For more than a combined period of five decades, as marketing practitioners and educators, we've been deeply involved in the planning processes of many corporations. Some of these firms have been *Fortune* 500 companies. Some were firms with less than 20 employees. Some dealt with products, some with services. Some had very sophisticated planning processes. Others lacked even rudimentary budgeting. This book, *Marketing Planning in a Total Quality Environment*, is the product of what we've learned over the years from working with these many and diverse corporations and their executives.

It provides a step-by-step process, check sheets, and formats to simplify your marketing planning process. After you finish the book, you'll know exactly how to go about marketing planning. You'll have formats which will help structure your thinking and presentation. And, you'll also know how to prepare a plan that you can follow throughout the year.

This book is divided into four sections: Introduction; The Eight Planning Steps; Retrospect and Expectation; and Appendixes.

Here's a brief explanation of each of these sections.

SECTION I:
INTRODUCTION

Section I explains the need to build total quality into your marketing plan; the need for a formal marketing planning process; the key to successful planning; how to make your plan a living document; the "ideal" method of planning; an illustrative case; the role of the marketing plan in the overall business plan; and an overview of the marketing planning process.

SECTION II:
THE EIGHT PLANNING STEPS

Eight planning steps are the framework and focus of any serious marketing planning effort. We give you pragmatic, detailed instructions for completing each step. As you move through the process, you'll learn how to develop a marketing plan that's fact-based and focused clearly on your target market and your competition. Furthermore, you'll master the art of implementation and control, enabling you to keep your plan on track.

The eight steps are:

Step 1. SWOTs (Strengths, Weaknesses, Opportunities, Threats): Present
Step 2. SWOTs: Present (continued)
Step 3. SWOTs: Present (continued)
Step 4. SWOTs: Future
Step 5. Gap Analysis
Step 6. Examination of Strategic Options and Strategy Selection
Step 7. Strategy Documentation and Evaluation
Step 8. Fleshing out, Documenting, and Formatting the Annual Marketing Plan

SECTION III:
RETROSPECT AND EXPECTATION

Here, highlights of the book are reviewed. Then, there's a brief warning about the new environment you'll be facing and approaches you should take to handle these new developments.

SECTION IV:
APPENDIXES

There are five Appendixes to supplement your information:

Appendix A: Forecasting Techniques
Appendix B: How to Adjust Financial Statements for Inflation
Appendix C: The Fact Book
Appendix D: The Annual Marketing Plan (Single Product/
Service-Single Target Market Booklet)
Appendix E: The Annual Marketing Plan (Summary
Format Booklet)

Several cautions:

This book assumes that you want to prepare and use a marketing plan for given product(s)/service(s)-target market(s).

A marketing plan presumes existence of a business plan. While the business plan meshes the plans of production/operations, human resources, finance, marketing and other major functional areas, the marketing plan spells out marketing's role in the overall business plan.

But, in many cases, the persons responsible for developing marketing plans will not have recourse to overall business plans simply because such plans do not exist. Of course, most companies have detailed budgets, but these budgets are a far cry from agreed-upon business strategies. Lacking business strategies, then, the planners fully recognize that they can't develop "pure" marketing plans. As a result, in developing their marketing plans, they have to go through some of the steps that are theoretically associated with business planning. Therefore, this book follows a strategic approach necessary for business planning.

If your company lacks an articulated strategy, then follow all of the steps outlined in this book. And get people involved. Make your approach to planning conform to, as nearly as possible, that of planning in a total quality environment.

If, on the other hand, you're from a company that follows a strategic planning process, but not in a total quality environment, then this book will show you how to help move your firm in that direction.

The planning process in this book is designed for developing and using a marketing plan for a product/service that has some sales history. Yet, with some modifications, it can also be used for developing a marketing plan for a new product/service.

Acknowledgements

Although there were many people who helped with the preparation of this book, we'd like to give special thanks to Rajan Chandran, P. J. duPlessis, Edward E. Emanuel, Robert D. Hamilton, Harold E. Klein, Mike Perry, Laurence G. Poli, Chris F. Van Veigeren, and James B. Wiley, whose reviews provided many valuable suggestions. In addition, our thanks to the members of our department, Nancy M. Childs, Joel S. Dubow, Joseph O. Eastlack, Richard J. George, Patrick J. Kirschling, Richard H. Kochersperger, William F. Leahy, and John B. Lord, who have made valuable suggestions, cajoled us, were patient with us, and, most of all, encouraged us. Our thanks also to Rita Memmo, who aided us in many ways. Finally, our enduring gratitude to Carol N. Gallagher and Karen A. Labenz, who were most helpful in editorial assistance.

SECTION I:

INTRODUCTION

INTRODUCTION

 The Need to Build Total
Quality into Your Marketing Plan

The Need for a Formal
Marketing Plan

Involvement: The Key to Successful
Total Quality Planning

How to Make the Plan a Living
Document

The "Ideal" Method

The Micron Case

The Role of the Marketing Plan
in the Business Plan

The Marketing Planning
Process–An Overview

The Need to Build Total Quality into Your Marketing Plan

This need may seem obvious. But building total quality into your marketing plan is not as straightforward as it seems. How do you define quality?

One guru compared defining quality to defining sex:

Everyone is for it. (Under certain conditions, of course.)

Everyone feels they understand it. (Even though they wouldn't want to explain it.)

Everyone thinks execution is only a matter of following natural inclinations. (After all, we do get along somehow.)

Most people feel that all problems in these areas are caused by other people. (If only *they* would take the time to do things right.)[1]

Unfortunately, the guru is right. Definitions of quality vary. Some are even downright silly. Like contrasting "quality" with "low price."

Take a look at the cartoon in Figure 1.1. Seem ridiculous? Of course. Imagine a person with a splitting headache answering the question, "We have high quality or low prices. Which do you want?" with "I don't care whether the aspirin will cure a headache or not. I just want aspirin that doesn't cost much."

Are we stretching a point? Absolutely not! Think for a moment about some of the advice you've had over the years. Or what you've read in marketing publications, particularly the pre-1990 vintage. "Concentrate on quality or low price."

It's time to trash such either/or notions. "Quality" can't be di-

FIGURE 1.1

"We have high quality and low prices. Which do you want?"

vorced from low-priced products/services any more than it can be married to high-priced products/services.

QUALITY DEFINED

We like Drucker's definition:

"Quality" in a product or service is not what the supplier puts in. It is what the customer gets out and is willing to pay for. A product is not "quality" because it is hard to make and costs a lot of money, as manufacturers typically believe. That is incompetence. Customers pay only for what is of use to them and gives them value. Nothing else constitutes "quality." [2]

That's why we also like Garvin's eight dimensions of quality.[3] They, too, highlight that there are no absolutes when it comes to defining quality.

- *Performance*. The performance of a product or service involves basic-use characteristics. It's difficult, however, to develop an overall performance ranking because a product or service might have basic-use characteristics not universally needed or wanted. Take Velcro, used in both industrial and consumer products. Auto manufacturers use Velcro to hold the interior lining against roof panels. The desired performance characteristic is extreme adhesiveness. Velcro straps can also be used instead of laces for kids' shoes. Use the same adhesive quality for those straps as is used for auto interior linings, and kids would sleep with their boots on.

- *Features*. The features of a product or service include characteristics that supplement basic-use characteristics. Recently, one of the authors bought a washer/dryer for a rental condominium. How many features do you suppose he wanted? Some people want VCRs only for rental movies. Two week multiple recording capabilities mean nothing to them. But to others?

- *Reliability*. Reliability is the functioning of a product or service within a specific time frame, such as the mean time to first failure, the mean time between failures, and the failure rate per unit of time. To some automobile owners, reliability is key. For others, quality means high performance. "So what if the car has to be taken to the garage after a few hundred miles? They'll come and get it. I've got other cars."

- *Conformance*. To what degree does a product's design and operating characteristics meet established standards? For example, do dimensions for parts and purity of materials fall within industry standards? Failure to conform to standards can be measured by the number of defects found through inspection. But, acceptable tolerances often vary from company to company. ISO 9000 is mandatory in the EC. But in America?

- *Durability*. Durability is a measure of the use a consumer gets before a product breaks down and has to be replaced. Some customers want products that will last a lifetime. Not others. Students and young marrieds equipping their first apartment may look for furnishings as temporary as their quarters. They'll likely head for Ikea.

- *Serviceability*. People have different standards of what constitutes acceptable service and differing thresholds of tolerance for breakdowns. For example, many direct-marketing businesses, such as *Time-Life* books and videos advertised on TV, use their 800 lines for much–or perhaps all–of their revenue-generating activity. Telephone downtime cannot be tolerated. For other firms, several hours downtime is not that critical.

- *Aesthetics*. This is purely subjective. Stereo sound can be quantified in decibels. But the level that teenagers find appropriate can be enough to cause adults to let out a few decibels of their own.

- *Perceived Quality*. (We prefer to call this the intangible product or service asset.) Buyers will pay only for what they believe to be quality. But buyers' perceptions of quality may be the result of your signals, such as the appearance of your salespersons, your advertising and brochures, and your physical facilities. And here's where it gets sticky. What some people find impressive might seem ostentatious to others.

So, as the eight dimensions point out, quality comes in many different forms. Furthermore, customer opinions as to what is "quality" are transitory. Markets are continually shifting. And splintering. As they change, so will concepts of quality. There are absolutely no absolutes.

Consider TV sets. In the late 1940s, for most people, a quality TV was a fashionable piece of wood furniture. The larger the console–even though the screen was small–the better. It was more important that everyone was able to see that you had a TV, than it was to watch TV. Today, for many people, a quality TV is defined by size of screen, picture fidelity, stereo, and so forth, not by the size of the cabinet.

So it's continually–repeat, continually–back to "'Quality' . . . is what the customer gets out [of the product/service] and is willing to pay for." Unfortunately, in too many companies "quality" is determined by engineers who set conformance characteristics, rather than by the wants of the target market.

Notice that we're *not* just talking about the core–the basic–product or service, but the whole bundle of amenities that surround it, such as aesthetics, or credit terms, or delivery times. In other words, the *augmented* product or service.

So when we refer to a product or service, we're always referring to it as the *augmented* product or service, because that is what the customer is buying.

BUILDING TOTAL QUALITY INTO YOUR MARKETING PLAN (AN OVERVIEW)

Producing quality products/services, as defined by the customer, doesn't just happen. It must be planned.

Total quality demands three key elements (see Figure 1.2).[4] As we go through the marketing planning process, we'll explain how to build them into your marketing plan. But, for now, an overview will be sufficient.

1. Quality Planning

Target Marketing. You start with the customer. "'Quality' is what the customer gets out [of the product or service] and is willing to pay for." So answer these questions:

- Who are our customers?
- What is quality to our customers?

- What are we offering to these customers?
- What are the gaps that must be filled?

Your customers–your target market–is that part (segment) of the market which you elect to serve with a given marketing mix, like product/service, price, promotion, and place.

Recognize that you have a "cast of customers." Quality planning should not just be focused on the ultimate user. If you sell supplies to a university, your cast of customers might well include the purchasing agent, the administrators, the professors, and the students.

Each member of the cast has his/her own needs which are most likely very different from any other cast member. The quality of your product/service will be determined by the extent to which it satisfies the needs of each cast member. Be sure that your augmented product/service has some attributes that satisfy each cast member.

Develop Product/Service Features that Respond to Targeted Customers' Needs and Develop Processes to Produce These Features. Beyond the scope of marketing? In the traditional sense, yes. But you've got to work closely–and right from the start–with other functional areas. You've got to make sure that what you want delivered (the augmented product or service) to your target market can be done at a desirable cost and within a desirable time frame. Sometimes this will require process reengineering.[5]

Your present organizational structure is probably too functionally compartmentalized. Take the advice of Robert L. Callahan, president of Ingersoll Engineers, Inc. "Simply put together people who can get the job done." Use cross-functional teams. Callahan calls it "swarming."[6]

Employees swarm at Milacron. Faced with tough competition from the Japanese (so tough that bankruptcy was a possibility), Milacron formed a cross-functional team of people from manufacturing and engineering as well as from purchasing, logistics, and marketing. Their task: to design a plastic injection machine that would be competitive with one made by the Japanese. That meant cutting costs by 40 percent and increasing the machine's operating efficiency by 40 percent. And the allotted development time was one year, half the usual period.

FIGURE 1.2

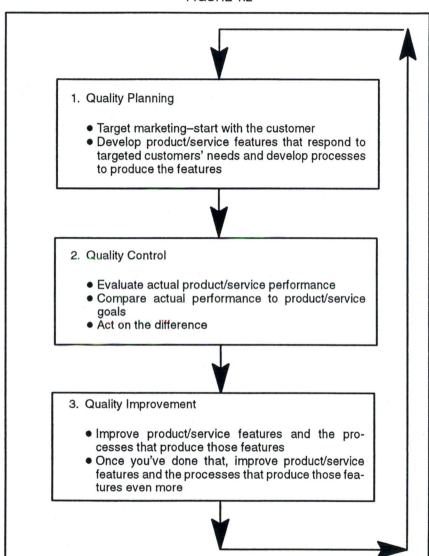

1. Quality Planning

   • Target marketing–start with the customer
   • Develop product/service features that respond to targeted customers' needs and develop processes to produce the features

2. Quality Control

   • Evaluate actual product/service performance
   • Compare actual performance to product/service goals
   • Act on the difference

3. Quality Improvement

   • Improve product/service features and the processes that produce those features
   • Once you've done that, improve product/service features and the processes that produce those features even more

Adapted from J.M. Juran, *Juran on Leadership for Quality* (New York: The Free Press 1989), p. 22.

The cross-functional team completed their assignment on time. And the product met all specifications. In the first full year of production, Milacron sold 2two and a half times more of this new model (Vista) than it had ever sold of Vista's predecessor.[7] A total quality environment demands employee involvement–and empowerment.

An Expanded View of Quality Planning. Now suppose you've figured out the product/service that will excite your target market. And, you've developed processes to produce these features.

Are you finished with total quality planning? No. What you've done is just for starters.

Total quality means more than just providing quality to your external customer. It's also satisfying your internal customers. So total quality means that you must improve significant processes within your marketing operation. This includes those processes that are working satisfactorily as well as those that are sadly in need of revamping.

Take a look at the diagram in Figure 1.3. View the diagram in a broad sense. This is the stuff your marketing department (like all departments) is made of. For example, let's assume it represents an internal operation. The supplier is a secretary who inputs sales data (the raw materials). The processor is a sales analyst who massages the data (the product), and the customer is the marketing manager who uses the product (massaged data) for decision making.

But which process should you improve? Ever hear "If it ain't

FIGURE 1.3

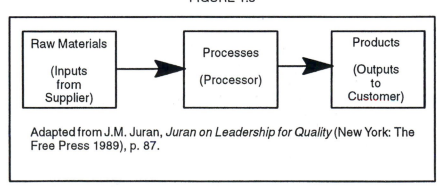

Adapted from J.M. Juran, *Juran on Leadership for Quality* (New York: The Free Press 1989), p. 87.

broke, don't fix it?" Follow that cliché and someday your firm will be "broke," thanks to your competitors' new efficiencies (just ask the multitude of U.S. companies steamrollered by the Japanese).

So, it's a matter of improving both the sick *and* the well. After all, you don't have to be sick to get better. Think in terms of "Even if it ain't broke, make it better."

A list of possible candidates:

- Reducing new product development time
- Improving product/service features
- Improving the measurement of advertising performance
- Reducing salesperson turnover
- Increasing on-time deliveries
- Reducing the number of complaints
- Increasing the response time for complaint satisfaction
- Improving marketing planning procedures

But, back to the question, "Which processes should you improve?" Count on SWOTs (Strengths, Weaknesses, Opportunities, Threats): Present (Steps 1, 2, and 3 of the planning process) to help you identify likely candidates. And, later on we'll suggest techniques to increase the quality of the outputs of these processes.

Of course, improvement of these processes will require education of your employees. Count on that.

2. *Quality Control*

The second key element of total quality is quality control. It consists of these three steps:

- Evaluate actual product/service performance
- Compare actual performance to product/service goals
- Act on the difference

This means that your marketing plan must be structured in such a way that you'll be able to evaluate, compare, and then act.

For example, suppose that part of your plan calls for hiring additional salespersons. You may have set up January tenth as a completion date for contacting applicants. Was this accomplished by this date? If not, then it's time to act on the difference.

We'll provide concrete examples later on (Step 8).

3. Quality Improvement

The third key element to "Total Quality" is continuous improvement. It's back to "Even if it ain't broke, make it better." And once you've done that, begin again. Don't, and you establish a culture of complacency. Which is a sure way to rocky times, or even Chapter 11.

When the Japanese cars first came to America they were junk. And that's being charitable. For example, in the 1960s, a Nissan dealer drove to one of the authors' homes to show off a new model. And what a show that was. The car looked shoddy. But it was not only looks that were at fault. As the dealer was driving out of the driveway, the left front wheel went sailing off.

But the Japanese, continually following their principle of *kaizen* (constant improvement through little steps), kept improving their cars. And then improved them some more. And some more . . .

Make *kaizen* your watchword.[8]

SO WHAT'S DIFFERENT ABOUT TOTAL QUALITY? (FOR THOSE OF YOU WHO DIDN'T READ THE PREFACE)

To some, planning for total quality might seem commonplace. Mundane. After all, isn't this what every firm does? Aren't all the activities of the firm really directed at total quality? As one executive said ". . . even though we might not call it planning for quality, the result of our business planning is higher quality. What do you think we're doing planning for–*lower* quality?"

But things are not always what they seem. In fact, doing business as usual may be quite different from total quality planning. The traditional business approach is to make the various functional areas as efficient as possible. For example, your shipping department might be evaluated in terms of total shipping costs, which is management's interpretation of efficiency. But that's not total quality planning.

The differences may be subtle, yet they are vast. Subtle in that departmental efficiencies are measured against standards. But if you're committed to total quality, your standards must be customer perception of quality, not management's interpretation of efficiency.

Total quality planning begins with the questions, "Who are our customers?" "What do our customers value?" "What are we offering them?" "Is there a gap between what our customers value and what we have to offer?"

The next step is developing product/service features that respond to targeted customers' needs and developing processes able to produce the product features.

Like Dell Computer did. Dell–a real "cloner" success story–used customer measure of quality to design its service department. They realized quality service meant overnight repair. While the service department could have been more efficient using traditional delivery, quality was built-in by meeting customer–not internal–standards.

Quality planning requires active change, something beyond mere lip service. Focusing on your customers will most likely require changes throughout the firm. Keeping focused will demand vigilance and resources. It will require employee involvement, empowerment, and education. And while the thought of recycling through the entire process again and again for areas of improvement will seem boring for some, but that's the way it's done.

WARNING

Some of you who read this book cover to cover will become total quality champions. You'll recognize that total quality is the differential advantage your firms need to remain competitive. But the total quality champion usually loses when the leadership of the company isn't also total quality oriented.

Look what happened at a Philadelphia bank a few years ago. Research on its target market indicated the bank's service was deficient. The marketing director commissioned its advertising agency to create a campaign stressing service.

The campaign, however, failed. Why? Because the marketing director just couldn't provide the service features advertised–or implied–in the campaign.

For example, he couldn't offer more conveniently located branches. That was branch banking's responsibility. He couldn't have the branches open earlier (or stay open longer). That was operation's responsibility. He couldn't put more tellers on duty. That, too, was operation's responsibility. He couldn't provide special training for tellers. That was human resources' responsibility. And all of these department managers had good reasons why they couldn't help implement the service strategy. The root cause was, of course, that they were being evaluated by other criteria, such as deposits per teller.

In fact, the only thing the marketing director *could* do was run the advertising campaign, promising service that was not being delivered.

This is what happens in many firms. Marketing programs offering improved quality–as defined by the customers–often conflict with traditional reward systems. Cooperation with other functional areas is lacking.

The total quality mentality cannot and will not spread upward. It will be thwarted, and the total quality champion will lose.

Do you think things would have been different at the Philadelphia bank if the CEO had been a champion for the improved customer service program? No question about it! The operations person would have found a way to keep the bank open. Because if he didn't, he would have had to find a new job. The manager of human resources would have found a way to train the tellers, and so forth.

Building total quality into the marketing plan, to succeed, must start at the top. The system must (1) support the functional interaction that must take place in total quality, (2) shift from traditional mandated activities of reporting and control to reporting and control of quality improvement activities, and (3) change rewards to match shifts in priorities.

Therefore, while we want to convince you of the importance and benefits of building total quality into the marketing plan, we also want to warn you that "total quality" is just that–*total*. And that requires commitment to total quality from corporate leadership.

So, what if you don't have–and for now, can't get–total quality commitment from your leadership? First, recognize your sphere of influence. Be cautious–very cautious–about developing programs that count on the volunteer assistance of other departments.

But within your sphere of influence, you can build at least certain elements of total quality into your marketing plan. Let's return to the three key elements of total quality.

1. Quality Planning

Even if you lack total commitment from other functional areas, you still can better answer these four questions:

- Who are our customers?
- What is quality to our customers?
- What are we offering to these customers?
- What are the gaps that must be filled?

And, to a certain extent, you can develop product/service features that more closely respond to your targeted customers' needs. For example, you might be able to change the frequency of salesperson's visits, or product information.

Going beyond your external customers, you can insist on total quality for your internal customers, such as sales data in a more usable form for the marketing manager. Or a training manual more suitable for the sales manager.

If you have people reporting to you, you can get them involved. You can empower them and you can make sure that they are properly trained.

2. Quality Control

Within your sphere of influence, you can:

- Evaluate actual performance
- Compare actual performance to product goals
- Act on the difference

For example, using your plan to improve the presentation of sales data for the marketing manager, you can examine the revised product. Does it meet the standards proposed in the quality plan? Similarly, evaluate the training manual. Does it meet the standards you established?

3. Quality Improvement

Total quality planning is never a one shot (or one-year) deal. Within your sphere of influence, make *kaizen* your watchword. On a scheduled basis, continue to refine the improvements already under way. Seek ways to upgrade all the activities under your control and reward subordinates accordingly.

If you are a total quality champion surrounded by doubters, don't give up. Make your operation first-rate. Lead by example. Just perhaps, others–hopefully top management–will catch on.

POINTS LEARNED

1. "A product is not 'quality' because it is hard to make and costs a lot of money . . . Customers pay only for what is of use to them and gives them value. Nothing else constitutes 'quality.' " (Peter F. Drucker)
2. Quality has a number of dimensions. Among them are performance, features, reliability, conformance, durability, serviceability, aesthetics, and perceived quality.
3. There are absolutely no absolutes when it comes to quality.
4. View your product/service as more than just the core product. Consider your product/service as the whole bundle of amenities that surround it.
5. Total quality demands three key elements: quality planning, quality control, and quality improvement.
6. Total quality means more than just providing quality to your external customers. It's also satisfying your internal customers.
7. If you don't have–and for now can't get–total quality commitment from your leadership, you can build at least certain elements of quality into your marketing plan within your sphere of influence.

LOOKING AHEAD

We hope you are thinking: "Why, total quality is nothing more than common sense. Everybody should do it." Exactly, but most companies don't do it. Total quality doesn't just happen. It must be systematized into a formal marketing plan.

INTRODUCTION

The Need to Build Total
Quality into Your Marketing Plan

 The Need for a Formal
Marketing Plan

Involvement: The Key to Successful
Total Quality Planning

How to Make the Plan a Living
Document

The "Ideal" Method

The Micron Case

The Role of the Marketing Plan
in the Business Plan

The Marketing Planning
Process–An Overview

The Need for a Formal Marketing Plan

WILL FORMAL, SYSTEMATIZED MARKETING PAY OFF FOR YOU?

You bet! Consider these three questions.

1. Is Your Intuitive "Good Enough" Marketing Plan Really Good Enough?

Perhaps not. A more systematic approach to marketing may reveal that you're missing out on lucrative sales. For example, a computer software company had no system for annual marketing planning. Business seemed to be good enough and top management was satisfied with its product managers . . . until one resigned. This manager was replaced by a former product manager from a food manufacturing company known for its marketing planning system. The new manager proceeded to increase sales and profits by 150 percent.

The company learned that it had failed to measure the potential of many markets. It needed a more formal, systematized approach. It needed an approach that would allow it to maximize *all* of the potential marketing opportunities for its products.

2. Does Your Present Marketing Planning Process Detect Unexpected Successes?

During the Great Depression, Cadillacs were not selling. General Motors wanted to eliminate the line. What saved it? Peter Drucker, in his *Adventures of a Bystander*, tells the story.

Nicholas Dreystadt, a middle manager, made an analysis of who bought Cadillacs and why. He discovered that Cadillac was neglecting an entire marketing segment, that of wealthy black entertainers, doctors, and lawyers. A Cadillac was an important success symbol to these affluent blacks, since they were denied access to other symbols such as luxurious housing and vacation resorts. Dreystadt developed this neglected market segment and eventually made Cadillac into a big moneymaker.[9] Nothing offers a richer chance to increase sales and profits than does the *Unexpected Success*. A formal marketing plan, by analyzing each product/service-target market, often uncovers such opportunities.

3. Does Your Present Marketing Planning Process Help Pinpoint the Shifts that Are Taking Place in the Market?

A common explanation for the failure of a product or service to live up to expectations is, "We were doing all right, but these other people started selling to customers we'd never even heard of and all of a sudden they had the market."[10]

Big companies, as well as small, continually have to identify, appraise, and react to new competitors, technologies, customer needs, and laws. Xerox, for example, lost a significant part of the copier market to the Japanese because of change in the product/market environment. Xerox failed to react to two things: (1) the emergence of new market segments, and (2) the emergence of new competitors.

Xerox focused its efforts on its very profitable segment: the buyers of large machines. It did not develop separate products and marketing programs for the small users: CPAs, doctors, lawyers, and small offices. Thus, market creaming and failure to practice differentiated marketing made Xerox vulnerable to competitive attack.

The Japanese started to make copiers that met the needs of this low-usage market segment. They did not compete directly with Xerox. Nor did they offer a machine with the speed and clarity of Xerox. Instead, they flanked Xerox by providing small users with the low-cost, simple machine that this low-usage segment wanted.[11] Today these new competitors have honed their manufacturing skills, distribution channels, and marketing skills. And they haven't confined themselves to the low-usage segment either. They're producing and marketing large machines, taking away market share from Xerox's served market.

Like Xerox, every company must anticipate that its products and services will be used for a host of purposes other than those originally intended. New market segments always emerge. And these new customers are always willing to pay for a product/service that fulfills their specific needs. A company's major customers may, in fact, turn out to be groups not even considered when the business was first launched.

The answers to these three questions point out that intuitive marketing is not the answer. At best it results in missed opportunities. At worst, it can result in a misunderstanding of the marketplace. And in business failure.

GAIN FORMAL, SYSTEMATIZED MARKETING THROUGH A WRITTEN ANNUAL MARKETING PLAN

Each of the above-mentioned problems could have been avoided through careful development of a marketing plan—in writing.

The Annual Marketing Plan Defined

The marketing plan describes, in writing, the strengths, weaknesses, opportunities, and threats your company will face, and the strategies you'll use to achieve results through:

1. Product/service emphasis
2. Target markets
3. Pricing policies
4. Distribution policies
5. Promotion policies (advertising, personal sales, specialty advertising, and publicity)

The plan also includes a work program giving detailed assignments, defined goals with deadlines, and accountability for performance. For example: an advertising campaign is assigned to someone (perhaps you), who then specifies the actions and budget required to carry out the campaign. Completion dates and timing of budgeted expenditures are set for control purposes.

But the important thing to remember is that your plan must be committed to paper.

Why Your Annual Marketing Plan Should Be in Writing

You may be thinking: "I know it works in some cases. But my business is different. I can hardly predict what's going to happen tomorrow. Why should I get involved in putting together a written plan for a *year?*"

That's a fair question, considering among other things, the uncertainties of the economy, governmental regulations, and the competition. But you can't escape the future consequences of your present actions. You either expand your sales force, or you don't. You either invest in developing new markets, or you don't. Today's decisions determine if your firm will prosper, stagnate, or fail.

Planning is unavoidable, inescapable. Your only choice is whether you do planning intuitively or in a formal way–by putting it in writing.

To Improve Communication. A bank with $300 million in deposits had no written plans. The president doubted the need for such formality. "After all," he claimed, "there are three of us who are the real movers and shakers. No decision of any magnitude is made by anyone but us. We're in constant communication with each other. Why should we go through all this mumbo-jumbo of putting our plans in writing?"

A consultant asked them to write down what they thought the bank's five-year objectives for deposits should be. One executive wrote $400 million. The second put down $800 million. The third (the president) would not participate. He didn't think it was a good question. He wasn't sure that deposits should be a goal of the bank. Clearly there was no agreement about what the bank was trying to be. Or, what customers they should be serving. How, then, could there be any real consensus about designing a total quality plan for the bank?

To Force More Rigorous Thinking. While intuitive thinking can provide brilliant insights, it can also be vague and inconsistent. These weaknesses are exposed by the process of writing. Writing is a tough discipline. Holes show up quickly.

To Facilitate Coordination with Other Functional Areas. Since it is in writing, everyone can study the plan at length. Personnel can better evaluate the plan. And total quality demands effective communication between functional areas.

Under other systems of planning, marketing plans are often simply suggestions to production/operations as to what should be produced. In a total quality environment, functions work together in developing product/service features that respond to customers' needs and develop processes able to produce those process features.

To Help Gain Approval. A written document will help you explain what you plan to do and why you need funds.

To Assist in Management Development. Formal planning develops managerial skills. And having managerial depth helps build a dynamic, successful organization.

In a written plan, you are forced to spell out who does what, when, and at what cost. Ultimately, this will result in a better job of delegation, and expanded management time. And a sense of how important time is! The former Detroit Lions quarterback Bobby Layne used to say, "I never lost a ball game. I only ran out of time." How often do you just seem to run out of time?

To Assure that Planning Will Be Done. The formal process requires that planning and reviews be scheduled and completed at regular intervals. Of course, merely devoting adequate time and effort to the process won't guarantee thoroughness. But it does make thoroughness possible.

WILL A WRITTEN PLAN GUARANTEE SUCCESS?

Nothing guarantees success. If a not-too-smart group puts together plans in writing, they might just go broke in a more orderly fashion. But with reasonable intelligence and knowledge of the industry, formalizing the planning process gives that extra edge.

There is the classic story about the man who decided that the only way he could ever become successful was to win the lottery. Although not religious, he started going to church and praying to God to let him win the lottery. This went on for six months.

Then one Sunday, after leaving the services, he threw himself down on the church steps. He looked up to Heaven, and shouted,

"Oh God, why don't you let me hit the lottery? Why don't you give me a break? Why don't you give me a break?"

A booming voice from above roared down, "Why don't you give Me a break? The least you could do is buy a ticket."

Make sure that you've got a ticket. Put your marketing plan in writing. Follow the eight planning steps in this book.

POINTS LEARNED

1. Intuitive marketing plans are not good enough. You need a formal, systematized approach to help you maximize all the potential marketing opportunities for your products/services.
2. A formal marketing plan often uncovers the unexpected success.
3. A formal marketing plan helps you identify, appraise, and react to new environmental conditions.
4. Putting your marketing plan into writing improves communication, forces more rigorous thinking, facilitates coordination, helps gain plan approval, assists in management development, and helps assure that planning will be done.

LOOKING AHEAD

But to make total quality marketing planning pay off, you can't be a lone ranger. You've got to get others involved.

INTRODUCTION

The Need to Build Total Quality into Your Marketing Plan

The Need for a Formal Marketing Plan

Involvement: The Key to Successful Total Quality Planning

How to Make the Plan a Living Document

The "Ideal" Method

The Micron Case

The Role of the Marketing Plan in the Business Plan

The Marketing Planning Process—An Overview

Involvement:
The Key to Successful
Total Quality Planning

Chuck Knight, CEO of Emerson Electric, summed it up when he claimed, "People don't fail in planning, they fail in implementation. Why? Well, my fundamental belief is that they fail because of the lack of ability to get people involved and committed."

Experience shows that managers are more likely to implement a plan that they are involved in. After all, people who have played a role in drafting plans want to see those plans succeed.

For example, the director of marketing for a bank hired a consultant to develop a procedural model for locating branch banks. When the president saw the model, he thought it was a good procedure and told the director of marketing to implement it. Proudly, the director of marketing explained the procedure to the other departments (real estate, branch banking, etc.) so that all understood their roles.

A year later the model was junked. It failed because most of the bank's executives really didn't care whether or not it succeeded. In fact, because of existing rivalries, some were more interested in seeing it fail. After all, it wasn't their plan.

Remember, only people who are involved in drafting the plan are going to try their best to make the plan succeed. People don't like to see their plans fail. But the operative word is *their.* Each person should view the plan as his/her own personal plan, not someone else's.

And total quality requires involvement not only within the marketing function but with other function areas as well. No wonder one of the main findings of a major study conducted by the Conference Board was the importance of the integration of marketing planning with other functions.[12]

Besides getting people to buy into the plan, there is another major reason why you want involvement. Involvement also strengthens the plan itself. Others may have bits of information unknown to you. At the same time, understanding grows. People are better able to spot problems and see solutions.

Then, there's one more reason to seek involvement. Marketing activities are visible to everyone. A vice-president of marketing of a major bank put it this way, "In marketing you're operating in a fishbowl. Just have five people not like your ad and call the CEO . . . On the other hand, in finance they could boot one that would cost the bank a million dollars and only a few people would know about it." So you're always out on the limb. You might as well have a lot of people out there with you.

Involvement in planning. It's key. As an executive of an oil company told us, "The biggest benefit of our marketing planning process is not so much the plan as it is the involvement of all levels of management who contributed to the plans."

The eight planning steps will show you when and how to get others involved.

POINTS LEARNED

1. Only people who are involved in drafting plans are going to try their best to make the plans succeed.
2. Involvement strengthens the plan. Others may contribute bits of information which will help the plan to be more successful. Understanding grows. People are better able to spot problems and see solutions.

LOOKING AHEAD

But your plan must be more than a shelf item. How can you make it a living document?

INTRODUCTION

> The Need to Build Total
> Quality into Your Marketing Plan

> The Need for a Formal
> Marketing Plan

> Involvement: The Key to Successful
> Total Quality Planning

> How to Make the Plan a Living
> Document

> The "Ideal" Method

> The Micron Case

> The Role of the Marketing Plan
> in the Business Plan

> The Marketing Planning
> Process–An Overview

How to Make the Plan a Living Document

How many times have you heard this? "We put together a marketing plan every year. And what a waste. We spend two weeks putting it together just to keep management happy. Then we get back to business and nobody ever looks at the plan again. Next year we go through the same 'rite of spring' again."

In fact, many marketing plans are nothing more than shelf items. Even then, however, not all the effort is wasted. Just putting plans on paper causes more rigorous thinking. And greater involvement.

But the value of a written marketing plan is increased tenfold if it becomes a working document, one that you refer to every day to track progress. Sometimes, of course, it will become necessary to modify the plan itself. That's okay. It still means that the plan is an active, living part of your day-to-day business.

One executive told us two books have all the answers he needed to get him through life. One was the Bible which provided answers on how he should behave and act in his personal life. The other book was the business plan. This told him how he should act in his business life. He read from both books almost daily.

The approach recommended throughout this book will help you develop living marketing plans. For now, concentrate on these two guidelines.

KEEP YOUR MARKETING PLANS SHORT

The first trick in developing your plan is to keep it short. Too much detail detracts from important facts and disrupts an orderly flow. Also, shorter plans are easier to adapt and change. General Eisenhower once said that "planning is everything, but plans are nothing." Plans will often have to be changed. And lengthy plans don't get changed. They're just too cumbersome.

Keeping the plan short doesn't mean that you shouldn't spend time assembling and analyzing facts concerning past performance and future projections. We want to make this clear: If you don't study the facts, forget about formal planning. But you don't want most of the results of this fact-finding in the plan itself. There's another place for it–in a fact book. (We'll discuss the fact book later.)

BUILD YOUR CONTROL MECHANISMS
INTO YOUR PLANS

Your marketing plan should specify exactly what you want to achieve. Built into the plan should be, for example, action plans and sales objectives (see Step 8 for an example). These will provide reasons to refer to the plan. Significant deviations from the plan will signal that it's time to revise it. In this way, control mechanisms will be part of your plan.

The eight planning steps will show you how to keep your plan short and how to build in controls. If you follow the steps, your plan will become a truly living document, an indispensable aid to you in implementation *and* control.

POINTS LEARNED

1. The value of a written marketing plan is increased tenfold if it becomes a working document.
2. Keep your marketing plans short. Store the results of your fact-finding in a fact book.
3. Build control mechanisms into your plans.

LOOKING AHEAD

Okay. So your plan must be short. And control mechanisms must be built into it. But what is the ideal method of marketing planning?

INTRODUCTION

The Need to Build Total
Quality into Your Marketing Plan

The Need for a Formal
Marketing Plan

Involvement: The Key to Successful
Total Quality Planning

How to Make the Plan a Living
Document

 The "Ideal" Method

The Micron Case

The Role of the Marketing Plan
in the Business Plan

The Marketing Planning
Process—An Overview

The "Ideal" Method

IS THE MARKETING PLANNING PROCESS PRESENTED IN THIS BOOK "IDEAL"?

No single method of planning or plan format applies to all companies. What will work best for your firm depends on:

Management's Comfort Zone. Is your management* more comfortable with a by-the-numbers procedure or with a shirt-sleeve approach? A radical shift from one planning style to another should be made gradually. If your management has experience in formal planning, it is likely to be more at ease with sophisticated techniques than management that is new to the process.

Product/Service Diversity. If your firm produces a single product or service and sells it to a single market, one marketing plan is all you'll need. However, if your firm sells a variety of products or services to a number of target markets, then you'll need to put together several marketing plans and consolidate them into a master plan.

Data, Staff, and Time Availability. In some industries, hard data is difficult to come by, making the analysis phase of marketing planning most challenging. Then too, staff allocated to research activities may be limited in even the largest of corporations. Time, of course, is always scarce.

Management Involvement. Do you have a company-wide total quality planning process? If so, very little explanation and justification of strategies will be necessary because management will be directly involved in the planning process. But if you're operating in a company without such a management commitment, then you'll probably have to sell them on your plan.

Present Planning Formats. If your firm already has an established format, you'll probably find it best to follow the old format as closely as possible.

---

*Throughout this book, the term management refers to the person you report to–whether that person is, in your case, a group brand manager, a marketing manager, the president of the company, or even the board of directors.

Company Jargon. There's a lot of jargon around. What some companies call objectives, other companies call goals. Some firms use the term "strategy" only at the corporate or business unit level. Others use the term at all levels within the firm. It's better to adopt company jargon. You'll have one less battle to fight.

So, there's no such thing as the "ideal" method or format. Furthermore, the ideal method and format for you today will be obsolete tomorrow: your management will become more experienced in planning, your company will grow and offer more products and services, you'll serve more target markets, and your database will improve.

YOUR UNIQUE COMPANY

Your company is unique. You can't expect off-the-rack planning procedures and formats to suit your needs perfectly. But there are enough similarities between companies that we can discuss procedures and formats which you can easily adapt to your situation.

Common Features of Most Marketing Plans

Examine Figure 1.4. Note the similarity of features among service firms and industrial and consumer product manufacturers. So even though your firm is unique, it's likely that you can follow a prescribed format if you make some modifications.

Common Marketing Planning Situations

The one type of plan that you and all other firms must develop is the product/service-target market plan. You must decide what product/service should be offered to a given target market and plan accordingly. This is real guts of the marketing planning process.

Planning would be greatly simplified if you had to develop a marketing plan for only one product or service for one market. But it's usually much more complicated. You probably sell a number of different products/services to a number of different markets. As a

FIGURE 1.4

Topics Included in Top Management's Directive

	Manufacturers of Industrial products	Consumer products	Service firms
Profit goals	69%	73%	73%
Sales goals	56	53	52
Budget constraints	52	56	79
Choice of target markets	42	33	46
Market share goals	39	46	42
Pricing strategy	39	42	50
New product/service development	39	33	35
Market penetration strategy	30	20	23
Cash flow goals	29	26	25
Product or service positioning	26	33	50
Production contraints	26	18	17
Distribution strategy	24	26	31
Advertising and promotion strategy	23	27	27
Number of respondents	109	66	48

*Howard Sutton, *The Marketing Plan in the 1990s,* (New York: The Conference Board, 1990), p. 52. Reprinted with permission. *The Marketing Plan* is an excellent book describing companies' planning procedures. Includes overviews of practices and a number of planning forms from industrial and consumer product and service firms. If you'd like more background, be sure to check this book.

result, you must develop a marketing plan for each product/service and then integrate them into an overall plan. Therefore, this book will show you: first, how to develop a marketing plan for one product/service-target market; and second, how to integrate them into an overall marketing plan.

PLANNING FORMS

We've included a number of checklists and formats. Now don't get us wrong. We don't believe that planning is merely "filling in the squares." On the contrary. Planning requires creativity. And lots of it. So why the checklists and formats?

One reason: They are a way to help jog your memory, to improve the likelihood that you don't forget some critical aspect. They serve the same purpose that checklists serve airline pilots. Think of a USAir captain of a Boeing 737. In a year, this captain will make hundreds of takeoffs and landings. Still, he/she uses a checklist prior to takeoff or landing. Why? To make absolutely sure that nothing has been forgotten. So consider the checklists and formats as reminders of the common elements that you *must* consider. There's a lot of opportunity within these checklists and formats for you to handle your unique planning situation and to express your creativity.

Another reason for forms: Since you're being systematically guided through the process, you can do the job more efficiently and quickly. Just like the captain of a Boeing 737.

Also, you may be approving plans that your subordinates have prepared. Or you'll be developing one of the many plans that your boss will be approving. Checklists and forms provide standardization, which makes plans easier to review.

Still another reason: Suppose that you have people reporting to you who are inexperienced in marketing planning, yet they're responsible for developing marketing plans. Forms will help train them to know what to look for. As the catcher and later coach of the New York Yankees, Yogi Berra, once said, "You can see a lot by looking." Our corollary: "If you know what you're looking for."

A final reason (actually there's yet another reason, but we're saving it for later on): You'll be using the plans throughout the year, checking progress and noting if changes need to be made. Since you'll probably be working with more than one plan, plan standardization will make the control process much easier. Again, this is a real time saver. We've included two types of forms, those for a fact book and those for marketing plans (see Appendixes C, D, and E).

The Fact Book

In preparing a marketing plan for a single product/service-target market, creating a "fact book" is an important part of the planning process (see sample forms in Appendix C). Your supporting documentation–including all of the data you will gather and analyze–

should be stored here in an orderly, easily accessible manner. In this way, the data is available if it needs to be reexamined. And when you go about planning next year you will have the historical data in ready-to-use form. Also, orderly record keeping makes your progress apparent at a glance, and builds confidence in your analysis.

These forms will guide you through the planning process. An explanation of how to complete these forms will be given in Steps 1 through 7. You will sometimes need more space than that given in the forms. This may well occur, for instance, for "4.3. Economic" in the Performance Profile in Step 3. In such a case, merely put the data behind that page and label it "4.3.1." If you wish to add subsections under general headings, then extend the numbering system. Example: 4.3.1.1, 4.3.1.2 , and so on.

Annual Marketing Plan Formats

Included in Appendixes D and E are sample forms for product/service-target market annual marketing plans and for consolidating these plans into a master plan. Step 8 will show you how to complete these forms.

POINTS LEARNED

1. There is no such thing as an ideal method of planning. What will work best depends upon, among other things: management's comfort zone; product/service diversity; data, staff and time availability; management involvement; present planning formats; and company jargon.
2. Even though your company is unique, it's likely you can follow our prescribed format if you make some modifications.
3. Checklists and formats will simplify and speed up your planning. They'll jog your memory. They'll provide standardization, making plans easier to review and control. And, they'll help train managers to become better planners.

INTRODUCTION

The Need to Build Total Quality into Your Marketing Plan

The Need for a Formal Marketing Plan

Involvement: The Key to Successful Total Quality Planning

How to Make the Plan a Living Document

The "Ideal" Method

The Micron Case

The Role of the Marketing Plan in the Business Plan

The Marketing Planning Process–An Overview

The Micron Case

This case will be referred to often throughout the book. It is not a complicated case. It is an adapted case designed to be quick and easy to comprehend. Its only purpose is to provide an example to explain the steps in the planning process–the same steps that you'd follow in both service- and product-oriented companies. We used a product-oriented company since it's easier to think about an unfamiliar product than it is to think about an unfamiliar service.

MICRON, INC.

Micron, Inc.[13] was founded by a former employee of a large research think tank. Aware of the potential future of research oscilloscopes, he developed his own highly sophisticated model. In 1976 he founded Micron, Inc. in order to market this device. Sales, however, did not materialize. In 1985, after a decade of frustrations, he sold his company. The purchaser was Silco, Inc., a small, diversified company with annual sales of $37 million.

THE SITUATION AT THE END OF 1992

The Market

The price of a research oscilloscope generally ranges from $40,000 to $45,000. Instruments in this price range are used for routine analysis in the less technical laboratories. However, some models cost about $200,000, including accessories. Micron's units, with accessories, sell for approximately $190,000 each, slightly below (by about 5 percent) the other competitors' products.

The users of Micron's instruments are highly sophisticated government, university, and research laboratory scientists who demand extensive applications and performance. Since 1987 Micron has sold a total of 38 instruments.

The total annual industry sales (of all research oscilloscopes) have risen from $96 million in 1987 to nearly $250 million by the end of 1992. Micron's share is about 1.6 percent. Industry sales are expected to reach between $400 and $425 million by 1997.

Looking specifically at the high-end research oscilloscopes, it's estimated that since 1987, the number of units sold has increased by about 10 percent.

The Competition

There are a variety of manufacturers, including some of the largest firms in the world. Four of these are in the *Fortune* top 100 industrials (worldwide). These companies have worldwide service networks and far more extensive sales coverage than Micron. They are very aggressive competitors; however, they sell research oscilloscopes exclusively in the $40,000-$45,000 range.

Two companies, IMPRO Industries and Moltec, Inc., are selling to the same target market as Micron. Each company has sales equalling about one-half of Micron's. IMPRO is the more aggressive of the two. It has a larger sales force than Micron, and its sales support is more extensive. Moltec's sales force is the same size as Micron's.

Both firms are in poor financial condition. IMPRO's financial condition, however, has been steadily improving. It is believed that in a year or two IMPRO's financial problems could be over. Moltec, on the other hand, seems to be just hanging on financially. It might not survive, at least as an independent company, for more than a year.

In spite of their relatively weak financial conditions, both IMPRO and Moltec have steadily increased their market shares over the past five years. Micron has the leading edge in technology, but there is evidence that IMPRO and Moltec are rapidly closing this gap.

Micron's Marketing Strategy

Micron maintains a continuing research and development program. Its annual R&D budget has been as much as $500,000. Micron's oscilloscope is considered the best on the market. It is more versatile, accurate, and more reliable than those offered by IMPRO and Moltec. All the scientists who have used Micron's oscilloscope praise the instrument and give excellent references. Reliability of the product is so high that there has been no need for service of any of Micron's oscilloscopes.

Two salesmen are charged with selling Micron's research oscilloscopes throughout the world. They do not do direct canvassing, but follow up leads from trade shows and advertising response. Until early 1992, a third salesperson was employed. However, to increase profitability, this person was released.

In some instances, sales have been lost because prospects could not justify the cost of a Micron unit. However, when superior versatility, accuracy, performance, and reliability are important buying criteria, Micron has an excellent chance of making a sale (see Table 1.1).

There has been some sales resistance to Micron's oscilloscopes because all servicing would have to be handled from its Boston facility. Some American prospects are reluctant to purchase Micron's oscilloscopes, in spite of their trouble-free history, because Micron does not have a nationwide service network. These American prospects have purchased from either IMPRO or Moltec, depending on whose plant was closer to their facilities.

Environmental Assessment (1982-1986)

The following eight major market trends have been identified:

1. Research oscilloscope technology is becoming more widely known and more widely accepted.
2. Continued rapid growth (at about the same rate as the past five years) is projected for applied research oscilloscopes ($40,000-$50,000 range). Demand for oscilloscopes for the most sophisticated research laboratory use ($200,000 range) is projected to grow 25 percent between 1993-1997.
3. Proof of high performance and specific problem solving has

been and will continue to be necessary to generate sales, especially for the higher-price research oscilloscopes.

4. Rapidly changing applications constantly require new accessories and some instrument redesign, especially for the higher-price research oscilloscopes.

5. The most aggressive competitors, those selling research oscilloscopes in the low-price range, are likely to follow these strategies:

   •a sales approach which emphasizes the size and dependability of the company;

   •professional marketing and sales promotional techniques;

   •underpricing the competition.

6. The four major producers (the four in the *Fortune* top 100 industrials) are not expected to enter into the high-end market. This is because of (1) the rapid growth in the low-end market; (2) the small size of the high-end market, and (3) the relatively slow growth in the high-end market.

7. IMPRO and Moltec, to the extent that their finances permit, will

TABLE 1.1

Micron's Comparative P & Ls (in $1,000)

	1987	1992	$ Change 1987-92	% Change 1987-92
Sales	2,000	2,400	+400	+ 20
Cost of Goods Sold	920	1,100	+180	+ 20
Gross Profit	1,080	1,300	+220	+ 20
Expenses				
R&D	300	180	-120	− 40
Selling	340	200	-140	− 41
Advertising	50	60	+ 10	+ 20
Administration Exps	200	210	+ 10	+ 5
Total Expenses	890	650	-240	− 27
Contribution to Corporate	190	650	+460	+242

follow very aggressive product and market strategies. IMPRO probably will acquire Moltec in 1993.

8. Inflation is projected to average 3 percent throughout the 1993-1997 period. It is believed that these increases can be passed on to the purchasers.

INTRODUCTION

The Need to Build Total
Quality into Your Marketing Plan

The Need for a Formal
Marketing Plan

Involvement: The Key to Successful
Total Quality Planning

How to Make the Plan a Living
Document

The "Ideal" Method

The Micron Case

The Role of the Marketing Plan
in the Business Plan

The Marketing Planning
Process–An Overview

The Role of the Marketing Plan
in the Business Plan

HOW THE MARKETING PLAN
TIES IN WITH THE BUSINESS PLAN

Talking about marketing plans gets confusing unless you focus on a specific organizational level. This book is about how to prepare and use the marketing plan in a total quality environment for a business unit or a single-industry firm (the procedures, however, can be applied to many varied marketing planning circumstances). So it's a must to understand the marketing plan in relationship to the business plan.

The "Ideal" Method

Let's look first at the "ideal" method of planning in a single-industry firm, or in a business unit of a diversified company. We'll use the Micron case as an example.

Micron was functionally organized as shown in Figure 1.5. The president assumed the responsibilities of finance and administration. Although responsibilities were delegated to functional managers, the president was very involved with day-to-day activities in design and engineering, manufacturing and marketing.

Corporate (Micron's parent company, Silco, Inc.) had specified that Micron was to develop a comprehensive one- and five-year business plan. Although corporate did not specify sales or profit performance goals, the executives at Micron had a pretty good idea of corporate's expectations: 20 percent sales and profits increases over the next five years.

First, Micron's planning team developed a one- and five-year business plan. This business plan was to give overall direction to the

FIGURE 1.5

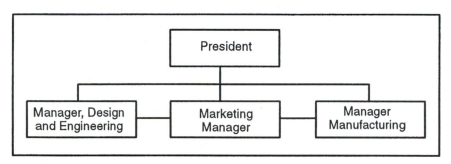

various functional areas, who then were to develop their annual plans.

Micron's planning team consisted of the president and the three functional area managers. In developing the business plan, the three managers, along with the people reporting to them, made detailed analyses of SWOTs: Strengths, Weaknesses, Opportunities, and Threats), Present and Future for their areas.

Then, the planning team discussed these findings at an all day meeting. They compiled a composite list of the firm's strengths, weaknesses, opportunities, and threats. They also developed a most-probable-case future. Next, they estimated the gap between corporate's performance goals and their forecasted sales and profits under a no-change strategy. Even allowing for good luck, the prognosis was gloomy. By the end of the five-year period, projected sales, compared to corporate's expectations, would be (a shortfall of about $800,000). Projected profits revealed a gap of about $160,000. There was no question that a new strategy was necessary.

Over a period of several weeks they studied possibilities. From time to time, the functional managers met with people who reported to them. Sometimes these were formal meetings, but mostly they were informal. These meetings produced ideas for viable strategies as well as feelings of plan ownership.

After deciding on the basic strategy to meet the one- and five-year performance goals, the planning team then started to flesh out the business plan. This business plan was to serve two purposes. First, it would detail the steps Micron needed to take to reach its one- and five-year performance goals for both sales and profits. Second, it would specify those quality criteria necessary to keep Micron on strategy so the one- and five-year performance goals could be reached. Once more, all of the managers consulted with the people reporting to them.

After considerable discussion and negotiation, the planning team put together a rough business plan. This plan specified, for instance, sales objectives for marketing and production volumes expected of manufacturing. Then each functional manager prepared detailed annual plans. Marketing's annual plan included actions essential to meet its required sales and profit volumes and specified required resources.

Figure 1.6 illustrates the process (note that in a larger organization there would be additional levels of planning). Remember that in this case there was extensive involvement of those reporting to the functional managers, creating a sort of "bottom up-top down process." Also recall that the functional managers worked together in developing the business plan before each of them developed his/her own annual plans. The rough business overall plan that emerged was exactly that–a rough draft with the sole purpose of serving as a guideline for the managers.

While the managers were developing their annual plans (again working with people reporting to them), it became evident that parts of the business plan had to be changed. For example, when marketing was fleshing out its annual plan, it realized that the timing of its sales would likely differ from the original estimate. The planning team then met for replanning and negotiations.

Sometimes changes in one functional area's plans were minor, yet affected another functional area. Then the two managers got together to try to resolve differences.

Finally, when the business plan was on target with differences resolved, functional areas finalized their annual plans.

You'll note that, as illustrated above, planning resulted in two basic kinds of plans:

1. The business plan–the overall marketing, manufacturing, design and engineering, and financial and administration strate-

gies and plans, using a comprehensive five-year planning horizon with one- and five-year financial and quality goals.
2. The functional plans–detailed annual plans for the four functional areas.

And also note that planning was carried out in a total quality environment.

Here's how the three key elements of total quality were integrated into the marketing plans, as well as into other functional area plans (specifics will be given in Steps 6 and 7).

FIGURE 1.6

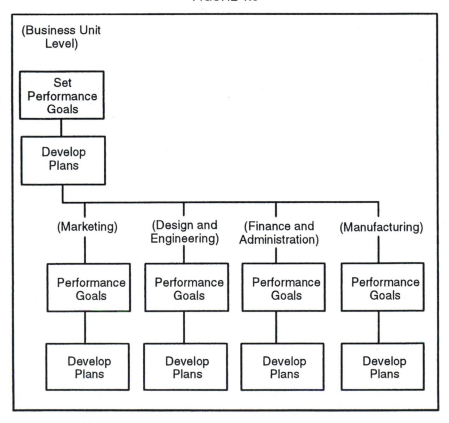

1. Quality Planning

Micron's planning team started with their customers. Marketing's SWOTs: Present and Future answered these four questions:

- Who are our customers?
- What is quality to our customers?
- What are we offering to these customers?
- What are the gaps that must be filled?

The next step was to develop product/service features that would respond to their targeted customers' needs and to develop processes able to produce the product/service features. The planning team (marketing, engineering, manufacturing, and administration), by working together in developing the strategy, made realistic plans, and the process saved time. For example, marketing did not develop a strategy only to find out that it wasn't feasible from a manufacturing point of view, and so on.

2. Quality Control

Each functional area had set, for various activities, targets for appropriate time periods throughout the year. As part of marketing's plan, for instance, specific targets were set for sales, profits, and for activities leading to achieving required sales, profits, and quality criteria. Targets were later measured against actual performance. Any deviations from the plan were analyzed and corrections would were made.

3. Quality Improvement

Central to the whole planning effort was constant improvement. It was recognized that ". . . this is a race where there is no finish line." Each functional area determined activities that should be improved. Work schedules were then set up to make sure that improvements would be made. They also realized that in the next year, further improvements would be made.

Other Methods–Less than Ideal

The development of the Micron marketing plan was the result of the "ideal" process. All of the major powers of the firm had a say in devising the strategy and annual business plan.

But that's not the way it's always done. In some firms the business plan is driven by the marketing plan. Marketing decides what to produce or what services to offer. Manufacturing/operations and finance have little opportunity to contribute, and that's too bad. Usually other functional area managers have valuable insights about the firm and its markets, which would make the plan more realistic. Furthermore, if marketing calls all the major shots, there will be a weak management team. What strong manufacturing/operations manager would put up with such secondary status?

In some firms the business plan is driven by the manufacturing/operations plan. Manufacturing/operations decides what can be produced, and then it's up to marketing to sell it. All of the drawbacks shown above apply, and then some.

Some planning procedures, on the surface, seem even more bizarre. In one firm each functional area develops an overall plan and then submits it to the CEO. The CEO then decides which plan to follow and functional areas then develop their plans to meet the accepted overall plan. This method involves a lot of unnecessary plan preparation. Furthermore, this procedure shuts off valuable interchange between functional areas that could take place during the planning process.

HOW THE MARKETING PLAN TIES IN
WITH THE DIVERSIFIED COMPANY'S
PLANNING PROCESS

The organizational structure in a business unit or a single-industry company usually follows functional lines. Top management understands the industry and is very involved in planning the firm's strategy.

On the other hand, in a highly diversified company, top corporate managers usually have little involvement in developing a business unit's strategy. Members of top corporate management may have had extensive experience in one or two industries. But, in general, they will know less about specific industries than the business units' general managers. Or, when the number of businesses of the company is great, sheer magnitude may keep top corporate management from extensive involvement in strategy development for each of the businesses, although business units' plans are, of course, subject to corporate approval.

Let's take a look at the most common practice of planning in a diversified company. For simplicity, let's assume a corporation with just two tiers, the corporate and the business unit (see Figure 1.7).

Corporate top management provides business units with statements spelling out broad areas of businesses in which they can operate, commonly called "mission statements." Corporate top management also provides general economic guidelines (such as GDP and inflation), planning formats, and timetables. Business units then develop plans to meet the sales, profit, and cash flow goals.

Sometimes corporate top management sets sales, profit, and cash flow performance goals for business units. But more often it's up to business unit managers to set these goals themselves (they usually have a good idea what corporate top management expects). Planning at the business unit level is then carried on essentially the same way as in the Micron example.

The business units' completed plans are then sent to corporate. Corporate top management may require modifications or may even reject some plans. Through this process corporate decides: (1) the resource allocation among business units; (2) that some units should be divested; and/or (3) that acquisitions are needed for the corporation to achieve its goals.

Compromise Methods

How corporate planning is carried out can vary widely. Here are two examples of differently structured planning teams.

Company A has two business units, one with sales of $25 million, the other with sales of $5 million. In this case, the corporate level, consisting of the chairman of the board and the president, is actively involved in the planning of both business units.

FIGURE 1.7

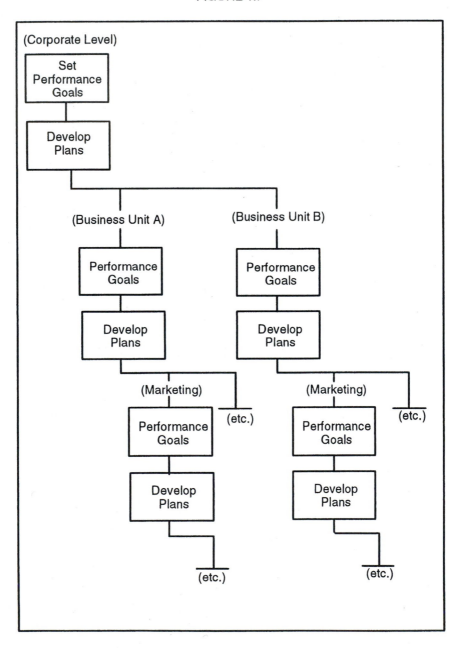

Another diversified firm, Company B, has four business units. However, one unit accounts for 90 percent of the firm's sales and profits. The CEO is very involved in planning with this major business unit. Planning for the other business units is carried out similarly to the common practice described in Figure 1.7. Given the specifics of these situations, there's nothing wrong with either of these planning approaches.

WHAT IS MARKETING'S ROLE AT THE CORPORATE LEVEL?

If there is a marketing person at the corporate level, his or her usual role will be to review the business units' plans from a marketing perspective. Most often the development of the units' marketing plans is the responsibility of each business unit, although the corporate marketing executive may assist. The more diverse the company, the less likely it is that there will be a corporate marketing executive.

POINTS LEARNED

1. In a single-industry company or a business unit of a diversified firm, the business plan consists of strategies and plans for the company (or business unit).
2. The business plan provides direction for the annual plans of the functional areas–including marketing.
3. Total quality planning requires that functional areas work together in developing the business plan.

LOOKING AHEAD

Next, let's take a look, specifically, at the marketing planning process.

INTRODUCTION

The Need to Build Total
Quality into Your Marketing Plan

The Need for a Formal
Marketing Plan

Involvement: The Key to Successful
Total Quality Planning

How to Make the Plan a Living
Document

The "Ideal" Method

The Micron Case

The Role of the Marketing Plan
in the Business Plan

The Marketing Planning
Process–An Overview

The Marketing Planning Process: An Overview

Marketing planning is a process. The process is finding the answers to six questions. Answer these questions and you will have your annual marketing plan.

Question 1. Where are you now?

Question 2. Where will you be if you continue your present strategy and operating plans?

Question 3. Where do you want to be? Will there be a gap between where you'll be and where you want to be if you continue your present strategy and operating plans?

Question 4. What should be your overall strategy to achieve your short- and long-term performance goals?

Question 5. What should you be doing next year to make sure you're on strategy and that you'll accomplish your short-term performance goals?

Question 6. How should you monitor your plan's performance?

Let's look more closely at each of these six questions.

Question 1. Where Are You Now?

To determine this, you must examine your strengths, weaknesses, opportunities, and threats as they exist today (hereinafter referred to as SWOTs: Present). SWOTs: Present provides you with knowledge about the current status of your markets, distribution channels, competition (both direct and indirect), and technology, about the economy and government regulations, and finally about your company itself.

In general, SWOTs: Present highlights today's major opportunities and problems. It is the base for planning, both strategic and annual. In fact, this is probably the most important part of the planning process. How you perceive yourself–your current problems and opportunities–is the foundation of the remaining sections of the marketing plan. If an error is made here then you're "building a house on a foundation of sand."

But do companies usually have a good understanding of their current situations? Take these case examples:

- The president of a medium-sized manufacturing company had been pleased with his company's sales and profit growth rates. But he was stunned to find that once sales and profits were adjusted for inflation, his company's increases were almost flat.
- A bank was considering closing a branch located on the ground floor of a high-rise office building. The branch had $200 million in deposits. Management believed loss of deposits would be minimal since the branch was located only one block from the bank's main office. Most depositors would probably switch to the main office. Still, because of the size of the potential loss, they brought in a consultant to do a feasibility study. The consultant's findings projected that the bank would lose over one-half of its deposits if it closed the branch. Most of the large depositors were lawyers located in the building, who, because of its convenience, used the branch to deposit funds for trust accounts and the like. If the bank closed the branch, it would be at a location disadvantage to two other banks (in fact, three, if another bank placed a branch in the vacated space). Consequently, the bank did not close down the branch.

  The bank was wise in bringing in a consultant for this study. But one wonders at the opportunities the bank might have missed–and would still be missing–because of a similar lack of understanding of other parts of its business.

- A glass manufacturer had been allocating a sizeable percentage of its marketing budget to advertising. Management was surprised to learn (as a tangential result of a consultant's study) that its large advertising budget was totally ineffective in stimulating dealers to specify its brand of glass. The advertising (in fact, the entire marketing program) was not directed toward its target market's key buying motives.

How could these companies have developed realistic marketing plans without understanding their current situations? It's easy to see that they might overlook both market opportunities and ways to improve their operating efficiency.

But are these isolated examples? Surprisingly, many firms do not have a solid grasp of present problems and opportunities. An executive vice-president of a large market research company once commented on this puzzling fact. Many of his company's clients, he said, lacked well-organized data bases. In fact, many did not even have a list of their key customers.

Of course, in all companies there's no shortage of beliefs about the firm's marketing strengths and weaknesses. Unfortunately, too many of these beliefs are myths. The myths may have been fact at one time. But what is "believed to be" and "what is" no longer match.

All action stems from the SWOTs: Present, no matter whether the examination is analytical or intuitive. Don't underestimate the importance of a thorough SWOTs analysis. Bruce Henderson, the founder of Boston Consulting Group, said it best when he said, "The successes [and conversely, failures] of the present must be fully understood before any constructive change can be made."[14]

SWOTs: Present, then, is to be a "snapshot" of the marketing strengths and limitations of your firm as they exist today. Of course you'll probably go back several years to establish trends–many companies use a five-year time span.

To answer "Where are you now?" first examine your company's (or business unit's) overall performance. This information will help you better understand the situation facing your company, thus placing your task in a sharper perspective.

Next, determine your major sources of volume. Which products/

services are increasing in importance? Which are decreasing? Then, what target markets are you now serving with your current products/services? Where should you concentrate your planning efforts?

Finally, develop performance profiles for each of your products/services-target markets. More specifically, each performance profile will include:

- *The Marketplace* (the target market, distribution channels, direct competition, and other external market forces)
- *Internal* (your company's performance relating to this product/service-target market)
- *Critical Summary* (issues of major importance generated by The Marketplace and Internal performance profiles)

The end result of your SWOTs: Present analysis, the *Performance Profile: Critical Summary*, must be more than a collection of facts. It must suggest corrective action, what needs to be done concerning major problems and opportunities. Of course, it's too early to recommend action now. You must first take a look at SWOTs: Future.

If you've done a thorough job on your SWOTs: Present analysis, you'll likely know more facts about the product/service-target market than anyone else in the firm. The value? *In a country of blind people, a person with one eye is king.*

Question 2. Where Will You Be if You Continue Your Present Strategy and Operating Plans?

To determine this, you must examine your strengths, weaknesses, opportunities, hereinafter and threats as they will be in the future (after this referred to as SWOTs: Future).

SWOTs: Future provides an understanding of your future operating environment. More specifically SWOTs: Future is a projection of industry conditions: the target market; distribution channels; competition (both direct and indirect); technology; economy; and governmental regulations.

Then, assuming that you follow a no-change strategy, SWOTs: Future will also highlight your future competitive position and will provide estimates of your sales and profits.

Unfortunately, too many marketing managers underestimate the importance of SWOTs: Present and SWOTs: Future. Consequently, they do not spend adequate time analyzing them. Instead, they jump into developing strategies and action plans without a proper base.

The result: flawed plans. It's just like painting a wall that hasn't been properly prepared.

> The preparation of the wall–crack filling, smoothing and sanding–is the all-important stage. [SWOTs: The Present and Future]. However, it is time-consuming, tedious and not obviously productive.

> Painting the wall is fun–a tangible achievement . . . [Plan Development]. However, if the objective was to provide a smooth, glossy finish, it will be impossible to achieve without good preparation.[15]

Question 3. Where Do You Want to Be? Will There Be a Gap Between Where You'll Be and Where You Want to Be if You Continue Your Present Strategy and Plans?

Gap analysis is the process of comparing your forecasts, assuming *no* change in your present strategies and operating plans, with management's performance goals (usually sales and some measure of profit).

There will usually be a gap. Gap analysis shows the degree of change required in order to achieve goals (either mandated or set by yourself). It answers the question, "Why should we change?"

Question 4. What Should Be Your Overall Strategy to Achieve Your Short- and Long-Term Performance Goals?

Given a planning gap, what should your game plan be in light of your present and future strengths, weaknesses, opportunities, and threats?

Now your firm, like all firms, has a longer-range plan. Sometimes it's clearly articulated. Sometimes it's not. But it's there. If it's not explicitly stated, make sure you know what it is.

In a total quality environment, management's participation helps ensure an understanding of the firm's long-range plan. But regardless of your situation, while developing your annual marketing plan, give thought to your firm's longer-range plan. No sense going off in the wrong direction.

Question 5. What Should You Be Doing Next Year to Make Sure You're on Strategy and That You'll Accomplish Your Short-Term Performance Goals?

The business plan, whether it is explicit or implicit, provides the general direction for achieving performance goals. Your annual marketing plan, which is derived from the business plan, tells you what to do throughout the next year. Your marketing plan must show how you will meet your short-term performance goals while also conforming to the business plan's strategy. Your marketing plan will include, for example, sales targets, detailed action plans, documented timetables and responsibilities, and budgets.

Question 6. How Should You Monitor Your Plan's Performance?

Your annual marketing plan must provide the scheme for monitoring performance throughout the year. Your plan format must lend itself to control purposes. At a minimum, there must be a written plan for every product/service-target market, including those elements mentioned above (Question 5). Then, if you are developing marketing plans for more than one product/service-target market, you'll also need a summary plan to better enable you to monitor overall operations.

Answering these six questions is marketing planning. The remainder of this book is organized to help you get and organize your answers–by following eight planning steps.

Six Major Questions	*The Eight Planning Steps*
1. Where are you now?	Step 1. SWOTs: Present. Gain an overall perspective by historical analysis of total sales, expenses and profits, and of sales and profits by products/services.

Step 2. SWOTs: Present (continued). To help decide where to concentrate planning efforts, list markets currently served with present products/services and analyze by sales and profits.

Step 3. SWOTs: Present (continued). Develop performance profiles for each product/service-target market.

2. Where will you be if you continue your present strategy and operating plans?

Step 4. SWOTs: Future. For each product service-target market, forecast market environment, target market's demand and your sales and profits (assuming you continue your present strategy).

3. Where is it you want to be? What will be the gap if you continue your present strategy and operating plans?

Step 5. Gap Analysis.

4. What should be your overall strategy to achieve your short- and long-term performance goals?

Step 6. Examination of options and and strategy selection.

Step 7. Strategy documentation and evaluation.

5. What should you be doing next year to make sure you're on strategy and that you'll accomplish your short-term performance goals?

Step 8. Fleshing out, documenting, and formatting the annual marketing plan.

6. How should you monitor your plan's performance?

In actual practice, the planning process seldom moves neatly from Step 1 through Step 8. Backtracking may be required. The annual marketing plan, for instance, may reveal that you can't meet performance goals given the current strategy. If so, you'll have to go back to Step 6 and develop a strategy that can meet your desired performance goals. Or you'll have to return to Step 5 and work with management to develop more realistic goals.

POINTS LEARNED

1. Eight planning steps make up the planning process.
2. Although these steps are presented 1-8, rarely does the planning process move in sequence. Backtracking is usually required.

LOOKING AHEAD

We're ready to start on the eight planning steps. The first step: SWOTs: Present.

SECTION II:

THE EIGHT PLANNING STEPS

THE EIGHT PLANNING STEPS

Step 1. SWOTs: Present. Gain an Overall Perspective by Historical Analysis of Total Sales, Expenses and Profits, and of Sales and Profits by Products/Services

Step 2. SWOTs: Present (cont.). To Help Decide Where to Concentrate Planning Efforts, List Target Markets Currently Served with Present Products/Services and Analyze by Sales and Profits

Step 3. SWOTs: Present (cont.). Develop Performance Profiles for Each Product/Service-Target Market

Step 4. SWOTs: Future. For Each Product/Service-Target Market, Forecast Market Environment, Target Market's Demand, and Your Sales and Profits (Assuming You Continue Your Present Strategy)

Step 5. Gap Analysis

Step 6. Examination of Strategic Options and Strategy Selection

Step 7. Strategy Documentation and Evaluation

Step 8. Fleshing Out, Documenting, and Formatting the Annual Marketing Plan

Step 1. SWOTs: Present

Gain an Overall Perspective by Historical Analysis of Total Sales, Expenses and Profits, and of Sales and Profits by Products/Services

BUSINESS-UNIT ANALYSIS

Examine your business-unit data first. If you're in charge of marketing, you do this as a matter of course. But make an overall analysis of your business unit even if your responsibility is limited to preparing an annual marketing plan for a product or service. Such an analysis will give you a better understanding of your business unit's growth, profits, and cash flow. You'll gain a sharper perspective of the financial opportunities and threats facing your business unit. And, you'll be able to compare the performance of your product/service to that of the overall performance of the business unit.

Examine Financial Statements

You'll want to analyze three statements: profit-and-loss, balance sheet (if you're examining company data), and cash flow. You can learn a lot from looking at one year's statements. But analyzing historical trends usually yields better insights.

Looking at the profit-and-loss statements, what does the sales trend suggest? If sales growth has been stagnant or declining, there may be great pressure to increase sales. What about gross margins? Are they being squeezed, year by year? What's the trend of expenses? Return on sales?

Turning to the balance sheets, what's the trend of key ratios, such as leverage (debt/equity), liquidity (current, quick), and activity (inventory turns and average collection period)?

Examine your statements of cash flow. Is the cash situation satisfactory? Is it improving? Or is it getting worse?

Make Industry Comparisons

Business unit statistics and ratios, such as order backlog and inventory turnover, can by themselves be helpful. However, additional insights can usually be gained by comparing company statistics and ratios with industry averages. For example, even if your sales and profits have been increasing, how do they look in relation to comparative companies.

Your products/services and target markets probably will not be exactly comparable with the composite of the firms that make up the industry average. Still, a comparison of statistics and ratios may point out that you're doing far better than most, indicating that, at least in this industry, you're doing many things right. Or, conversely, these comparisons may show that you're below average, signaling that change is probably warranted.

Sources for industry averages include Dun & Bradstreet and your industry association.

Adjust Financial Statements for Inflation

Perhaps your business unit does not adjust sales, profits, etc., for inflation. If so, think about making such compensations. (See Appendix B for methodology.)

Inflation can distort information. For example, in 1983, the president of a small firm was shocked to learn that between 1973-1982 his company's sales, when adjusted for inflation, were down over 50 percent. He had thought sales were merely flat because he had been monitoring them using nominal dollars instead of constant dollars.

In another case (see Figure 2.1), a wholesaling company's current sales were overstated by 24 percent because of inflated dollars. Furthermore, these inflated dollars made other analyses misleading. To wit, sales (in dollars) per employee (a critical measurement for wholesalers) was overstated by $20,000. This led management to believe that the sales (in dollars) per employee ratio was satisfactory. In fact, employee productivity had declined by 27 percent.

FIGURE 2.1

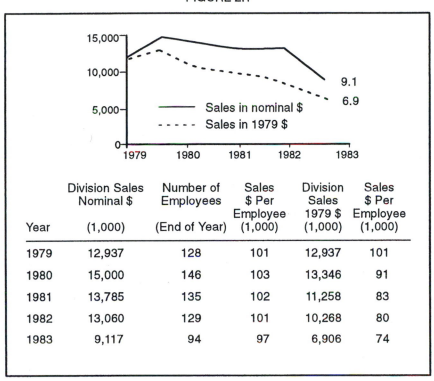

Year	Division Sales Nominal $ (1,000)	Number of Employees (End of Year)	Sales $ Per Employee (1,000)	Division Sales 1979 $ (1,000)	Sales $ Per Employee (1,000)
1979	12,937	128	101	12,937	101
1980	15,000	146	103	13,346	91
1981	13,785	135	102	11,258	83
1982	13,060	129	101	10,268	80
1983	9,117	94	97	6,906	74

A look at the Micron case also shows the importance of dealing with dollars adjusted for inflation. A comparison of FY '87 and FY '92 P & Ls (unadjusted) points out how, among other changes, sales have increased by 20 percent. (Note Figure 2.2.) However, when adjusted for inflation, using the CPI-U, All Items, the picture changes, as Figure 2.3 points out.

Sales, instead of increasing by 20 percent, have declined by 2 percent. Furthermore, the decline in expenditures for R&D and selling are greater than indicated by nominal dollar comparison. In fact, $407,000 of Micron's $416,000 (about 98 percent) increase in contribution to corporate can be attributed to cutbacks in R&D and selling expenditures (versus 57 percent under nominal dollar comparison).

FIGURE 2.2

P & L (in $1,000)	1987	1992	$ Change 1987-92	% Change 1987-92
Sales	2,000	2,400	+400	+20
Cost of Goods Sold	920	1,100	+180	+20
Gross Profit	1,080	1,300	+220	+20
Expenses				
R&D	300	180	−120	−40
Selling	340	200	−140	−41
Advertising	50	60	+10	+20
Administration Expenses	200	210	+10	+5
Total Expenses	890	650	−240	−27
Contribution to Corporate	190	650	+460	+242

Inflation, even in years of relatively low inflation–say 4 percent–does add up. If you're using a five-year analysis, that amounts to, compounded, 21.7 percent. For many companies that would create quite a distortion.

PRODUCT/SERVICE ANALYSIS

Examine the present and historical sales and profits of products/services (more detailed analyses, such as by sales persons, territory, or customers, will come later). Ideally, you'd have pretax income for each product/service. But most likely that will not be the case. You'll have to use some lesser measure of profit, such as gross profit.

Set up your analysis so you can make comparisons from year to year. See Figure 2.4 (this table assumes that you can measure gross profit for each product/service). Again, constant dollars will give you a better perspective. But suppose that you have a number of products/services that you market as a line of products, such as varieties of canned soup? Then analyze these as a group.

How Accurately Does Your Organization Measure Costs?

Be sure to analyze allocated costs. The way your organization is allocating costs may be a suitable procedure for custodial purposes, such as profit-and-loss reports for income tax purposes and share-holder reports. But for analyzing the profit and loss of products and services it may fall woefully short.

Here's why. For example, suppose your organization follows traditional full-cost accounting, utilizing allocated costs. This is the way it works:

Full-Cost Accounting

Sales

  − Cost of Goods Sold (Purchases of components, raw materials and direct and indirect manufacturing costs)

  = Gross Profits

  − Operating Expenses (Including general and administration overhead allocation)

  = Pretax Income

Such an accounting procedure may send false signals. Examine the statement found in Figure 2.5, which shows year-end earnings for the ABCD Industrial Company (fictitious).

At first glance it appears that ABCD's private label group should be dropped, since it has caused a $624,000 drain on company earnings. Yet closer examination reveals that the private label group has absorbed $879,000 of allocated costs–$667,000 of manufacturing overhead and $212,000 of general and administrative costs. Could manufacturing overhead and general and administrative costs be cut back by $879,000 if the private group were discontinued? In many cases allocated costs are fixed or sunk and may or may not be directly related to whether a particular product group is or is not discontinued.

Activity-Based Costing (ABC)

Sometimes called activity-based accounting, ABC is a better approach to determining profitability than traditional full-cost accounting.

If your organization has adopted activity-based costing (ABC), you can skim the rest of this step. But be sure you carefully analyze major cost drivers and how costs are allocated.

FIGURE 2.3

P & L (in $1,000)	1987 (nominal)	1987 (adjusted to '92 $$)	1992	$ Change 1987-92	% Change 1987-92
Sales	2,000	2,460	2,400	−60	−2
Cost of Goods Sold	920	1,132	1,100	−32	−2
Gross Profit	1,080	1,328	1,300	−28	−2
Expenses					
R&D	300	369	180	−189	−51
Selling	340	418	200	−218	−52
Advertising	50	61	−60	−1	−2
Administration Expenses	200	246	210	−36	−15
Total Expenses	890	1,094	650	−444	−41
Contribution to Corporate	190	234	650	+416	+178

ABC is defined as:

A system that focuses on *activities* as the fundamental cost objects and uses these building blocks for compiling the costs of products and other cost objects.[1]

Costs are calculated, individually, for each activity. To do this, major cost drivers are determined within each activity. And here are the basic differences between ABC and traditional full cost accounting: (1) No single factor, such as labor, determines manufacturing/operations costs, and (2) Activities cut across department lines. The product or service cost is then "built up" from the cost of the various activities required to manufacture the product or deliver the service.

A "rudimentary" ABC example is given in Figure 2.6. Note how the costs of "miles to store" and "yard time" were split apart. Under traditional full-cost accounting, this would probably not have been done. (If you'd like an excellent easy-to-get source on ABC, see Terrance P. Pore, "A New Tool for Managing Costs," *Fortune*, June 14, 1993, pp. 124-129, which provides a good overview of ABC, giving examples of how companies have used ABC to more accurately determine costs.)

FIGURE 2.4

PRODUCT/SERVICE SALES AND PROFITABILITY	19 ___ $ Volume	19 ___ % Total	19 ___ $ Volume	19 ___ % Total	19 ___ $ Volume	19 ___ % Total	19 ___ $ Volume	19 ___ % Total	% Change $ Volume	% Change % Total
PRODUCT/SERVICE (										
SALES										
PROFIT										
PRODUCT/SERVICE (										
SALES										
PROFIT										
PRODUCT/SERVICE (										
SALES										
PROFIT										
PRODUCT/SERVICE (										
SALES										
PROFIT										
PRODUCT/SERVICE (										
SALES										
PROFIT										

FIGURE 2.5

STATEMENT OF EARNINGS BY COMPANY/PRODUCT GROUP
THE ABCD COMPANY
YEAR ENDED DECEMBER 31, 19

(in $1,000)

| | Total Company | Product Group | | |
		Consumer	Industrial	Private Label
NET SALES	$20,273	$3,413	$13,671	$3,189
Cost of Goods Sold				
Variable Expenses (Material & Labor)	$10,184	$1,561	$ 6,216	$2,407
Fixed Expenses (Manufacturing Overhead)	2,876	309	1,900	667
	$13,060	$1,870	$ 8,116	$3,074
Gross Profit	$ 7,213	$1,543	$ 5,555	$ 115
Gross Margin (%)	35.6	45.2	40.6	3.6
Selling Expenses				
Promotion	$ 2,860	$ 437	$ 2,043	$ 380
Freight	662	113	446	103
Other	819	158	617	44
	$ 4,341	$ 708	$ 3,106	$ 527
GENERAL & ADMINISTRATIVE EXPENSES	$ 1,364	$ 232	$ 920	$ 212
BEFORE TAX PROFIT	$ 1,508	$ 603	$ 1,529	$(624)
RETURN ON SALES (%)	7.4	17.6	11.1	(19.6)

FIGURE 2.6.

'Rudimentary' ABC efforts yield big results for Spartan

For several years, Spartan Stores Inc., Grand Rapids, Mich., has been quietly building a respectable reputation as a wholesaler whose size belies a driving commitment to innovative thinking and practices.

Like many companies, Spartan has been re-engineering or reorganizing itself to stay competitive and become more efficient. Spartan President and Chief Executive Officer Patrick M. Quinn told *Grocery Marketing* the wholesaler has achieved significant savings through what might be called a "soft entry" into the world of Activity Based Costing.

"The example I use of how we began this kind of thing in a very rudimentary way is how we changed our freight (rate) system around about three months ago," he said.

Challenged by the necessity to develop a more realistic rate structure, Quinn said Spartan faced a series of tough questions.

"How do you make it fair?" he asked. "How do you make it realistic? And how do you charge people for what they use?"

The solution was to apply some of the principles of ABC to the problem. "We assigned a cost of so much for yard time and so much per mile to the store," Quinn said.

Unlike a pure ABC approach that would establish an actual per truck cost figure for yard time, Spartan used an approximate or "averaging" approach to fixing yard time cost. However, the wholesaler put considerable effort into determining the specific cost involved in having a truck sitting at a retailer's back door. The result of that analysis opened the door to significant savings.

"What we found," Quinn explained, "was that to have that truck at your door costs 67 cents a minute."

Spartan began billing its customers for this unloading time and, as Quinn explained, "The burden (for unloading efficiency) shifts to the retailer whose big concern becomes 'How fast can I get this truck out of here?'"

"We had (initially) projected a one hour and 10 minutes average unloading time, which would have still created a significant savings," Quinn added. "But the real average (for a Spartan customer to unload a truck) is actually 38 minutes."

Obviously the speeded-up unloading significantly reduces the wholesaler's costs, but Quinn was quick to add: "What this lets us say is, 'Here's what we're dealing with (in terms of cost), now how can we improve together.'"

Through ABC, he added, "You actually understand costs that nobody knew they had."

In response to the new policy, several Spartan customers have already adjusted their operations–reorganizing back rooms, reducing inventory and, as a result, reducing labor–and have begun to achieve significant cost reductions.

Of course, change is never universally well received. "When we first did this we had stores calling us saying, 'This is terrible, we can't do it,'" Quinn said, recalling a retailer who was unloading his deliveries by hand.

"We have one customer who took between seven and seven and a half hours to unload a truck," he said. "He didn't have a forklift and wasn't too happy with the new system.

"But when he called up I told him 'Put a pencil to it and, at 67 cents a minute, figure out exactly how long your payback period is if you buy a forklift.'"

The savings for the warehouse have been immense. Drivers' wages during the initial phase of the new policy were reduced by $195,000.

Ryan Mathews, "'Rudimentary' ABC Efforts Yield Big Results for Spartan," *Grocery Marketing*, August, 1993, p. 12.

ABC is not limited to process-costing systems. It can also be used for job orders. And ABC can be used by both service companies and manufacturing firms.

But what if your firm doesn't use ABC? Then, to examine historical costs, be sure to closely analyze how these costs were allocated. And, until your organization effectively implements ABC, consider analyzing profitability by using either contribution accounting or merchandising profit.

Using Contribution Accounting and/or Merchandising Profit

Contribution Accounting. Examine the illustration below.

Contribution Accounting

Sales

– Cost of Sales (Variable–purchases of components, raw materials and variable manufacturing costs directly traceable to this product)

= Gross Profit

– Operating Expenses (Other variable expenses directly traceable to this product)

= Contribution Margin

Note that implementing contribution accounting is not necessarily easy to do. In some firms you may need a rather sophisticated accounting system to isolate variable expenses. Then, too, contribution accounting is only acceptable for internal accounting purposes, which means extra work and expense for the accounting department.

Merchandising Profit. If you're dealing only with marketing expenses, consider merchandising profit–based mainly on factors you control, such as price and controllable marketing expense.[2]

Merchandising Profit

Sales

— Cost of Sales (Variable–purchases of components, raw materials and variable manufacturing cost directly traceable to this product)

= Gross Profit

— Controllable Marketing Expenses

= Merchandising Profit = Product Margin

The same drawbacks apply to merchandising profit as they did to contribution accounting.

POINTS LEARNED

1. Gain an overall perspective by examining your business unit first.
2. Look at three key statements: profit and loss, balance sheet, and cash flow.
3. Make industry comparisons.
4. Adjust financial statements for inflation. Even a moderate inflation rate–say 4 percent a year over a five-year time span–can cause major distortion during periods of sluggish growth.
5. Next, analyze present and historical sales and profits of products/services.
6. Consider using contribution accounting or merchandising profit if your firm does not use activity-based costing.

LOOKING AHEAD

Your next step is to analyze the sales and profits of each target market that each product/service serves. It's a necessary step to help you allocate your planning efforts.

THE EIGHT PLANNING STEPS

Step 1. SWOTs: Present. Gain an Overall Perspective by Historical Analysis of Total Sales, Expenses and Profits, and of Sales and Profits by Products/Services

Step 2. SWOTs: Present (cont.). To Help Decide Where to Concentrate Planning Efforts, List Target Markets Currently Served with Present Products/Services and Analyze by Sales and Profits

Step 3. SWOTs: Present (cont.). Develop Performance Profiles for Each Product/Service-Target Market

Step 4. SWOTs: Future. For Each Product/Service-Target Market, Forecast Market Environment, Target Market's Demand, and Your Sales and Profits (Assuming You Continue Your Present Strategy)

Step 5. Gap Analysis

Step 6. Examination of Strategic Options and Strategy Selection

Step 7. Strategy Documentation and Evaluation

Step 8. Fleshing Out, Documenting, and Formatting the Annual Marketing Plan

Step 2. SWOTs: Present (cont.)

To Help Decide Where to Concentrate Planning Efforts, List Target Markets Currently Served with Present Products/Services and Analyze by Sales and Profits

If you're only developing a marketing plan for one product/service-target market, you can skip this step. But if you're putting together a marketing plan for a number of products/services-target markets, then this step is essential.

Here's why. You know you're not going to have the time you'd like to devote to planning. So you're going to have to make compromises. You'll do what's logical. You'll spend your time planning for those products/services-target markets that are most important. Like those that promise the largest sales and profit volumes (no doubt the 80-20 principle is at work). Or those products/services-target markets that seem to be the real comers. Or those that are in trouble. The other products/services-target markets will receive lesser attention.

Allocating your planning efforts in this manner is pure common sense. It's something you'd do intuitively. But you need facts to help you make better judgments, and you need to put these facts together in a systematic way so you can better communicate your opinions and get inputs from others. This is vital in total quality planning. And this is what Step 2 is all about.

THE PROCESS

List Present Target Markets Served by Your Present Products/Services

Disregard (for now) what might be the ideal target markets. State what you're presently doing, not what you should be doing (you do that in Steps 6 and 7).

List your products/services-target markets according to your current practices on Figure 2.7. Note that Figure 2.7 is similar to Figure 2.4, except that Figure 2.7 includes a break out of products/services by target markets.

Your present practice may be to develop marketing strategies and programs for a group of products to be sold to a given target market; for example, varieties of canned condensed soup. In such situations, place each group of products/services under a single product/service-target market classification.

For some products/services, you may be selling the same product/service to more than one target market. If you've developed distinct marketing programs for each of these target markets, then list these target markets separately under each product/service.

For example, a manufacturer of a small diameter motor was selling the same motor to six different target markets. Because each market had differing technical and marketing assistance requirements, price sensitivities, and purchase quantities, the manufacturer had developed separate marketing programs for each of the six target markets. In completing Figure 2.7, this manufacturer would list these six markets separately.

Make sure you sufficiently describe each target market so that you will be able to distinguish one from another as you go through the planning steps.

All that you've done so far in Step 2 is describe your present target marketing practice for each product/service.

Track Sales, Profits, and Percentages of Totals

For each product/service-target market, record sales, profits, and percentages of total sales and profits. As you did in Figure 2.4, use constant dollars.

POINTS LEARNED

1. You're not going to have the time you'd like to have for planning. Help decide where to concentrate your planning efforts by analyzing your present products/services-target markets.

2. First, list present target markets served by your present products/services.
3. Then, for each product/service-target market, record sales, profits, and percentages of total sales.

LOOKING AHEAD

Now for each product/service-target market, here's what needs to be done:

Step 3.   SWOTs: Present. Develop performance profiles.

Step 4.   SWOTs: Future. Forecast market environment, target market's demand, and your sales and profits (assuming you continue your present strategy).

Step 5.   Gap Analysis. Where is it you want to be? Will you be able to get there with your present strategy and operating plans? If not, how big a gap must you close?

Step 6.   Examination of Strategic Options and Strategy Selection.

Step 7.   Strategic Documentation and Evaluation.

Step 8.   Fleshing Out, Documenting, and Formatting the Annual Marketing Plan.

These steps are covered in forthcoming sections.

OVERCOMING CONCERNS

If you're like some managers, right now you have two major doubts about this approach. First, you may know that your current marketing programs aren't satisfactory. Changes will have to be made. So you ask, "Why go through all the bother of studying what has been and what exists today?" Remember, "The successes [and conversely, failures] of the present must be fully understood before any constructive changes can be made.[1]

Let's look at an analogy. After being shellacked (or winning victoriously), what's the first thing a football coach would do in

FIGURE 2.7

	19___		19___		19___		19___		% Change	
	$ Volume	% Total	$ Volume	% Total	$ Volume	% Total	$ Volume	% Total	$ Volume	% Total
PRODUCT/SERVICE										
TARGET MARKET ( )										
SALES	— —	— —	— —	— —	— —	— —	— —	— —	— —	— —
PROFIT	— —	— —	— —	— —	— —	— —	— —	— —	— —	— —
PRODUCT/SERVICE										
TARGET MARKET ( )										
SALES	— —	— —	— —	— —	— —	— —	— —	— —	— —	— —
PROFIT	— —	— —	— —	— —	— —	— —	— —	— —	— —	— —
PRODUCT/SERVICE										
TARGET MARKET ( )										
SALES	— —	— —	— —	— —	— —	— —	— —	— —	— —	— —
PROFIT	— —	— —	— —	— —	— —	— —	— —	— —	— —	— —

preparation of the next game? You're right. The coach would re-view game films. And that's what you're doing by going through SWOTs: Present. So much for the first apprehension.

Now let's look at the second concern. In looking ahead, you saw that for each product/service-target market Steps 3 through 8 had to be completed. And given the number of marketing programs you have to develop . . . well, that's a lot of work. Reconcile yourself to the fact that you're already following these steps–only intuitively. So now you're just putting them in writing. And you know the advantages of making things explicit.

Make this approach practical by following these three guidelines:

1. If possible, subdivide the work. Can you set up product/ser-vice, brand, or market managers?
2. Only perform thorough examinations on the most important product/service-target market classifications. These would be those determined by sales and profit analysis. Examine such variables as source of volume, source of profitability, and whether sales and/or profits are rapidly growing or rapidly declining.
3. For less important products/services-target markets, follow the same steps, only less thoroughly. You're already doing these steps intuitively. But use the forms and checklists. They'll force more rigorous thinking and facilitate communication, and they will save you time.

Now all this may appear a little overwhelming when you realize that you have to repeat this process for each of the products/services-target markets you have, and then consolidate all the plans into one overall plan. One way to make the process easier is to make the system we just outlined into a step-by-step process. We will use the analogy of the loose binder with dividers. The first time you begin the planning process, you have a main section of the binder which is the old or original way of planning, and the other divided sections will be the new product/service-target market planning approach for *one* or *two* of the most important products/services-target markets. The main section will still be the largest of the sections. The process should be less intimidating since you are working on one or two planning units, and for the bulk of the planning you use the "same old method." Then next year, you pick another one or two products/ services-target markets to use the new approach on, and repeat the process on the products/services-target markets from the previous year. Each year, you are reducing the number of planning units in the main section and adding more dividers with the new plans. After this process is repeated a number of times, the main section becomes less important and each of the divided sections becomes more important.

Now you can keep this process up until all the product/service-target markets are now separately planned, or you can quit with some of the less important products/services-target markets left in the main section (no longer really the main section). Regardless, this process of using a notebook with dividers lets you break down the task into smaller steps, and most importantly, lets you focus your planning attention on the most important products/services-target markets first.

THE EIGHT PLANNING STEPS

Step 1. SWOTs: Present. Gain an Overall Perspective by Historical Analysis of Total Sales, Expenses and Profits, and of Sales and Profits by Products/ Services

Step 2. SWOTs: Present (cont.). To Help Decide Where to Concentrate Planning Efforts, List Target Markets Currently Served with Present Products/ Services and Analyze by Sales and Profits

 Step 3. SWOTs: Present (cont.). Develop Performance Profiles for Each Product/Service-Target Market

Step 4. SWOTs: Future. For Each Product/Service-Target Market, Forecast Market Environment, Target Market's Demand, and Your Sales and Profits (Assuming You Continue Your Present Strategy)

Step 5. Gap Analysis

Step 6. Examination of Strategic Options and Strategy Selection

Step 7. Strategy Documentation and Evaluation

Step 8. Fleshing Out, Documenting, and Formatting the Annual Marketing Plan

Step 3. SWOTs: Present (cont.)

Develop Performance Profiles for Each Product/Service-Target Market

COMMON PROBLEMS IN ANALYZING THE PRESENT

Too frequently this step is done poorly. For example, take a look at Figure 2.8. This chart typifies the problems of so many SWOTs: Present analyses. Assume that there are no other elements of the marketing mix that should be included. Further, assume that the ratings of competitive advantage, however obtained, are accurate.

There are at least two things wrong with this type of analysis: failure to indicate key success factors and failure to specify how the company compares with individual competitors.

Failure to Indicate Key Success Factors

For any market segment there are few quality dimensions, perhaps only one, in which a firm must excel to be successful. Now look again at Figure 2.8. Let's assume that for this product/service-target market that the quality dimension of accessibility (hours) is key. But what does the chart show?

It implies that the company's technical advice (training) and delivery capability are its weakest links. But what if these quality dimensions already met (or exceeded) acceptable quality standards? The company would pursue the wrong path if, as a result of this analysis, it began to skew its focus toward improving technical advice and delivery capability. The company would be far better off by improving its accessibility.

Failure to Specify How the Company Compares with Individual Competitors

Since competitors usually have varying strengths and weaknesses, your overall marketing strategy is likely to be more effective if you have a competitive plan of action for each major competitor. Sometimes you do not need to beat all of your competitors to meet your marketing objectives.

For example, there is the story of two men who were on safari in Africa. Foolishly they strayed from their Land Rover. Suddenly they spotted, off in the distance, a lion charging down upon them. One of the men sat down and started to put on his running shoes. The other shouted, "Are you crazy? You can't outrun the lion even with running shoes." The person putting on the running shoes, with a sly grin on his face, replied, "I don't have to outrun the lion. I only have to outrun you."

These are just two common pitfalls. There are a number of other traps, all of which can keep your SWOTs: Present from serving as a valuable tool for developing your marketing plan. We'll show you how to avoid these traps. Essential to preventing problems is organizing and analyzing critical factors and relationships in a systematic way. And to do this, performance profiles provide powerful guides.

FIGURE 2.8

Quality Dimensions:	Competitive Advantage Among the Best			Neutral Average			Competitive Disadvantage Below Average		
	10	9	8	7	6	5	4	3	2	1
Accessibility (Location)			✔							
Accessibility (Hours)			✔							
Technical Advice (Training)					✔					
Delivery					✔					
Extended Credit Terms		✔								

DEVELOPING PERFORMANCE PROFILES

You will need to complete three major types of performance profiles–*The Marketplace, Internal,* and *Critical Summary.*

Included in the text are completed performance profiles, using the Micron case as an example. Since the amount of data in the Micron case is limited, these profiles contain less information than would normally be expected.

You'll note that the performance profile forms include columns for both the present and the future (with the exception of *Performance Profile: Internal*). For now, ignore the future columns. These are to be completed during SWOTs: Future.

The Performance Profile: The Marketplace

In completing this profile you will analyze four key elements:

- The Target Market
- Distribution Channels (other than direct sales force)
- Direct Competition
- Other External Forces

1. The Marketplace: The Target Market

Let's walk through the steps included in Figure 2.9. Note that each of the sections below, 1.1 through 1.4, explains how to complete corresponding numbered sections on Figure 2.9.

1.1. Target Market (description). Fully describe the target market you're now serving. This description should enable you to tell at a glance how this segment differs from other market segments. For example, Micron's target market was "highly sophisticated scientists at universities, government and research laboratories," which differed from the other market segment, "laboratory technicians that perform routine analysis in less technical laboratories."

1.2. Key Buying Motives. Keep in mind that your target market is not purchasing products/services. Rather it is buying benefits. Solutions to problems. Think in terms of quality as defined by the target market.

FIGURE 2.9

PERFORMANCE PROFILE: The Marketplace
1.   Target Market

Category	The Present 1992	The Future 19__
1.1 Target Market (description)	Highly specialized research scientists at universities, government and industry research laboratories	
1.2 Key Buying Motives	Extensive Applications High performance and reliability Immediate service	
1.3 Other Factors	Mature Stage	
1.4 Target Market Demand	Trend to Date (describe) and Volume (if available) ≅ $4,800,000 Demand flat has increased 10% in the past five years.	Forecast: 19__ _____ 19__ _____ Inflation Adjustments

Although the target market has a number of purchasing motives, some are more important than others. In Micron's case, the key buying motives are extensive applications, high performance, reliability, and immediate service.

What about price? Micron's target market is not highly price sensitive. The acceptable price band is relatively wide. In some other markets, of course, it's a different situation. For example, ready-mix cement sold to contractors is so highly price sensitive that the price band is usually a single point. In this situation, price would be a key buying motive.

To help identify key buying motives from other decision criteria, Rausch has suggested ranking buying motives on a scaled chart.[1] Figure 2.10 is an adaptation from Rausch, using as comparisons the buying motives of the two market segments from the Micron case.

If you have trouble ranking buying motives, and you cannot find satisfactory answers by questioning your target market, consider using conjoint analysis. In this technique, respondents rank various packages of attributes (different aspects of quality) for a given product/service. A computer program facilitates packaging of the attributes as well as ranking the results. A more detailed explanation of conjoint analysis can be found in almost any current book on marketing research.[2]

You may find, for example, that some customers in your target market are highly price sensitive while others are not. If so, you are probably serving a target market that is too broadly focused. You may be trying to be all things to all people. When it comes time to develop your strategy and annual marketing plan (Steps 6-8), you will want to consider resegmenting your market.

1.3. Other Factors. Besides key buying motives, there may be other noteworthy factors. Let's look at three.

Where is the product/service on the life cycle curve? Its location on this curve can be a valuable indication of the most suitable marketing strategy. You may find that you are close to a transition point, such as moving from maturity to decline. If so, a change in strategy may soon be necessary.

Have the target market firms shifted to different geographic areas, such as the Sun Belt?

FIGURE 2.10

Buying Motives, by Market Segment		
Laboratory technicians		Highly Sophisticated Scientists
	Most Important	
Price	10	Extensive application, high performance, reliability
	9	
	8	Immediate repair service
	7	
Immediate repair service	6	Price
	5	
Extensive application, high performance, reliability	4	
	3	
	2	
	1	
	0	
	Less important	

Who is involved in the decision-making process? In many marketing situations, the actual buyer is not the only one involved. For example, in an industrial plant the purchasing agent may write the order, but several engineers (influencers) may recommend which product/service to buy.

The check sheet in Figure 2.11 includes these, and other factors, that you might wish to include in your analysis.

Data from the Micron case suggest that the product's stage (maturity) on the life cycle curve is the only entry for the *Target Market (Other Factors)* check sheet. This entry was considered important enough to be highlighted on Figure 2.9.

FIGURE 2.11

PERFORMANCE PROFILE: The Marketplace (continued)

1.3 Target Market (Other Factors)

Characteristics of Target Market	Trend to Date	The Present 1992	The Future 19____
Position of Product/ Service on Life Cycle Curve	*[life cycle curve graph: Introduction, Growth, Maturity, Decline; Total Industry Sales vs. Time]*	Maturity	
Cyclical Factors	Same/Changing		
Seasonal Factors	Same/Changing		
Geographical Location	Same/Changing		
Size of Target Market Firms	Larger/Same/Smaller		
Concentration of "Key Accounts" in Industry	Increasing/Same/ Decreasing		
Backward Integration	Extensive/Same Non-Existent		
Bargaining Power	Greater/Same/Less		
Rate of Growth of New Customers in Target Market	Increasing/Same/ Decreasing		
Number of Customers in Target Market	Increasing/Same/ Decreasing		
Purchasing Influencers	Non-Existent/Same/ Changing		
Other Characteristics (Specify)			

1.4. Target Market Demand. The target market's demand for a given type of product/service is the target market's total purchases of this type of product/service from both you and your competitors. This should not be confused with industry demand. For example, in the Micron case the oscilloscope industry demand was $250 million. But the industry consists of two segments: the "high-end ($200,000) users" and the "low-end ($40,000-$45,000) users." These are two distinct markets. Knowledge of the oscilloscope industry's demand would not be very helpful to Micron in developing a marketing plan for the high-end segment. The two segments which make up the industry have quite different sales and growth rates.

You may be able to get relatively accurate numbers to determine your target market's present demand and its past growth rate. If so, consider yourself fortunate. More likely, you'll have to resort to using rough approximations. If you know, for example, that the trend has been up, but you do not know the percentage, simply indicate the trend by use of an arrow and make a rough approximation (such as 10 percent-30 percent a year).

Appendix A discusses various types of forecasting techniques, some of which may be appropriate to help you to determine the past and present purchases of your target market.

2. The Marketplace: Distribution Channels
(Other than Direct Sales Force)

If you and your competitors sell direct to your target market, skip this section (your direct sales force will be examined while completing the *Performance Profile: Internal*).

Examine the check sheet in Figure 2.12. Assume that you, or your competitors, have a multistep distribution channel; for example, manufacturer–wholesalers–target market. Then analyze each stage of the distribution channel. (Since Micron sells direct to its target market, no example is provided.)

2.1. Sales by Distribution Channels. What distribution channels do you and/or your competitors use to reach your target market? If more than one type is used, for example, brokers and agents, list each type separately.

FIGURE 2.12

PERFORMANCE PROFILE: The Marketplace (continued)

2. Distribution Channels (other than direct sales force)

Category	The Present			The Future 19____		
	% of Market	Trend ↑; -or ↓	Your Market Share	% of Market	Trend ↑; -or ↓	Your Market Share
2.1 Sales, by Distribution 2.2 Channels						
_____	_____	_____	_____	_____	_____	_____
_____	_____	_____	_____	_____	_____	_____
_____	_____	_____	_____	_____	_____	_____

Distributor Channel Analysis (Channel _____)

2.3   Key Buying Motives   _____   _____

_____   _____

_____   _____

_____   _____

2.4   Other Factors

Distributor Channel Analysis (Channel _____)

2.3   Key Buying Motives   _____   _____

_____   _____

_____   _____

_____   _____

2.4   Other Factors

2.2. Percent of Market, Trend, and Your Market Share. What is each channel's percentage share of the total sales to the target market (target market demand)? What are the trends to date? What is your market share of each channel's sales? Again, you probably don't have exact information. Make your best estimates.

2.3. Key Buying Motives. For each of the channels you listed above, what are the key buying motives? Determine these in the same manner as you did for your target market.

Make sure that you really understand the channels' key buying motives. Too often there's a lack of understanding. Furthermore, not much effort is spent trying to determine them. In fact, less than 1 percent of manufacturers' research budgets is spent to gain a better understanding of trade buyers' key buying motives.[3] And this is too bad. Conditions now often require more trade promotions. For instance, in 1987 it was reported that of the $100 billion that companies spent on promotions, approximately two-thirds of this was spent on trade promotion incentives.[4]

2.4. Other Factors. What major changes have taken place within each distribution channel, such as size, sophistication, and/or frequency of purchases? Figure 2.13 provides a more complete list.

3. The Marketplace: Direct Competition

Refer to Figure 2.14. (Again we pick up the Micron example).

3.1.1. Identify Direct Competitors. Direct competitors are those selling similar products/services to the same target market as you are. Be sure the competitors you list really are direct competitors. Many companies may offer somewhat similar products/services, but serve different market segments. As we have seen, this is true of the Micron case. The large firms servicing the market for the low end research oscilloscopes are not really in direct competition with Micron. They are selling a different product to a different market segment.

Determining direct competitors is usually quite easy. You probably already know who they are. But if you don't, find out by talking with a representative sample of your target market. Identify those three to four competitors who can do you the most competitive damage. Those competitors who could "blow your socks off on any given day."

FIGURE 2.13

PERFORMANCE PROFILE: The Marketplace (continued)

2.4 Distribution Channel (Other Factors)

Distribution Channel _____

Characteristics of Channel	Trend to Date	The Present	The Future 19____
Size of Middleman	Larger/Same/Smaller	_____	_____
Sophistication	Same/Greater	_____	_____
Backward Integration	Extensive/Same/Non-Existent	_____	_____
Forward Integration	Extensive/Same Non-existent	_____	_____
Bargaining Power	Less/Same/Greater	_____	_____
Frequency of Purchases	More Concentrated/Same/Less	_____	_____
Inventories Carried	Larger/Same/Smaller	_____	_____
Financial Strength	Stronger/Same/Weaker	_____	_____
Purchasing Influencers	Non-Existent/Same/Changing	_____	_____
Other Characteristics (Specify)			

FIGURE 2.14

PERFORMANCE PROFILE: The Marketplace (continued)

3.1 Direct Competition (The Present) *1992*

		Your Firm MICRON	Competitor IMPRO	Competitor MOLTEC	Competitor
3.1.1					
3.1.2	Key Success Factors	(Ratings of Comparative Key Success Factor Strengths: High = 3; Average = 2; Low = 1 and trend by ▲ ; —; or ▼)			
	1. R&D	3↓	2	2	
	2. Highly specialized Sales engineers	1-2↓	3	1-2	
	3. Immediate service capability	2	2	2	
	4. Production quality control	3	?	?	
	5.				
3.1.3	Management's Current Major Emphasis	(List Key Success Factors)			
		—	Highly specialized sales engineers	?	
3.1.4	Market Share	(%, and Trend ▲ ; —; or ▼)			
		50%↓	25%↑	·25%↑	
3.1.5	Target Market's Rating of Augmented Products/ Services	(Superior, Above Average, Average, Below Average, Inferior)			
		Superior	Average to Above Average	Average to Above Average	
3.1.6	Relative Financial Strength	(Very Strong =3; Average = 2; Weak = 1 and Trend ▲ ; —; or ▼)			
		3	1↑	1↓	
3.1.7	Company Commitment	(Aggressive = 3; Holding = 2; Divestment = 1)			
		2-1	3	3	
3.1.8	Other Factors				

Some firms have many direct competitors and for them to list each competitor would be impractical (if not impossible). If this is true in your case, you should place competitors into strategic groups. For example, a small advertising agency claimed it had hundreds of competitors. The dilemma was resolved by placing these competitors into several groups: industry specialists (full service), industry specialists (limited line), generalists, and boutiques. (In Micron's case, its direct competitors were IMPRO and Moltec.)

3.1.2. Determine Key Success Factors. A critical few factors will determine your success or failure to serve a given target market. Let's look again at the cement example. A firm selling ready-mix cement to large builders on a bid basis usually will find that superior service and above-bid specifications mean very little unless the firm also turns in the lowest bid. In this case the key success factors are those resources that facilitate competitive pricing and profitability.

Identification of key success factors will provide you with two important pieces of information: (1) your sources of competitive advantage, and (2) how you can direct your marketing efforts to those tasks that really matter. Of course you cannot disregard other required functions of your business. You must meet minimum acceptable levels for these.

Following through with the example of the ready-mix cement firm: if the company, for instance, does a very sloppy job on delivery, it may find itself being excluded from the lists of qualified bidders. A firm must do an acceptable job on all marketing tasks. But it must be superior on the one, two, or several critical elements–the key success factors.

Key success factors must be factors you can measure against your competitors. For example, although "low price" is of some guidance, it's all encompassing. It does not pinpoint sources of competitive advantage. Low price could be the result of a number of factors, such as volume purchasing, favorable supplier location, long production runs, low cost labor, and cost efficient promotion.

Usually identification of key success factors is straightforward. Key success factors stem from key buying motives. In Micron's case, the key buying motives are extensive application, high performance, reliability and immediate repair service. It's apparent that the key success factors are research and development, production quality control, highly specialized sales engineers, and immediate service capabilities.

Rate Competitive Position

Your company's effectiveness, within a given market segment, depends on how well you measure up against direct competition. Rate your company's strengths on key success factors in relation to each of your competitors.

If you have placed your competitors in groups (such as in the above case of the advertising agency), rate yourself against the best-in-class of each group.

3.1.3. Management's Current Major Emphasis. Compare those key success factors on which your firm and competitors are concentrating to determine if your firm and your competitors are following different strategies.

3.1.4. Market Share. Determine (or estimate) market shares and trends for your firm and your competition. Total sales may be less meaningful than market share. Although your sales may be climbing, your market share may be eroding.

Make sure that you consider only your market share for a given product/service-target market. For example, in Micron's case, its market share for its product/service-target market was 50 percent, not 1.6 percent of the total oscilloscope industry.

3.1.5. Target Market's Rating of Augmented Products/Services. Rank how the target market perceives, relatively, your firm's and your competitors' product/service and the whole bundle of amenities surrounding the product/service (the augmented product service). After all, customers do not buy merely the core product/service. Rather, they are also purchasing the amenities that accompany the product/service, such as reputation of the vendor, image of the product/service, credit terms, and delivery times. To get these rankings, survey your target market.

Having an overall rating is useful, but it's far more helpful if you also know how you compare with your competitors on each key buying motive. To help rank your augmented products/services, benchmark your products/services against your competition. Figure 2.15 shows how it could be done for Micron. (Note: This information was not in the case.)

FIGURE 2.15

Buying Motives			Competitive Ratings 10 = high / 1 = low		
Primary	Secondary	Tertiary	MICRON	IMPRO	MOLTEC
Extensive Applications (capable of solving a VARIETY of research problems)	High power Laser research	Can capture and digitalize transient data	8	7	6
	Practical physics research	Can record non-repetitive high voltage fast rise doses	8	6	7
Reliability (Failure rate)	Mean time to first Failure	~~~	10	9	9
Immediate Service	Equipment back in operation 24 hours after Failure	~~~	2*	2*	2*

* Service varies directly with the proximity of the customer's location to the manufacturer's plant.

Adapted from J.M. Juran, **Juran on Planning for Quality**, (New York: The Free Press) 1988, pp. 38-42.

Since the key buying motives for the high-end research oscilloscopes were extensive application, reliability, and immediate service, these key buying motives have been subdivided into primary, secondary, and tertiary needs.[5] Subdivision of the key buying motives enables you to better understand the customers' key buying motives. In some cases, such as immediate service, one subdivision may be enough (equipment back in operation within 24 hours after failure). In others, such as extensive application, it might take two subdivisions.

Besides addressing key buying motives, looking at secondary buying motives is also helpful. This list can be quite lengthy, and each buying motive requires specific quality planning. For involved planning projects, you may have quite a large book of, say, LOTUS 1-2-3 spreadsheets. So if you're just starting in total quality planning, consider for now just working with key buying motives.

3.1.6. Relative Financial Strength. Estimate the relative financial strength of your firm in relation to other competitors. Do your competitors have the financial resources necessary to carry out aggressive–or even maintenance–programs?

3.1.7. Company Commitment. Rate your company's and your competitors' relative commitments: are they in an aggressive, holding, or divestiture posture? Micron had cut back on R&D and had eliminated one sales position. So it was estimated that, at best, Micron's commitment was "holding."

3.1.8. Other Factors. What major changes have taken place among your competitors? Have they, for example, increased in number, size, or sophistication? Figure 2.16 suggests other characteristics you might wish to include in your analysis.

The competitor analysis for key success factors and target market's ratings should be considered in light of the competitor's entire portfolio of business units. Shared production facilities, R&D, salespersons, and the like often result in synergistic effects. Among others, these could result in lower costs, providing one-stop shopping, enhanced product image, and more responsive service.

Figure 2.14 has been filled out for Micron. Note that question marks signify that certain information was unknown (and, of course, points to holes that should be filled).

FIGURE 2.16

PERFORMANCE PROFILE: The Market Place (continued)

3.1 Direct Competition (Other Factors) 1992

Characteristics of Direct Competitors	Trend to Date	The Present	The Future 19___
Number of Competitors	<u>More</u>/Same/ Fewer	2	___
Structure (size)	Larger/Small Smaller	Both IMPRO and MOLTEC about ½ the size of MICRON	___
Management Sophistication	<u>Same</u>/More	About the same as MICRON	___
Product/Service Offerings	More/<u>Same</u>/ Fewer	One product	___
Channels of Distribution Used	<u>Same</u>/Changing	Direct	___
Marketing Practices	<u>Same</u>/Changing	___	___
Research and Development	Same/Changing	?	___
Other Characteristics (Specify)			

Direct Competition–Summary Sheet

Managers frequently find that going between two sets of forms–
such as *Direct Competition (The Present)* and *Direct Competition
(The Future)*–is confusing. Even worse, important elements are
often missed.

Figure 2.17 is used to consolidate important competitive data. Its
sole purpose is to facilitate comparing the present with the future.
Take information from Figure 2.14 and consolidate it under "The
Present" (you'll complete the future column later on).

Since this is a summary sheet, use it to highlight key items,
adding no new information, of course. Again, the Micron case is
used as an example.

Direct Competition (Distribution Channels)

If you sell through distribution channels, rate your competitive
strengths. The charts in Figures 2.18 and 2.19 are similar to those
for *Direct Competition* (Figures 2.14 and 2.17) with one major
exception: Instead of "Target Market's Ratings of Products/Ser-
vices," here it is "Distribution Channel's Perception of Company/
Competitors."

What if you sell through a distribution channel in which you are
the exclusive supplier? Complete the chart solely for your company
with the exceptions of "Market Share" and "Relative Financial
Strength." Fill out the chart to show how you rate in absolute terms.
(For insights for filling out "3.2.8. Other Factors," see Figure 2.13.)

Complete one of these profiles for each distribution channel that
you use.

4. The Marketplace: Other External Forces

This section covers those forces beyond direct competition which
have an impact on your business: indirect competition, technological, economic, and governmental forces.

4.1. Indirect Competition. What substitute products/services are
you competing against? For example, typewriter manufacturers are

FIGURE 2.17

PERFORMANCE PROFILE: The Marketplace (continued)
Direct Competition (Summary Sheet) *1992*

Category	The Present		The Future 19___	
Key Success Factors	R & D Highly specialized sales engineers Immediate service capability Production quality control			
Direct Competitors	Market Share	Augmented Product/Service	Market Share	Augmented Product/Service
Your Firm	50% ↓	Superior		
IMPRO	25% ↑	Average to Above Average		
MOLTEC	25% ↑	Average to Above Average		
Comments (emphasis, financial strength, and/or commitment)	MICRON - Holding (or divestment); Relatively strong financially; Losing market share			
Comments on General Trends	IMPRO - Aggressive, Relatively weak financial condition but improving; Gaining market share; Strong sales force MOLTEC - Aggressive; Very weak financial condition; But gaining market share			

FIGURE 2.18

PERFORMANCE PROFILE: The Marketplace (continued)

3.2   Direct Competition/Distribution Channel _____ (The Present)

3.2.1	Your Firm	Competitor	Competitor	Competitor
3.2.2 Key Success Factors	(Ratings of Comparative Key Success Factor Strengths: High = 3; Average = 2; Low = 1 and trend by ▲ ;—; or ▼)			
1.				
2.				
3.				
4.				
5.				
3.2.3 Management's Current Major Emphasis	(List Key Success Factors)			
3.2.4 Market Share	(%, and Trend ▲ ; —; or ▼)			
3.2.5 Distribution Channel's Perception of Company/Competitors	(Superior, Above Average, Average, Below Average, Inferior)			
3.2.6 Relative Financial Strength	(Very Strong =; Average = 2; Weak = 1 and Trend ▲ ; —; or ▼)			
3.2.7 Company Commitment to the channel	(Aggressive = 3; Holding = 2; Divestment = 1)			
3.2.8 Other Factors				

FIGURE 2.19

PERFORMANCE PROFILE: The Marketplace (continued)

3.2 Direct Competition/Distribution Channel _____(Summary Sheet)

Category	The Present	The Future 19____
Key Success Factors		

Direct Competitors	Market Share	Channel's Perception	Market Share	Channel's Perception
Your Firm				

Comments (emphasis, financial strength, and/or commitment)

Comments on General Trends

in competition with computer manufacturers. While not in direct competition because the products are so different the advent of computers has had a devastating effect on typewriter sales just the same.

What other industries are you competing against? How are they impacting the demand for your product/service? In the case of Micron, its indirect competition was those manufacturers who produce research oscilloscopes in the price range of $40,000 to $45,000. So far, these indirect competitors have not been a factor in the upper end of the market.

4.2. Technological. Technical innovation bears a close relationship to indirect competition. Monitoring innovation is difficult because so many new ideas come from outside the industry.

A study by Cooper and Schendel of 22 companies in seven industries (locomotives, vacuum receiving tubes, fountain pens, safety razors, fossil fuel boilers, propellers, and leather) found that in the majority of cases the first commercial introduction of an innovation occurred outside the industry. The study further revealed a prevalent pattern that sales of old technologies did not decline immediately, but usually continued to increase in the short run. Initially, the new technology captured a series of submarkets and, on the average, it took from five to 14 years for the sales (dollar) volume of the new technology to exceed that of the old technology.[6]

The danger here, of course, is that replacement technologies may emerge and grow while firms utilizing the old technology remain complacent because of near-term growth and prosperity. The chart in Figure 2.20 illustrates how this evolutionary process might take place.

Two examples which point out the swiftness of market penetration and filling of the niches are (1) electromechanical cash registers, holding 90 percent of the market in 1972, yet only 10 percent in 1976; and (2) bias-ply tires, which had 70 percent of the market in 1977, yet only 8 percent in 1980.[7] Carefully consider any technological changes which are occurring that may impact your industry. Remember, these changes are likely to develop outside of your traditional industry.

Some companies make it a point to monitor technological displacement rate. For example, examine Figure 2.21. Assume that

FIGURE 2.20

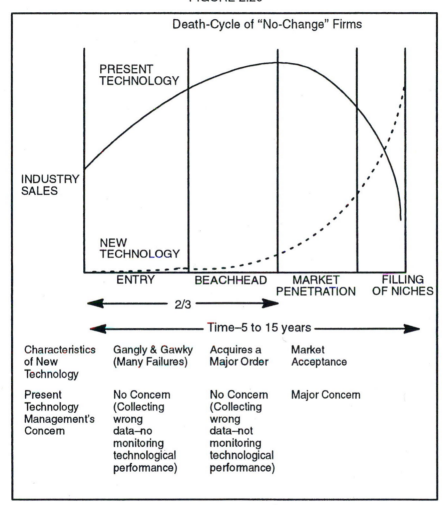

industry x is selling glass bottles to industry y. Although industry x's sales to industry y are increasing, the technological displacement ratio indicates that industry y's product (glass bottles) is being displaced (plastic bottles). The rapid increase in the industry's sales masked this decline.[8]

4.3. Economic. The economy, through inflation or deflation, may distort your data. A very brisk expanding economy may mask prob-

FIGURE 2.21

Year	Industry x's Sales to Industry y	Industry's Sales	Technological Displacement Ratio
1983	10M	100M	10.00%
1984	12M	200M	6.00%
1985	15M	300M	5.00%
1986	17M	400M	4.25%
1987	20M	500M	4.00%
1988	18M	600M	3.00%
1989	20M	700M	2.80%
1990	22M	800M	2.75%
1991	24M	900M	2.66%
1992	26M	1000M	2.60%
1993	28M	1200M	2.33%

lems, such as an erosion of market share while sales figures rise. On the other hand, an economic downtown may cause a sales slump. This could conceal gains in competitive strength.

4.4. Government. For example, does your target market include companies or agencies funded by government funds? Then, governmental legislation may affect sales.

4.5. Other Forces. Any factor, unique to your industry, which has not been included as yet should be analyzed here.

A *Performance Profile*: *Other External Forces* filled out for Micron is shown in Figure 2.22.

As we pointed out previously, you'll sometimes need more space than the forms provide. This may well occur, for instance, for "4.3. Economic" (see Figure 2.22). In such a case, merely put the data behind that page and label it "4.3.1." If you wish to add subsections under general headings, then extend the numbering system. Example 4.3.1.1, 4.3.1.2, and so on.

The Performance Profile: Internal

You've looked at the market place (target market, channels of distribution, direct competition, and other forces). Upon reflection, you'll realize that the information you've gathered here would be the same regardless of whether you or your competitors had com-

FIGURE 2.22

PERFORMANCE PROFILE: The Marketplace (continued)

4. Other External Forces

Category	The Present *1992*	The Future 19____
4.1　Indirect Competition:	Widespread use of low cost oscilloscopes; field dominated by large aggresive competitors with wide sales and service networks	
4.2　Technological:		
4.3　Economic:		
4.4　Governmental:		
4.5　Other Forces:		

pleted the analysis. After all, you've just been describing the market place.

The second major performance profile is *Performance Profile: Internal.* Here examine only those factors and activities which relate solely to your company.

Cover significant areas. These will vary by product/service line, target market, and company. The list in Figure 2.23 suggests categories that many companies have found to be significant. This is an imposing list but let's show you how to make this manageable.

First, looking again at Figure 2.23, we'll start with 5.1.1. *Product/Service Line* listed under 5.1. *Sales and Profit Analysis.*

5.1.1. Product/Service Line. You will need more than sales and bottom line figures. If all you can tell is that sales and profits are off by 10 percent, you simply don't have enough to work with. Let's take a look at the Micron case.

Suppose we were to do a financial analysis of Micron's product/service-target market. (As it turns out–intentionally–financial analysis of Micron is straightforward and simple. The company consists of only one products/services-target market. So the financial analysis of the company is the same as the financial analysis for its product/service-target market. Naturally, you'll have more, probably many more, products/services-target markets. But the principle for examining one or many producst/services-target markets is the same).

Figure 2.24 shows what Micron's data (adjusted for inflation) looked like. Looking at the data, we can say:

- Sales and gross profits are down by 2 percent.
- Because sales and gross profits are down by the same percentage, gross margin also has remained constant.
- R&D expenses are down by 51 percent.
- Selling expenses are down by 52 percent.
- Advertising expenses are down by 2 percent.
- Administrative expenses are down by 15 percent.
- Total expenses are down by 41 percent.
- Contribution to corporate is up by 178 percent. However, $407,000 of Micron's $416,000–or about 98 percent–increase

FIGURE 2.23

	Type of Analysis	
5.1	*Sales and Profit Analysis*	*Purpose: To identify sales and profit and growth rates*
	5.1.1 Product/service line	Overall financial performance
	5.1.2 Product/service-line items	Relative importance of various items in the product/service line
	5.1.3 Customers	Importance of key customers, customer characteristics, e.g., turnover rate
	5.1.4 Distribution channels	Distribution channels which are contributing most to company sales and profit
	5.1.5 Salespersons	Salespersons who are contributing most to company sales and profit
	5.1.6 Markets (industry)	Markets where present customers are concentrated
	5.1.7 Geographic areas	Importance of various geographic areas to company
5.2	*Order Backlog*	*Purpose: To identify trends in unfilled orders*
5.3	*Expense Analysis*	*Purpose: To identify productivity concerning:*
	5.3.1 Advertising/sales	Advertising expenditures to overall sales
	5.3.2 Employee/sales	Sales per employee
	5.3.3 Inventory/sales	Inventory turnover
	5.3.4 Sales promotion/sales	Percentage of sales promotion to sales
	5.3.5 Physical distribution/ sales	Percentage of physical distribution costs to sales
	5.3.6 Square footage/sales	Sales per square footage
	5.3.7 Bad debt loss/sales	Bad debt loss percentage
	5.3.8 Accounts receivable/ sales	Age of accounts receivable
	5.3.9 Marketing overhead/ sales	Percentage of marketing overhead costs to sales
	5.3.10 Marketing research/ sales	Percentage of marketing research to sales

FIGURE 2.23 (continued)

5.4 Marketing Activities	Purpose: To identify efficiency concerning:
5.4.1 Marketing programs (general)	Successful/unsuccessful programs; trends
5.4.2 Sales coverage	Adequacy of representation
5.4.3 Sales calls	Productivity
5.4.4 Advertising/public relations	Productivity
5.4.5 Order processing, assembly, and delivery	Time and cost
5.4.6 Inventory control	Turns and cost
5.4.7 Technical assistance/repairs	Speed, quality, extent
5.5 Organizational Factors	Purpose: To identify:
5.5.1 Management's orientation	Feasibility of alternative strategies
5.5.2 Resources	Feasibility of alternative strategies

FIGURE 2.24

P & L (in $1,000)	1987 (nominal)	1987 (adjusted to '92 $$)	1992	$ Change 1987-92	% Change 1987-92
Sales	2,000	2,460	2,400	−60	−2
Cost of Goods Sold	920	1,132	1,100	−32	−2
Gross Profit	1,080	1,328	1,300	−28	−2
Expenses					
R&D	300	369	180	−189	−51
Selling	340	418	200	−218	−52
Advertising	50	61	−60	−1	−2
Administration Expenses	200	246	210	−36	−15
Total Expenses	890	1,094	650	−444	−41
Contribution to Corporate	190	234	650	+416	+178

in contribution to corporate can be attributed to cutbacks in R&D and selling expenditures.

Since you'll probably be dealing with multiproducts/services-target markets, you won't have exact figures to deal with for categories such as administrative expenditures and the like.

Consequently, you'll have to work with allocated costs. That's tricky at best. So instead of constructing a P&L, you may wish to set up your analysis, as we pointed out in Step 1, by contribution or merchandising profit.

5.1.3. Customers. Let's use customer analysis as another example. Possibly your present target market should be redefined into smaller segments. Your customer base is probably *not* homogeneous. Wipe out the concept of "our average customer." If 20 percent buy every week and 80 percent just occasionally–say every three months–does that mean your "average customer" buys about once every three weeks?

Likewise, if 50 percent of your customers are crazy about your product or service and 50 percent feel just so-so about it, does this mean that your "average customer" thinks your product or service is pretty good? (Someone who believes that probably wonders how a person could drown in a lake with an average depth of only three inches.)

GTE Service Corporation found that its customers' key buying motives varied. Start-up companies wanted technical assistance, while mature firms wanted technical advances in products and services. The solution: GTE designed packages of servicing options from which individual accounts could choose.

Here are 13 questions to examine the appropriateness of your present segmenting strategy for a given product or service. While going through these questions, continually ask yourself, "Have I segmented this market finely enough? Or am I trying to be all things to all people?" You will probably uncover facts that, when you're developing your strategy for the next year, will direct you to more profitable avenues.

1. Who are your heavy users? The 80-20 rule probably applies to your product/service-target market.
2. Who are your heavy, heavy users? You may have a small

percentage of your heavy users who purchase a very large percentage of your product or service.

3. Who are your light users?
4. Are some customers expanding their purchases?
5. Are some customers purchasing less?
6. Where are your customers located? Are there geographic differences of use? Urban? Rural? Regional? National? International?
7. Which of your customers can you most profitably serve?
8. What is the frequency of purchases by users? Is the pattern the same among all users? Or do some users purchase quarterly, while others purchase on a weekly basis? Such differences could lead to, for example, different strategies in pricing, shipping, and/or credit.
9. What promotion best appeals to your various customers? For example, is it a person-to-person sales approach? Or would some method such as direct mail sweepstakes be more effective?
10. Who makes the purchasing decision? Is it the purchasing agent? Or the user? Is there an influencer that must be reached? Are the purchases made by one person or are they the result of group buying? Is there reciprocity involved?
11. Do your customers buy your whole line of products and services?
12. How price-sensitive are your different customers? Quite frequently there's a rather wide range of price sensitivity among a company's customer base.
13. What nonprice features do your customers really value? What are their key buying motives? If you find that your customers have different *key* buying motives, it probably indicates that you have not segmented the market finely enough. To help detect differences of key buying motives among your customer base, use the charts in Figures 2.25, 2.26, and 2.27. These are guides to help isolate key buying motives for users/consumers of professional services, industrial products, and packaged foods, beverages, and drugs. If one of these guides does not match your particular product/service, then use them to help you design an appropriate one.

FIGURE 2.25

KEY BUYING MOTIVES: PROFESSIONAL SERVICES

Performance (Primary, measurable characteristics of a service. Examples: prompt service and absence of waiting time).

_____   _____

_____

Features (Measurable characteristics of a service that supplement performance. Example: location and hours).

_____   _____

_____

Conformance (The degree to which a service meets established standards).

_____   _____

_____

Serviceability (Certainty of continuity of service).

_____   _____

_____

Aesthetics (Users' tastes, such as appearance of report).

_____   _____

_____

Perceived Quality (Users' impression of the service stemming from, for example, general reputation of the firm, exclusivity, customer list, quality of advertising and salespersons, and loyalty toward salespersons).

_____   _____

_____   _____

Reciprocity   _____

Awareness   _____

Tradition (habitual behavior)   _____

Low Price (including deals)   _____

Trial Offer   _____

Billing Procedure/Credit Terms   _____

Referral   _____

FIGURE 2.26

KEY BUYING MOTIVES: INDUSTRIAL PRODUCT

Referral   _____

Performance (Primary, measurable operating characteristics
of a product. Examples: a lift truck's load capacity, acceleration,
and handling).

Features (Measurable characteristics of a product that supplement   _____
performance. Examples: air conditioning on a lift truck,
technical advice, training, and adaptability for technical upgrade).

Reliability (The probability of a product's not failing within a   _____
specified period of time).

Conformance (The degree to which a product meets established   _____
standards).

Durability (Use one gets from a product before it breaks down   _____
and replacement is preferable to continued repair; also
trade-in/resale value).

Serviceability (Maintenance costs, availability of replacement parts   _____
and service, cost of service, ease of servicing, extent of downtime
required for servicing, and certainty of continuity of service).

Aesthetics (Users' tastes, such as preference of design and   _____
appearance).

Perceived Quality (Users' impression of the product stemming   _____
from, for example, general reputation of the firm; exclusivity;
customer list; quality of advertising and salespersons; and loyalty
toward brand, salespersons, dealers, distributors).

Reciprocity   _____
Awareness   _____
Availability (hours, location)   _____
Tradition (habitual behavior)   _____
Low Price (including deals)   _____
Trial Offer   _____
Billing Procedure/Credit Terms   _____
Delivery   _____

FIGURE 2.27

KEY BUYING MOTIVES:
PACKAGED FOODS, BEVERAGES, AND DRUGS

Performance (Primary, measurable characteristics of a product. Examples: Flavor, essence, nutrition/healthfulness, freshness, and shelf life).

Features (Measurable characteristics of a product that supplement performance. Examples: convenience of use and packaging).

Conformance (The degree to which a product meets established standards).

Aesthetics (Users' tastes, such as preference of design and appearance).

Perceived Quality (Users' impression of the product stemming from, for example, general reputation of firm; exclusivity; customer list; quality of advertising and salespersons; and loyalty toward brand, salespersons, dealers, distributors).

Reciprocity   _____
Awareness   _____
Availability (hours, location)   _____
Tradition (habitual behavior)   _____
Low Price (including deals)   _____
Trial Offer   _____
Billing Procedure/Credit Terms   _____
Delivery   _____

*Adapted from Ronald R. Gist, *The Executive Course in Marketing Management* (seminar) (Denver, 1987), and David A. Garvin, *Management Quality* (New York: The Free Press, 1988), ch. 4.

5.1.5. Salespersons. Let's use "Salespersons" as another example. You may find that 14 of your 40 salesmen account for 85 percent of your company's sales. But analysis can't stop here. Additional information is needed before you can take corrective measures. Some measures to consider in evaluating past performance of salespersons are presented in Figure 2.28.

Again, a more meaningful analysis can often be made by examining trends. For example, what have been the salesperson's sales (adjusted for inflation) for the past five years? The salesperson's meeting of quotas? Contribution to profits?

You'll always put financial, customer, and sales-force data under

FIGURE 2.28

–Quantitative ratings:

Sales Volume (total sales volume)
Quota (level of expected performance)
Direct selling expenses (total of salesperson's salary and expenses)
Contribution to profits (sales minus cost of goods sold minus salesperson's salary and expenses)
Salesperson's share of the market (total territory purchases divided by salesperson's territorial sales)
Sales/key account ratio (% of sales accounted for by key accounts)
Number of new accounts secured
Number of lost accounts
Number of cancelled orders
Order size (total sales divided by number of orders)
Order/call ratio (number of orders divided by number of sales calls)
Call frequency ratio (number of sales calls divided by number of customers)

–Qualitative ratings:

Prospecting
Sales presentations
Ability to handle objections
Ability to close sale
Customer relations
Knowledge of customers
Knowledge of products
Personality
Work scheduling

close scrutiny. But there's a myriad of other areas you should examine. So how should you allocate your time?

Here are some criteria. Examine those areas that:

1. Have a big impact on performance, such as:
   - Key (or critical) success factors as determined by your customers' key buying motives.
   - Critical factors in terms of cost. If your logistics function represents 60 percent of your total costs, then a 10 percent reduction of logistics costs would have a very significant impact on your profitability. On the other hand, if the logistics function only constitutes 6 percent of your total costs then a 10 percent reduction would have negligible impact on total cost reduction.
2. Are in need of improvement. No doubt you have a pretty good idea of where there's slack in your company. These are areas worthy of close scrutiny.
3. Are capable of being improved. Some activities may be carried out inefficiently. Yet they are difficult (or perhaps impossible) to improve because of internal politics, governmental regulation, and the like.
4. Are small enough so that you can get your arms around them. Better not try to solve the world hunger situation. Rather, bite off chunks that you can chew.
5. Are capable of being implemented within a reasonable amount of time. It may be questionable to start analyzing something that will take a decade or so to pay off. After all, you're developing an annual marketing plan.
6. Are within your resource availability.

After you have completed your internal analysis, place those significant action-oriented findings on the *Performance Profile: Internal* sheet in Figure 2.29. You'll note that only "The Present" column appears on this sheet. The future, of course, will depend upon actions taken by your company. Again, the Micron case serves as an example.

The Performance Profile: Critical Summary

The final step in SWOTs: Present is to prepare a critical summary. Although cataloging the data in the two previous performance profiles, *The Marketplace* and *Internal,* is necessary for analysis and documentation, only a few issues will be of major importance. List these on the *Performance Profile: Critical Summary* sheet.

These critical issues must be more than a collection of facts. They must suggest corrective action, what needs to be done concerning major problems and major opportunities. This prevents the *Performance Profile: Critical Summary* from becoming a list of meaningless facts. You've probably seen lists that included such statements as "Strong management team," or "Good customer relations." These are the kind of say-nothing comments that should be avoided.

Of course, it's too early to take action now. Unless it is something critical that requires immediate action, you will want to hold off deciding what to do until after you have completed SWOTs: Future. Figure 2.30 shows some examples of critical issue statements which suggest specific, meaningful activity.

While putting together the *Performance Profile: Critical Summary* always ask yourself "What possible actions could I take to capitalize on the opportunity or to reduce the problem that this statement presents?" If you cannot come up with any actions, reconsider placing the issue on the form. Again, remember that such hypothesized actions are just tentative. To make sure that you are dealing with critical issues, limit the summary to one page.

Figure 2.31 is a *Performance Profile: Critical Summary* completed for Micron.

PRACTICAL GUIDELINES FOR CONDUCTING THE SWOTS: PRESENT

This analysis can be overwhelming unless managed carefully. The following guidelines will help make a manageable project out of a possible nightmare.

FIGURE 2.29

PERFORMANCE PROFILE: Internal

Category	The Present *1992*
5.1.1 Overall Financial	Sales have remained flat over the past two years (2% decrease); Gross margin remained the same; R&D has been cut back $189,000 (51%); Selling expense by $218,000 (52%). Dramatic increase in contribution to corporate ($414,000--177%) but 98% of this has come from cutbacks in R&D and selling expense.
5.4.2 Sales Performance	Cutback in one salesperson in late 1981 (to increase profitability). Two salesmen handle all field sales.
5.4.3 Sales Performance	Evidence of poor prospecting.
5.4.7 Customer Service	Micron's instruments have been trouble free.

FIGURE 2.30

STATEMENTS	SUGGESTED ACTION (Not to be placed on form, but included here to show how the statements suggest possible action steps.)
One service accounts for 90% of profits	Design new program to ensure service remains competitive; consider expanding line to reduce vulnerability
4 salespersons (out of 20) bring in 70% of sales	Implement a key salesperson retention program
6 salespersons' (out of 20) gross profits do not cover their salaries, commissions, bonuses, and expenses	Retrain, relocate (perhaps their territories lack potential), or dismiss
Employee productivity has declined by 28%	Increase productivity or decrease the number of employees
20% of the division's inventory has had zero turns in the first five months of the year (six turns a year is normal for the industry)	Get rid of "dead" inventory
23 customers account for 72% of the firm's sales	Develop a key customer account program

Always Be Collecting Data

The A-B-C-D Rule of getting the job done is that you should "always be collecting data." If you wait until two weeks before you start putting together your marketing plan, you'll never get the job done.

First, you probably won't get the two weeks. But even if you do, a two-week time frame is simply not long enough. You might need secondary information and you'll have to write for it. Or, it might be essential to talk to a particular key customer who just happens to be on vacation. Or, after you get part way into the SWOTs: Present analysis, you might realize that it's vital to conduct a field study.

FIGURE 2.31

PERFORMANCE PROFILE: Critical Summary

The Present 19__22__	The Future 19_____
Major Problems (Negatives)	**Major Problems (Negatives)**
In past two years, MICRON's sales have been flat (-2%); Severe cutbacks in R&D and selling expenditures, yet both are key success factors.	
Evidence of poor prospecting.	
Lack of service network has cost sales.	
Competition is Aggressive, esp. IMPRO. IMPRO has a larger sales force and more extensive sales support.	
In past 5 years MICRON has lost market share to both IMPRO + MOLTEC.	
Major Opportunities (Positives)	**Major Opportunities (Positives)**
MICRON's instruments have been trouble free.	
Competitors are financially weak; IMPRO's condition is improving; MOLTEC's is worsening.	
MICRON has 50% of the market and is in good financial condition.	
In spite of cutbacks in R&D, MICRON's oscilloscope is still rated as superior.	
Current Target Market Demand	**Forecast of Target Market Demand**
≅ $4,800,000	19____ _____
Demand has increased by 10% in the last five years	19____ _____
	Inflation Adjustments

A successful SWOTs: Present analysis results from many bits of information gathered here and there over a period of time. It doesn't come from a sudden "bolt of lightning" resulting from a gigantic, last-minute study.

Here's an easy way to follow the A-B-C-D Rule. When you come across an interesting article, clip it out. Put it in your fact book. Do the same with all relevant bits of information. Then, when it comes time to put together (or revise) your plan, your SWOTs: Present is almost completed.

Decide on Data Needed and Set Up Timetables

Decide at the outset when the SWOTs: Present must be completed. The length of time for this job depends, of course, on a host of variables: the nature of the business, difficulties in retrieving information, the scope of the analysis, and so on.

In addition to setting a SWOTs: Present completion date deadline, you must decide what information you need to gather. Your forms will help you pinpoint missing data. Next, determine how you're going to get the data. Planning ahead can save you time. And lots of it. For example, you may decide that the best way to find out about your competitors' product line is through personal examination. That can probably best be done at an appropriate trade show.

Set up timetables for each major task. If you allow a nebulous period of time to complete a job, you invite procrastination. Decide on what needs to be done. Set dates for every step. For example, if you wish to make an analysis of your key customers, decide at the beginning when this task must be finished. Then adhere to the timetables you have set.

Examine Secondary Data First

You may have to go out in the field to determine customer product/services preferences, competitive prices, and the like. But be sure that you don't go through the painstaking and costly trouble of gathering information that is already available.

We mentioned earlier that possibly the most productive way to use your time is examining data that you have within the company. As

Horace S. Schwerin, then vice president of corporate planning for Campbell Soup Company said, "Company files are choked with data documenting the economic, demographic, and lifestyle changes affecting our society. What is rare today, and always has been, is an in-depth analysis of the problems and a search to see whether a careful and creative interpretation of existing data could provide most of the answers before the decision is made to go out and collect new data."[9]

After you have examined data that you have within the company, then examine published data. Trade associations, governments, computer data banks, and industry and business publications are often rich sources of information about the target market, industry financial ratios, and competitors.

Of course you can carry the search for secondary information to the extreme. It's necessary to have a basic understanding of the industry to optimize the value of field interviews. Yet, don't try to exhaust all published sources before getting into the field.[10]

Expect Redundancy

There will always be some overlap. When you're making a detailed analysis of price you cannot help but take competitors into consideration, although you may have examined competitor/price relationships in another context, such as, analysis of competition. However, repetition is often helpful as it may emphasize areas of opportunity and/or vulnerability.

Expect Blind Alleys

Action-oriented findings usually take considerable scanning, prying around, and scrutinizing. Often you come up with nothing. But that's the process. There is a story about a census taker who called on a home where the housewife said that they had 16 children. The census taker remarked how lucky they were. She replied, "Oh no, we're not lucky. Lots of times we do it and we get nothing."

Be Thorough in Collecting Data

Resist collecting data in slipshod fashion. Thoroughness will lead to accuracy. And accurate information is more likely to lead you to correct conclusions. Aside from that, others will be more inclined to accept your findings if they trust your methods. Thoroughness breeds confidence. Then, when you do it right the first time, there will be no need to backtrack (again and again) for information you should already have. Use your fact book. It will help you to be thorough.

Keep the Task Manageable

On the first time around, it will probably be impractical, if not impossible, for you to gather all the facts you'd like to have. Even if it were feasible, not all of the data would be relevant. Console yourself with the notion that the excessive data can obscure that which is truly important.

Gather only the information that you feel is essential. This creates a very positive psychological effect: the feeling that the planning process is relevant. Accumulating statistics whose usefulness is highly suspect can be very defeating.

In general, view the SWOTs: Present as an ongoing process. Follow the A-B-C-D Rule. After conducting the initial SWOTs: Present analysis and proceeding through the planning process, you may find that as part of overall strategy you need to expand your product line, for example. But before a sound decision can be reached, more detailed information about indirect competition is needed. Collect this information then.

Keep in mind that planning is a continuous process, something you do year after year. Through time your data base and methods of analysis will grow increasingly sophisticated. Most likely when you first start (on a formalized basis), you'll find areas where you lack information you'd really like to have, but you can't take the time to gather it. If this should happen, and it probably will, make plans to begin collecting data. You'll have it when you go through the next planning cycle.

Since you won't be able to examine everything the way you'd like to, "do the obvious first," as Peter Drucker put it. There are no hard-and-fast rules concerning the "obvious." But two common-sense rules offer a measure of assistance as to what should be examined and how detailed the analysis should be.

The first of these rules is: Take a hard look at those items that could really make a difference. The planning forms will help you to focus on the obvious, especially key buying motives and key success factors. Then, find–and examine–other strategic elephants. This guideline is rather obvious, but it's often not followed. For example, a company was facing a serious cash flow situation. Net sales could not be increased (the firm was on credit hold). Nor could gross margins be increased. Expenses had to be cut to restore the firm to profitability. Examine the income statement of one of the firm's branches in Figure 2.32. It's quite evident that of all the expenses listed, personnel was the only place where cutbacks could make a significant difference. Yet, management failed to see this. This shows how all too often the obvious may be overlooked.

The next common sense rule is to consider how thoroughly you know the various parts of your business, and to spend more time evaluating those areas that you don't know well. It may also help if you keep the following questions in mind: how much will it cost in terms of time and/or money to get this information? And how much might it cost in sales and profits if I don't?

Accept the fact that you'll have to make best estimates about many things. If you try to gather everything, you'll never finish the planning cycle. You'll have the same experience as the firm that zestfully started formal planning, but it never got any further than the SWOTs: Present because the president had insisted on gathering all the facts.

Regardless of what kind of information is gathered or how it is presented, it should not be viewed as busywork. Again, the best way to avoid ineffectuality here is to make sure your *Performance Profile*: *Critical Summary* suggests corrective action.

Do It Now

During the situation analysis, you may uncover some areas that require immediate action. Obviously, you don't need to wait until the plans are complete to take action. For example, during a SWOTs: Present analysis, a bank's manager discovered that one service accounted for almost 100 percent of its profits. Management

FIGURE 2.32

INCOME STATEMENT April 30, 19__		
NET SALES	$80,825.40	100.00%
COST OF GOODS SOLD	59,454.34	73.56
GROSS PROFIT	21,371.06	26.44
OPERATING EXPENSES		
Controllable Expenses		
Salaries and Bonus	7,433.11	9.20
Commissions	6,336.78	7.34
Payroll Taxes	2,582.03	3.19
Group Insurance	629.67	.78
Delivery Expense	2,278.15	2.82
Freight Out	909.97	1.13
Office Supplies and		
Postage	516.17	.54
Education and Training	.00	.00
Advertising	423.65	.52
Warehouse Supplies	471.00	.58
Telephone	1,437.38	1.78
Travel	445.25	.55
Sales Promotions	.00	.00
General Insurance	560.33	.69
Building and Equipment		
Repair	93.60	.12
Equipment Rent	53.04	.07
Building Rent and Utilities	2,432.16	3.00
Total	26,602.29	32.31
Before Tax Profit	(5,231,23)	(5.87)

decided, logically, that action had to be taken immediately to ensure the continued profitability of this service.

A Final Word

The first time through a formal SWOTs: Present analysis may be a frustrating experience for you. You may agree that the analysis suggested is necessary. Yet you don't have the necessary data.

Let me quote what the president of a small computer software company had to say (he was doing the SWOTs: Present analysis himself):

> At first I was discouraged. We just did not have the information in our files. Furthermore, there was not much published data available either on target market or on our competitors.
>
> But I began to poke around and I realized that I had more information than I had originally thought. For example, although there was not much secondary information on our target market, still there were data from general industry (broader target market) surveys, such as the *Quality Magazine* survey of 1,100 users. These gave us valuable insights regarding key buying motives and other information about our target market.
>
> Then, although our company records couldn't break out key customers *per se,* I was able to learn a lot by organizing customers according to billing discounts (quantity).
>
> I found that even though I had limited information, I was learning more about my business than I ever knew before. Even so, because I was starting to organize the information from "ground zero," I realized that I needed a plan for gathering information. So I drew up a chart containing the information needed, and goals–how and when–for getting this information.
>
> Furthermore, I've set up procedures to make sure that I'll have the information in the future. For example, for every software package sold, before it goes out the door, I insist that the following is recorded: SIC, company name and size, state, and source of inquiry. The SWOTs: Present analysis, even with limited information, has given me new perspectives about our business. It's been the most valuable part of the planning process.

CRITICAL REVIEW BY AN "OUTSIDER"

What do you see in the box below? Come up with an answer before you go on. You may say "Something that looks like four Chinese figures." Or, you may see the word "left."

Of course there is no right answer. But it's interesting to witness what happens to a person who first sees something like Chinese figures. Then, after being shown how the figure also represents the word "left," "left" is all the person sees. The person will not say, "I see the Chinese figures and the word left."

The point is that we don't see the world as it actually exists. Rather we see a distorted picture of it due to a number of factors, such as our past experience, our interests, our desires, and the like.

Sometimes it's hard to be objective. Following a structural procedure, as recommended here, will help you to see things as they are. Still, it's easy for you to bias your findings.

So after you have completed the analysis, have an "outsider" review your conclusions. In some instances the outside review is automatic: for example, a business unit has its review by corporate.

But for a single industry firm, such reviews are not automatic. Then, too, for some business units, even the corporate review may not be sufficient. Persons at the corporate level may not have the expertise in your industry to provide an accurate assessment. Or, for political reasons, they cannot do so.

If one of these above situations applies to you, then you might consider one or more of the following sources: accountants, lawyers, bankers, vendors, customers, "friendly" competitors, and consultants. Regardless of which you choose, make sure that the person is familiar with your industry. Such a person will have more realistic insights than an equally bright individual who has little knowledge of your industry.

MAKING SWOTS: PRESENT WORK IN A TOTAL QUALITY ENVIRONMENT

The ultimate purpose of SWOTs: Present for marketing planning is to provide insight into what the firm should do to be more successful in the marketplace. While marketing may play the key role in preparing the SWOTs: Present analysis, many of the recommended actions evolving from it will require the consent of other functional areas. These functional areas must believe the SWOTs: Present findings before they will be willing to go along with the changes.

Don't wait until the SWOTs: Present is complete to present your findings to other functional areas in your firm. If you do, they'll never be able to internalize the results. They must be a part of the ongoing SWOTs: Present process. And this requires that they be exposed to continual customer contact and briefings–something that will not take place unless it's planned.

Here are some ways to involve nonmarketing functional personnel.

Customer Contact

Arrange for them to:

- Go on sales calls with salespersons. Just to listen, to take notes. The primary purpose is to find out what the customers are like, what's important to the customers, and what's happening in the industry.
- Go on service calls. Find out why the product or service went wrong and how the customers react to these breakdowns and service calls.
- Work with the marketing research department. Interview customers.
- View focus group interviews.
- Work the booth at trade shows.
- Staff the 800 number.
- Use and compare your products/services with the products/services of your competitors.

Or, you may find that more intensive involvement is feasible. For instance, go to Tokyo's large appliance district, Akihabara. Who will you find manning the counters? Product designers and engineers. This is a great way to learn more about what customers want.

Or, how about "living" with customers while they use your products or services? One Japanese firm assigned an engineer to ride around with a bulldozer operator for a year–just to find out how to make the tractor more user-friendly.

Briefings

As a practical matter of developing SWOTs: Present, you will be following the A-B-C-D Rule. As you collect data throughout the year, you may make some significant findings. Don't wait until the end of the year to let relevant parties in on these findings. Maybe you'll do this informally, by phone or talks in the hall. Maybe it'll be through interoffice memos with appropriate sections highlighted. Maybe you'll use formal meetings or weekend get-togethers. Whatever you do, keep them informed.

Total quality planning requires the wholehearted effort of every functional area of the firm. Sharing significant information in this way will not only familiarize other functional units with the workings of SWOTs: Present, but will also help make believers of them. They'll begin to visualize new product/service features for targeted customers. They'll develop the processes needed to produce these features. And, best of all, they'll see that the processes work.

POINTS LEARNED

1. Complete SWOTs: Present for each product/service-target market.
2. Organize and analyze critical factors and relationships in a systematic way. Three performance profiles–*The Marketplace, Internal,* and *Critical Summary*–provide you with the needed structure.
3. In completing the *Performance Profile: The Marketplace,* you'll analyze four key elements:
   - *The Target Market.* Describe the target market, key buying motives, other factors, and the target market demand.

- *Distribution Channels.* List distribution channels used by you or your competitors. Then for each of these channels, state its percent of the total target market demand, trend, your market share, its key buying motives, and other factors.
- *Direct Competition.* Identify direct competitors. Determine key success factors. Determine market shares. Rate competitive positions, management's current major emphasis, target market's perception of products/services, relative financial strength, company commitment, and other factors.
- *Other External Forces.* Examine those forces beyond direct competition that have an impact on your business: indirect competition, technology, economic and governmental forces.

4. In completing the *Performance Profile: Internal,* examine only those factors and activities which relate solely to your company. Cover significant areas.

5. Although it's necessary for documentation and analysis to catalog the data in the two performance profiles, *The Marketplace* and *Internal,* only a few issues will be of major importance. List these on the *Performance Profile: Critical Summary* sheet. These critical issues must be more than a collection of facts. They must suggest corrective action, what needs to be done concerning major problems and major opportunities.

6. Practical guidelines for conducting the SWOTs: Present:
   - Always be collecting data.
   - Decide on data needed and set up timetables.
   - Examine secondary data first.
   - Expect redundancy.
   - Expect blind alleys.
   - Be thorough in collecting data.
   - Keep the task manageable.
   - Do it now.

7. After you have completed the SWOTs: Present have an outsider review your conclusions.

8. To make SWOTs: Present be effective in a total quality environment, make sure that other functional area personnel, as

well as those in the marketing department, are involved in the process.

LOOKING AHEAD

You can put many of SWOTs: Present findings into action next year if changes in competition and the like will not be radical. But, before you finalize what you should do next year, take a look at the short- and longer-range future. And that's the next step.

THE EIGHT PLANNING STEPS

Step 1. SWOTs: Present. Gain an Overall Perspective by Historical Analysis of Total Sales, Expenses and Profits, and of Sales and Profits by Products/ Services

Step 2. SWOTs: Present (cont.). To Help Decide Where to Concentrate Planning Efforts, List Target Markets Currently Served with Present Products/ Services and Analyze by Sales and Profits

Step 3. SWOTs: Present (cont.). Develop Performance Profiles for Each Product/Service-Target Market

Step 4. SWOTs: Future. For Each Product/Service-Target Market, Forecast Market Environment, Target Market's Demand, and Your Sales and Profits (Assuming You Continue Your Present Strategy)

Step 5. Gap Analysis

Step 6. Examination of Strategic Options and Strategy Selection

Step 7. Strategy Documentation and Evaluation

Step 8. Fleshing Out, Documenting, and Formatting the Annual Marketing Plan

Step 4. SWOTs: Future

For Each Product/Service-Target Market, Forecast Market Environment, Target Market's Demand, and Your Sales and Profits (Assuming You Continue Your Present Strategy)

THE PROBLEM

In a contest between you and the world, bet on the world.

–Franz Kafka

We asked the cyclone to go around our barn, but it didn't hear us.

–Carl Sandberg, from *The People, Yes*

The necessity of adapting to the world is well known. But there's a problem: predicting the future. Forecasting bloopers are legend, even providing rich material for cartoonists (see Figure 2.33).

Still, you can't escape the futurity of your present actions. You either build a plant or you don't. You invest money in R&D or you don't. You open new sales territories or you don't. What you're going to be tomorrow depends on what you do today.

This, of course, comes as no surprise to you. You're conscious of the futurity of your actions. In effect, every decision you make depends on how you view the coming years. If you think the future will be about the same as today, you'll follow marketing programs that have worked in the past. On the other hand, if you think the future will be radically different, you'll make corresponding changes in your marketing programs.

So forecasting is an inescapable activity. You forecast, either intuitively or consciously. Those are your only choices. Conscious, systematic forecasting has advantages similar to those of conscious, systematic planning. Step 4 shows how to use forecasting to increase the effectiveness of your plan.

THE TIME HORIZON

Make a long-range and a short-range (annual) forecast. You may say, "Just a minute. Sure a long-range forecast is necessary for a strategic plan. But, I'm only developing an annual marketing plan!" Even so, your market forecasts should include a long-range outlook. *Remember: you cannot escape the futurity of the actions you take today.* You can take some actions today–at little cost–which will make you better prepared for the more distant future.

FIGURE 2.33

"*. . . First I was a Keynesian . . . Next I was a monetarist . . . Then a supply-sider . . . Now I'm a bum . . .*"

Bill Schorr, Los Angeles Herald, Copyright © 1982. Reprinted with permission.

Still you may say, "Things are doing fine. Why should I go through all the bother?" Let's approach that answer indirectly, with an example of the rapid impact of exponential growth.

A farmer has a mill pond. It's his pride and joy. His cattle drink from it. His grandchildren fish in it. Suppose one day a beautiful lily pad appears in the pond. Although lily pads are pretty, he doesn't want his pond to get covered with them. If that should happen, the fish would die. Furthermore, the cattle would stomp down the banks trying to drink. The pond would become a mess.

To get the pads cleaned out, he must give a contractor seven days notice. Now suppose lily pads double in number daily. And suppose that the pond and the lily pads are of a size that in 60 days from the time the first lily pad appears, the pond will be completely full of lily pads. The question is: By checking the percentage of the pond covered with lily pads, how will the farmer know when he absolutely *must* call the contractor? Think about it for a minute.

To begin, the pond has one lily pad growing on it. But every succeeding day the number of lily pads doubles. On the second day, then, there are two pads, on the third day, four, and so on. Sixty days later, if growth is allowed to continue, the pond will be entirely full. It's relatively easy to understand that only half of the pond is free of lily pads on the next-to-last day, the fifty-ninth. But it's usually harder to grasp that on the fifty-third day, just a week before the pond is full, the pads cover only 0.8 of 1 percent of the surface. In other words, if the farmer doesn't call in the contractor when the pond is filled with *less* than 0.8 of 1 percent of lily pads, it's too late.

Unfortunately, complications that stem from faulty strategies often grow at an exponential rate. At first, faults in strategy are hardly detectable, but toward the end they close in remorselessly. It takes time to devise adjustments to your strategy, put them to work, and then turn things around. In fact, by the time it's obvious to everyone that your strategy is beginning to flounder, it may be too late to do anything about it.

To make matters worse, strategic decisions are not self-regenerative, in the way that operating decisions are. You are *forced* to make operating decisions every so often, but, unless you have a formal review process, this is not the case for strategic decisions.

Campbell Soup Company decided in 1921 to put soup in cans. While every year, can size, soup variety, label design, and so on was reviewed, changed, or modified, the basic strategic decision to put soup in cans was not seriously reviewed. However, changing life-styles, fast food restaurants, health issues related to the soldered seams, and new technology were all making that initial strategic choice less attractive.

After Campbell's experienced an eleven-consecutive-year de-cline in per capita soup sales, the company reviewed its strategy of "soup-in-the-can." Campbell's now makes dry soup, frozen soup, and refrigerated soup. And the list goes on.

Perhaps the outcome of your long-range environmental assess-ment is that you decide to continue to do what you've been doing in the past. In such a case, was the assessment a waste of time? Not at all. You will have systematically examined the opportunities and threats in your relevant environment and you are at least more aware of the risks and advantages of your present course of action.

However, examination of the product/service-target market's en-vironment may uncover concealed threats. You may find that your target market is decreasing in size, or that some of your customers may be defecting to a new product/service, thus posing current and future threats to yours. This happened to firms providing overnight letter delivery when the facsimile systems started to proliferate.

Or, you may find that your major product/service is slowly but surely becoming obsolete, due to increasing government regula-tions. For example, some states have passed legislation which makes the legal penalties for using radar detectors outweigh pos-sible gains through avoidance of speeding tickets. This legislation could spread from state to state. Then there's the federal govern-ment. The Federal Highway Administration has proposed that radar detectors, "bird dogs" in CB radio lingo, be made illegal for use in commercial vehicles weighing more than 18,000 pounds. (The Ad-ministration has no jurisdiction over cars.)[1]

Or, perhaps you are a smaller company that has developed a market, but now the market has grown big enough to attract larger firms. This could result in a reversal of fortune. For example, Johnson Products Company, Inc. pioneered personal grooming products for black consumers. Although the company started in the founder's basement, by 1974 Johnson's sales were over $30 million. But as Johnson's sales (which were also the industry sales) increased, the size of the market became attractive to larger firms in the cosmetics industry. Avon and Revlon, among others, entered the market. Johnson Products has had a tough time competing against new, extensively promoted products from the large, well-financed, aggressive competitors.

If you are confronted with such threats, you can now start shifting to a different market segment, changing products/services, and so on. The earlier you start, the more gradual and less disruptive the changes will be.

Don't wait until it's life threatening to act. Make time your ally, not your enemy. Look at what happened to a small bakery on the East Coast. They had strong brand loyalty and little competition in their regional market. A brand manager brought to the attention of top management that a very successful baked product was moving into the region.

"How much share do they have *now?*" asked the president.

"Less than one percent of the market," the brand manager responded.

"Then don't bother me with trivial issues," the president retorted.

Six years later, with the competitor's new product having 21 percent of the market, strong trade relations, good promotional programs, and established channels of distribution, the East Coast bakery decided something must be done. But now the competitor had a well-established beachhead.

Most firms do take into consideration a time period of longer than one year. One survey showed that out of 262 firms, only 22 percent developed marketing plans for just one year. The rest developed plans for one year plus a brief reference to later years (44 percent), or they developed a separate longer-range plan in addition to the one-year marketing plan (34 percent).[2]

How far into the future should you forecast? It depends on the type of industry you're operating in and the type of fixed commitments you have to make. However, five years seems to be the most common time frame. A five-year planning horizon gives you time to make gradual changes, yet is not so distant as to seem "blue sky." (You probably won't want, at this time, to follow Sony's example of creating a 100-year plan.)

Of course you must adhere to company constraints. Perhaps management has a time horizon of just one or two years. Keep in mind, "No manager who has a longer time horizon than his superiors can expect to survive."[3] This makes sense. Such a manager would be spending resources for long-range viability but his/her superiors would be looking for the maximum short-range payout.

THE NECESSITY FOR FORECASTING ENVIRONMENTAL CHANGES

Let's look at the Micron case again. Assume that Micron wants to make one- and five-year forecasts.

Suppose, by some means, Micron could forecast the target market demand for high-end oscilloscopes. Would this be the only forecast that Micron would need to develop a marketing plan? Of course not. Micron would need to know restructuring that might take place in the market environment. For example:

Target Market

Will there be changes causing shifts in your target market's key buying motives? What type of research will these companies be doing? Will this research require new/different accessories? Or even new oscilloscopes?

What about the number of companies in the target market? What about the size of the firms? For example, will there be larger firms in the target market? If so, will they have different purchasing patterns and credit needs?

And, will there be changes in geographic location? Industry classification?

Distribution Channels

Then, what about distribution channels? Will there be fundamental changes, such as competitors using manufacturers' representatives?

Direct Competition

Most certainly, Micron would need to know more about what their competitors will be up to. Will they be more aggressive? What about their R&D strategies? Service?

Then, will there be any mergers? Any new competitors? If so, what will be the nature of these new entrants? Will they be divisions of major corporations or small start-up companies?

Other External Forces

Micron would need to analyze its indirect competition, such as contract research agencies. Closely akin to indirect competition are technological changes. Are there any new developments that are causing the high-end oscilloscopes to become less in demand or, heaven forbid, obsolete? Forecasting these developments can be neglected because, as noted, changes often come from outside the industry.

Economic conditions and governmental policies will have their impact on demand for high-end oscilloscopes. Certain types of firms that purchase research oscilloscopes are almost recession-proof. Others are not.

As for the government, its allocation of research grants may have a great impact on demand. But beyond the number of high-end oscilloscopes demanded, changes in governmental support may also change the composition of demand. Universities, for example, may be more likely to purchase high-end oscilloscopes than industrial firms.

So, for your product/service-target market there's no question that you'll also need to forecast environmental changes for factors such as those suggested in the performance profiles.

FORECASTING IN A TOTAL QUALITY ENVIRONMENT

In total quality planning, other functional areas will have extensive customer contacts, and subsequently will help make forecasts more accurate. Manufacturing/operations personnel, because of their specialization, are more likely to pick up some clues that might go unnoticed by marketing. The same is true for finance, and so on. All of this input gives your planning team greater insights into your customers' future actions.

Albeit getting close to the customer doesn't ensure successful forecasting, it does help you to understand their needs and the marketplace better, and to be a little less naive in forecasting.

In many cases, true quality programs lead to relationships between suppliers and customers that encourage sharing of future plans. For example, let's look at what happened between a manufacturer of electric coffee makers and one of its customers. Rather than keep the manufacturer in the dark about its future, the customer shared with the manufacturer its strategic plan, along with its projections of growth and sales.

Do you think the manufacturer was better able to predict its future sales? You bet! And do you think the manufacturer's savings derived from better planning were passed on (in part) to the customer? Right again!

The Long-Range Forecast

First, let's take a look at the long-range forecast. In long-range forecasting, you're looking for trends to determine your strategy. You're more interested in general directions than in point values.

To organize your analysis of SWOTs: Future, use "The Future" columns on the *Performance Profile*: *The Marketplace* (beginning with Figure 2.9) as a guide. The categories include items that usually need to be forecasted. Any factors you feel should be forecasted that were not part of your SWOTs: Present can be placed on the forms under "other" categories. This should include factors *not* important today but which might be important in the future. For example, AT&T might not be considering factors related to telecommunications in home offices. But five years from now AT&T might expect home offices to be a major work site.

It's usually advisable to use "The Future" column for your most-distant forecast. For example, if you're using a five-year planning horizon, place your five-year forecasts in "The Future" column. Any changes that you think will occur in years one through four, just note in the margins.

"The Future" columns are placed next to "The Present" columns to give a better overall perspective. You'll be more likely to be realistic if you consider what has been–and what is now–happening. Furthermore, this juxtaposition facilitates comparisons of the present with the future, increasing the probability that you'll take into account the changing environment in your marketing strategies and plans.

You can be sure that for some of the categories, you won't have much confidence in your forecasts–regardless of the forecasting techniques you might have used. However, for now, use your most-probable forecasts. Later on we'll cover how to handle your uncertainties.

Although the categories to be forecasted are laid out sequentially, that's not necessarily the order in which forecasts should be made. For example, look at *Performance Profile: The Marketplace–Target Market* (Figure 2.9). You may have to forecast "1.3. Other Factors" before you forecast "1.2. Key Buying Motives." Then, since the target market demand is a derivative of other categories, such as indirect competition, economic conditions, and growth of the target market, it ("1.4. Target Market Demand") should be the last category you forecast.

For many companies, a good starting point is to determine if there is any relationship between general economic conditions, government activity, demographics, and/or other factors which are regularly forecasted, and target market demand. Even if you cannot find a good relationship, much is to be gained by focusing on those factors thought to influence target market demand.[4]

After you have completed the *Performance Profile: The Marketplace* (except for making projections of "1.4. Target Market Demand,") reevaluate your projections. Because of interrelationships and dependencies, you may find that some projections need to be changed. For example, originally you may have estimated that at the end of your planning horizon your product would be in the early stages of maturity on the life-cycle curve. However, after examining characteristics of substitute products, you might now believe that your product would be near obsolescence and in the decline stage of the life-cycle curve. This would, of course, affect your forecast of target market demand.

Figure 2.34 is a schematic, recommending various types of forecasting techniques. While these recommendations are generally valid, it is your sound assessment of your unique planning situation that will determine the appropriateness of a given technique. Information on forecasting techniques and methodology can be found in Appendix A. But for now, we'd like to mention one rule particularly applicable for long-range forecasting, that is: when forecasting target market demand, because of possible structural discontinuities–changes in the target market, competitors, governmental regulations, and the like–it's dangerous (if not foolhardy) to use techniques based solely on historical trends and relationships, such as time series. Instead, use a build-up approach. Forecast general economic conditions, characteristics of the target market, substitute products/services, changes in relevant technology, and so forth. Then make your target market demand forecasts.

Still, if you have a history of your target market demand, use a trend line as a reference point for your long-range forecast. If your build-up forecast is different from the trend line, make sure you know the reason why. And that it stands the test of logic. Then, too, because trend lines are easy to construct, management will have probably drawn one. If your forecast differs from the trend line projection, you'll want to have a ready explanation.

The Annual Forecast

Now let's take a look at annual forecasting. There's a major difference in long-range and annual forecasting, especially for products/services in the maturity and decline stages of the life-cycle curve. Since structural changes usually will be fewer in the short range, you can place a greater reliance on quantitative approaches. So if you have past target market demand data, consider starting with a trend line. Use the build-up approach as a check on your findings from this projection. Figure 2.35 recommends various types of forecasting approaches. Again, for specific details on these techniques and methodology, see Appendix A.

The annual forecast of target market demand will be the basis for your marketing plans *and* the plans of production/operations, personnel, finance, and the like. Once your program is underway, your short-range latitude for making adjustments is usually not very wide. Consequently, the annual forecast should be more precise than the long-range forecast. Ideally, your annual forecast of your product/service-target market's demand should be in point values.

Noting Your Annual Forecasts

You'll remember that it's recommended that the "The Future" column be used for the long-range forecast (with the exception of "Target Market Demand"). For example, while developing environmental forecasts for year five, you noted in the margins forecasted changes for years one through four. Now that you're looking at year one more closely, you may detect additional changes likely to occur. Also note these in the margins.

FINDING TIME FOR FORECASTING

Again, it takes time to do this sort of forecasting. Begin by making a list of those categories you need to forecast (similar to the one for SWOTs: Present). *Performance Profile: The Marketplace* is a good place to start (example: possible changes in key buying motives). Then, list how you're going to get the necessary information. Gather bits of information throughout the year. Follow the A-B-C-D Rule.

Doing it this way, as with SWOTs: Present, does stretch out the forecasting process but you'll usually wind up spending less time overall. For example, you may decide that the best way to find out some of your competitor's plans may be through a mutual supplier. Talk with purchasing and arrange to go out to lunch with the supplier the next time he/she calls on your company. As with SWOTs: Present, a successful SWOTs: Future analysis usually results from many bits of information gathered over a period of time, producing small insights here-and-there, rather than from a gigantic, last-minute study.

FORECASTS FOR YOUR SALES, COST OF GOODS SOLD, EXPENSES, AND PROFITS (UNDER A NO-CHANGE STRATEGY ON YOUR PART)

Here the assumption is that the environment may change, but for now you're holding your present strategy (and marketing program)

FIGURE 2.34

Recommended Techniques for 5-Year Forecasting

Key: Value of Technique
1 = Primary
2 = Secondary
3 = Reference Point
[] = Not Applicable

*Sales force composite and survey of buyers are used in a broad sense: compiling sales (or purchasing) estimates and gathering other market information

Variable to be forecasted	Forecasting Technique									
	Quantitative Techniques				Qualitative Techniques					
	Time Series			Regression Analysis	Executive Opinion	Expert Opinion	Sales Force Composite*	Survey of Buyers' Intention (Industrial)*	Survey of Buyers' Intention (Consumer)*	Syndicated Services
	Trend Line	Moving Averages	Exponential Smoothing							
Target Market (characteristics)	3				1	1	3	1		1
Target Market (demand)	3			3	1	1	3	2		1
Distribution Channels (characteristics)					1	1	3	2		1
Distribution Channels (demand)	3			3	1	1	3			1

Direct Competition (characteristics)			1	1	3	2	1
Direct Competition (sales)	3		1	1	3	3	1
Substitute Products—Existing (characteristics)			2	1	3	1	1
Substitute Products—Existing (demand)	3	3	3	1	3	1	1
Substitute Products—New (characteristics and demand)			3	1	3	1	1
Technological Innovation			2	1			1
General Economic Conditions			3	1			1
Governmental Regulations			3	1			1

FIGURE 2.35

Recommended Techniques for *1-Year Forecasting*

Key: Value of Technique 1 = Primary 2 = Secondary 3 = Reference Point [] = Not Applicable	Forecasting Technique									
	Quantitative Techniques				Qualitative Techniques					
Variable to be forecasted	Time Series Trend Line	Moving Averages*	Exponential Smoothing*	Regression Analysis	Executive Opinion	Expert Opinion	Sales Force Composite**	Survey of Buyers' Intention (Industrial)	Survey of Buyers' Intention (Consumer)*	Syndicated Services
Target Market (characteristics)					1	1	1	1		1
Target Market (demand)	1	1	1	1	1	1	1	1	2	1
Distribution Channels (characteristics)					1	1	1	2		1
Distribution Channels (demand)	1	1	1	1	1	1	2	2		1

Direct Competition (characteristics)					1	1	1	1	1
Direct Competition (sales)	1	1	1		1	1	1	2	1
Substitute Products—Existing (characteristics)					2	1	2	1	1
Substitute Products—Existing (demand)	1	1	1	1	3	1	3		1
Substitute Products—New (characteristics and demand)					3	1	3	1	1
Technological Innovation					2	1			1
General Economic Conditions					2	1			1
Governmental Regulations					1	1	2	2	1

165

constant to see what your sales and profitability results would be. Keep in mind that this forecast is based on your current strategy. This forecast is just to show you where you'd be if you continue to do what you're doing now. You are not bound to these findings. That's why you're planning.

Sales Forecasts

If you've done a thorough job in environmental forecasting, preparing this forecast should not be difficult. You've got projections on general market conditions including competitive activity and product/service-target market demand.

Your sales forecast, at this point in the planning process, need not be of pinpoint accuracy (although eventually it should be). All you are seeking, for now, is a broad picture. You'll develop an accurate sales forecast after you've decided on your marketing strategy and annual marketing plan.

A word about inflation. Even you feel it advisable to build inflationary changes into your plan, it's usually better to do this later on. Remember, right now you're just trying to see what would happen under a no-change strategy on your part. Inflated dollars often make it difficult to understand trends. For example, suppose you project an inflation rate of 5 percent per year. Also assume that you forecast your sales to be flat. Your sales forecasts would show a growth (albeit inflation-based) of 5 percent, possibly causing some confusion during a management review. Unless you have some compelling reason, such as a management requirement, just use current dollars only (in the Micron case, that would be 1992 dollars).

The following are two suggested procedures for sales forecasting.

Method 1. Sometimes you can quantitatively forecast product/ service-target market demand. If you can, you probably know your present market share. Estimate your market share for the years throughout your planning horizon, given your present strategy. To make adjustments for competitive advantage/disadvantage more realistic, think in terms of specific competitors, their likely structural and strategy changes, and the impact these changes would have given other forecasted environmental conditions. Ask these questions:

- Which competitors–or groups of competitors–are you going to take sales away from? How will your present strategy enable you to do this? When?

or conversely,

- Which competitors–or groups of competitors–are going to take sales away from you because of their new competitive strengths and strategies?

To get your new sales forecast (under a no-change strategy), multiply your projected market share by projected target market demand. This was the method used in the Micron case. It was predicted that the market demand would grow at the rate of 5 percent real growth per year, and that Micron would lose market share to IMPRO; Micron would have 45 percent in 1993, and 35 percent in 1997 (Micron's executives forecasted that their competitors, in spite of increased aggressiveness, would have a more difficult time increasing their market share since their earlier gains were from Micron's "fringe areas." This, of course, may have been a dangerous assumption). The sales forecast, then, for 1993 would be $5,040,000 × .45 = $2,300,000 (rounded); for 1997, $6,126,000 × .35 = $2,100,000 (rounded).

Method 2. But what if you can't quantitatively forecast target market demand? You can get a sales forecast by following these steps:

1. Plot your product/service-target market sales for past years (five years back is usually ideal).
2. Using a trend line, project your sales for the next five years.
3. Adjust this trend line by:
   - Forecasted changes in target market demand for year one and your most distant year. These would include increases or decreases in target market demand brought on by changes in the target market and/or other external forces, such as indirect competition, technology, economic, and government.

– Direct competition. To make adjustments for competitive advantage/disadvantage, follow adjustment procedures discussed in Method 1 above.

Be sure to list assumptions as part of the forecast. And, while you're at it, follow the advice given by a sports gambler: "Be careful betting on your home teams. They never are quite as good as you think they are. And, they're never as bad as you think they are." So watch that you don't overevaluate your competitive advantages. On the other hand, don't make your competitive disadvantages out to be worse than they really are.

Figure 2.36 shows what the forecast chart would have looked like had Micron used Method 2, given the following reasoning by Micron's executives: they believed that the market had been growing but Micron had been losing market share. They also reasoned that their competitors, in spite of increased aggressiveness, would have a more difficult time increasing their market share since their earlier gains came from Micron's "fringe areas." Still although the market would continue to grow, they estimated Micron's sales would decline about 3 percent a year over the five-year period, with a greater decrease in the first year–5 percent.

Figure 2.37 is a form completed for sales and profit forecasts for the Micron case. Numbers were rounded to avoid implying a higher level of forecast accuracy.

Cost of Goods/Services Sold and Expense Forecasts

There are three types of expenses you'll have to forecast: cost of goods/services sold, selling expenses, and administrative expenses. These forecasts are usually fairly simple to arrive at, since you're making projections for a no-change strategy.

Cost of Goods/Services Sold. Make an estimate of the costs of units/volume of services you expect to sell. For this forecast, get production/operation and finance involved.

Selling Expenses. Project what marketing expenses you'll have to cover to carry out your present strategy, such as advertising, personal selling, public relations, and the like.

Administrative Expenses. Here administration, finance, and accounting will be most helpful. You may not be able to make, with

FIGURE 2.36

Sales Forecast for Micron, Inc.
(in $1,000, 1992 dollars)

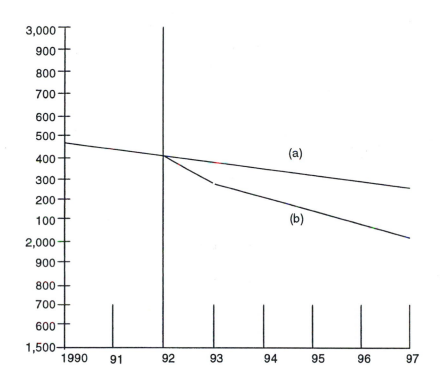

Key:

(a) Sales, under no-change company strategy, assuming target market demand to grow at the rate of 5 percent a year and no competitor strategy change.

(b) Sales, under no-change company strategy, assuming target market demand to grow at the rate of 5 percent a year, and competitors change strategies;

5 percent Loss of sales to competitors by end of 1993;
15 percent Loss of sales to competitors by end of 1997.

FIGURE 2.37

SALES AND PROFIT FORECASTS*

(Assuming You Continue Your Present Strategy, but Your Operating Environment Changes)

Forecast	1993 Annual Forecast	1997 Most-Distant Forecast
Sales Forecast	2,300,000	2,100,000
Profit Forecast (Contribution to Corporate)	600,000	490,000

Methodology:

Sales Forecast
Estimated (executive opinion, expert opinion) target market demand: *Real growth rate of 5 percent per year.*
Estimated (executive option) market share for Micron: 45 percent in 1993, 35 percent by 1997

Profit Forecast
Estimated (executive opinion) that gross margin, expenses will remain constant

*In $ 1992, rounded

any accuracy, cost allocations for a given product/service-target market. If so, you'll be better off using contribution accounting (see Step 1).

Profit Forecasts

You're now ready to put together a budgeted profit and loss statement (or contribution margin if you're using contribution accounting). If you've opted to give your sales forecasts in inflated dollars, your expenses should likewise be adjusted.

Examine Figure 2.38. Note that the cost of goods sold is the same percentage as in 1992 (45.8 percent), expenses are also held constant, and all figures are in 1992 dollars.

FIGURE 2.38

Pro-forma P & Ls* (in $1,000, 1992 dollars)		
	1993	1997
Sales	2,300	2,100
Cost of Goods Sold	1,050	960
Gross Profit	1,250	1,140
Expenses		
R&D	180	180
Selling	200	200
Advertising	60	60
Administration Expenses	210	210
Total Expenses	650	650
Contribution to Corporate	600	490
*Assumptions: gross margin, expenses will remain constant		

Profit forecasts were recorded on the Sales and Profit worksheet (Figure 2.37).

Completed examples of *Performance Profile: The Marketplace* and *Performance Profile: Critical Summary* for Micron appear in Figures 2.39-2.48.

FORECASTS WITH LESS-THAN-COMPLETE INFORMATION

You'll always be dealing with "grey" areas. What will happen to the economy? What will your competitors do? Will new technologies make your present products/services obsolete? And regardless of what techniques you use and how much time and money you spend, uncertainty will still cloud the accuracy of some of your forecasts. Unfortunately, if you miss on some of these forecasts, it will usually create havoc with your plans.

For many companies, uncertainty is a way of life which adds to the difficulties of the forecasting process. In Step 7 we'll talk about how to plan for an uncertain future using contingency planning.

FIGURE 2.39.

PERFORMANCE PROFILE: The Marketplace

1. Target Market

Category	The Present *1992*	The Future 19*97*
1.1 Target Market (description)	Highly specialist research scientists at universities, government and industry research laboratories	No change
1.2 Key Buying Motives	Extensive application High performance & reliability Immediate service	Rapidly changing demands will require new accessories and some instrument redesign No change
1.3 Other Factors	Mature Stage	No change
1.4 Target Market Demand	Trend to Date (describe) and Volume (if available) ≈ $4,800,000 Demand has increased by 10% in the past five years.	Forecast: 19__ **$5,040,000** 19__ **$6,126,000** Inflation Adjustments 3% in 1993 = $5,184,000 3% Average over 1994-97, 1997 = $7,618,000

FIGURE 2.40

PERFORMANCE PROFILE: The Marketplace (continued)

Target Market (Other Factors)

Characteristics of Target Market	Trend to Date	The Present 1992	The Future 19 97
Position of Product/ Service on Life Cycle Curve	*[life cycle curve graph: Introduction, Growth, Maturity, Decline; Total Industry sales vs. Time]*	Maturity	No change
Cyclical Factors	Same/Changing	_____	_____
Seasonal Factors	Same/Changing	_____	_____
Geographical Location	Same/Changing	_____	_____
Size of Target Market Firms	Larger/Same/Smaller	_____	_____
Concentration of "Key Accounts" in Industry	Increasing/Same/ Decreasing	_____	_____
Backward Integration	Extensive/Same/ Non-Existent	_____	_____
Bargaining Power	Greater/Same/Less	_____	_____
Rate of Growth of New Customers in Target Market	Increasing/Same/ Decreasing	_____	_____
Number of Customers in Target Market	Increasing/Same/ Decreasing	_____	_____
Purchasing Influencers	Non-Existent/Same/ Changing	_____	_____
Other Characteristics (Specify)			

FIGURE 2.41

PERFORMANCE PROFILE: The Marketplace (continued)

3   Direct Competition (The Present) *1992*

Key Success Factors	Your Firm MICRON	Competitor IMPRO	Competitor MOLTEC	Competitor
	(Ratings of Comparative Key Success Factor Strengths: High = 3; Average = 2; Low = 1 and trend by ↑;—; or ↓)			
1. R & D	3 ↓	2	2	
2. Highly specialized sales engineers	1-2 ↓	3	1-2	
3. Immediate service capability	2	2	2	
4. Production Quality Control	3	?	?	
5.				
Management's Current <u>Major</u> Emphasis	(List Key Success Factors)			
	—	Highly specialized sales engineers	?	
Market Share	(%, and Trend ↑;—; or ↓)			
	50% ↓	25% ↑	25% ↑	
Target Market's Ratings of Augmented Products/ Services	(Superior, Above Average, Average, Below Average, Inferior)			
	Superior	Average to Above Average	Average to Above Average	
Relative Financial Strength	(Very Strong = 3; Average = 2; Weak = 1 and Trend ↑;—; or ↓)			
	3	1 ↑	1 ↓	
Company Commitment	(Aggressive = 3; Holding = 2; Divestment = 1)			
	2-1	3	3	

Other Factors

FIGURE 2.42

PERFORMANCE PROFILE: The Marketplace (continued)

Direct Competition (The Future) *1997*   OUT OF BUSINESS ↓

Key Success Factors	Your Firm **MICRON**	Competitor **IMPRO**	Competitor **MOLTEC**	Competitor
	(Ratings of Comparative Key Success Factor Strengths: High = 3; Average = 2; Low = 1 and trend by ▲ ;—; or ▼)			
1. R & D	2↓	2↑		
2. Highly specialized sales engineers	1	3		
3. Immediate service capability	2	2		
4. Production quality control	2	2		
5.				
Management's Current <u>Major</u> Emphasis	(List Key Success Factors)			
	—	Highly specialized sales engineers	35% 1997	
Market Share	(%, and Trend ▲ ; ⟋ or ▼)			
	35%↓	65%↑		
Target Market's Ratings of Augmented Products/ Services	(Superior, Above Average, Average, Below Average, Inferior)			
	Average to Below Average	Superior		
Relative Financial Strength	(Very Strong = 3; Average = 2; Weak = 1 and Trend ▲ ; —; or ▼)			
	2	2		
Company Commitment	(Aggressive = 3; Holding = 2; Divestment = 1)			
	1	3		
Other Factors				

FIGURE 2.43

PERFORMANCE PROFILE: The Marketplace (continued)

3.4 Direct Competition (Other Factors)

Characteristics of Direct Competitors	Trend to Date	The Present 1992	The Future 1997
Number of Competitors	More/Same/ Fewer	2 Both IMPRO and MOLTEC about ½ the size of MICRON	Fewer (MOLTEC will be out of business)
Structure (size)	Larger/Same/ Smaller	———	Larger (IMPRO)
Management Sophistication	Same/More	About same as MICRON	More
Product/Service Offerings	More/Same/ Fewer	One product	Same
Channels of Distribution Used	Same/Changing	Direct	Same
Marketing Practices	Same/Changing	———	Same
Research and Development	Same/Changing	?	IMPRO will be spending more on R&D
Other Characteristics (Specify)			

FIGURE 2.44

PERFORMANCE PROFILE: The Marketplace (continued)

3. Direct Competition (Summary Sheet)

Category	The Present 1992	The Future 19 97
Key Success Factors	R&D Highly specialized sales engineers Immediate service capability Production quality control	Increased R&D capabilities SAME

Direct Competitors	Market Share	Augmented Product/Service	Market Share	Augmented Product/Service
Your Firm	50% ↓	Superior	35% *45% 1993	Average to Below Average
IMPRO	25% ↑	Average to Above Average	65% *55% 1997	Superior
MOLTEC	25% ↑	Average to Above Average	OUT OF BUSINESS	

	The Present	The Future
Comments (emphasis, financial strength, and/or commitment) Comments on General Trends	MICRON - Holding (or divestment); Relatively strong financially; Losing market share IMPRO - Aggressive, Relatively weak financial condition but improving; Gaining market share; Strong sales force MOLTEC - Aggressive; Very weak financial condition; But gaining market share	Under "NO-CHANGE MICRON STRATEGY" IMPRO will become market leader, IMPRO will probably acquire MOLTEC BUY OUT 1993

FIGURE 2.45

PERFORMANCE PROFILE: The Marketplace (continued)
4. Other External Forces

Category	The Present *1992*	The Future 19_97_
4.1 Indirect Competition:	Widespread use of low cost oscilloscopes; Field dominated by large aggressive competitors with world-wide sales and service networks	Relatively high growth in low-end-market, low growth (5% per year) in high-price market. For this reason, the major manufacturers are likely to stay in low price market. Expect these companies to be very aggressive in this low price market.
4.2 Technological:		
4.3 Economic:		
4.4 Governmental:		
4.5 Other Forces: (major)		

FIGURE 2.46

SALES AND PROFIT FORECASTS*

(Assuming You Continue Your Present Strategy, but Your Operating Environment Changes)

Forecast	1993 Annual Forecast	1997 Most-Distant Forecast
Sales Forecast	2,300,000	2,100,000
Profit Forecast (Contribution to Corporate)	600,000	490,000

Methodology:

  Sales Forecast

    Estimated (executive opinion, expert opinion) target market demand: *Real growth rate of 5 percent per year.*
    Estimated (executive option) market share for Micron: 45 percent in 1993, 35 percent by 1997

  Profit Forecast

    Estimated (executive opinion) that gross margin, expenses will remain constant

*In $ 1992, rounded

GAINING ACCEPTANCE OF FORECASTS

Sometimes marketing has a difficult time getting other functional areas to buy into forecasts. However, this is usually not a problem in a firm where functional areas are working together in total quality planning. Other functional areas will have had exposure to customers. They will be at least somewhat aware of industry trends. So the forecast will not come as a complete surprise.

However, if your product/service-target market is apt to be buffeted by turbulence and resulting discontinuities, reasonable forecasts could vary greatly, depending upon assumptions.[5] This is why you must keep upper management and other functional managers apprised of findings throughout the forecasting process.

With any assessment of high-change environments, believability is diminished when the forecasts are simply presented "on the table" to management. The reasoning that went into generating the

FIGURE 2.47

Pro-forma P & Ls* (in $1,000, 1992 dollars)		
	1993	1997
Sales	2,300	2,100
Cost of Goods Sold	1,050	960
Gross Profit	1,250	1,140
Expenses		
R&D	180	180
Selling	200	200
Advertising	60	60
Administration Expenses	210	210
Total Expenses	650	650
Contribution to Corporate	600	490
*Assumptions: gross margin, expenses will remain constant.		

forecasts may be obscured in the final summarization. It's also likely that management's perceptions of relevant environmental variables may differ considerably from your own. This is why it's important that management be involved at the outset of the process, rather than merely at its conclusion.

If you're in close and constant communication with management, it can be effective to get input informally. For instance, in the case of an industrial and farm equipment manufacturer, the informal approach works well because, as one planning manager explained, "The lines of communication in our company are very short. The total corporate staff is all located within 100 feet of each other. It's very easy for people to communicate and share. The officers of the company are very accessible to people doing this kind of work. So, typically, getting input is informal as opposed to 'Here's a questionnaire we want you to fill out.'"

For many firms, however, formal meetings seem to be a better way of getting management's input. Even firms that prefer the informal approach may find meetings necessary when there is a wide divergence of opinion among management. Meetings can be short or all-day sessions, held at the home office or away, one-time

FIGURE 2.48

PERFORMANCE PROFILE: Critical Summary

The Present 19 92	The Future 19 97
Major Problems (Negatives)	**Major Problems (Negatives)**

Major Problems (Negatives)

In past five years Micron's sales have been flat (-2%); Severe cutbacks in R&D and selling expenditures, yet both are key success factors.

Evidence of poor prospecting.
Lack of service network has cost sales.

Competition is aggressive, esp. IMPRO. IMPRO has a larger sales force and more extensive sales support.

In past 5 years MICRON has lost market share to both IMPRO & MOLTEC.

Major Opportunities (Positives)

MICRON's instruments have been trouble free.

Competitors are financially weak; IMPRO's condition is improving, MOLTEC's is worsening.

MICRON has 50% of the market and is in good financial condition.

In spite of cutbacks in R&D, MICRON's oscilloscope is still rated as superior.

Current Target Market Demand

≅ $4,800,000

Demand has increased by 10% in the last five years.

Major Problems (Negatives)

MICRON'S sales will drop by 17%; Contribution to corporate will decrease by 37%.

IMPRO will become stronger financially and will probably buy out MOLTEC. As a result of this and other aggressive market actions, IMPRO will become market leader.   BUYOUT 1993

MICRON'S market share will drop by 15%. Relatively slow market growth (5% per year)   5% market share drop in 1993

As a result, IMPRO, in an attempt to increase sales will be more aggressive.

R&D will become increasingly more important. Yet MICRON has cut back on R&D and sales force expenditures which may not enable MICRON to be competitive.

Major Opportunities (Positives)

Relatively slow market growth may discourage "majors" from entering the market.

Forecast of Target Market Demand

19____ $5,040,000

19____ $6,126,000

Inflation Adjustments

3% in 1993 = $5,184,000
3% Average over 1994 - 97
1994 - $7,618,000

or continuing affairs. In some companies, all it will take to provoke discussion is a brief initial statement of preliminary forecasts along with the underlying assumptions. Usually people will debate the assumptions and not the numbers.

Sometimes formal management approval is not necessary if managerial involvement has been intense throughout the process. But, usually some sort of approval process is necessary in order to ensure a perceptual match. Approval procedures may range from a simple presentation of the finished forecasts to management, to more significant managerial involvement in the process itself. Take the example of one firm, as reported by a manager. "We go over with management the most likely forecasts, then discuss other forecasts and why we rejected them. Often that results in some very lively discussion as different viewpoints are brought forward." Final agreement is reached at that (or subsequent) meetings.

If you have people reporting to you, also get them involved. They'll probably provide some good insights. Then, too, being asked to participate in a meaningful way will make them feel more like part of the management team, which is what you want to happen.

POINTS LEARNED

1. Forecasting is an inescapable activity. Conscious, systematic forecasting has advantages similar to those of conscious, systematic planning.
2. Develop a long-range and a short-range forecast even if you're only developing an annual plan. You can take some actions today–at little cost–which will make you better prepared for the more distant future.
3. Besides forecasting target market demand, also forecast possible changes in the target market, distribution channels, direct competition, and other external forces.
4. In total quality planning, other functional areas will have extensive contacts, and subsequently will help make forecasts more accurate.
5. In long-range forecasting, you're looking for trends to help

determine your strategy. You're more interested in general directions than in point values.

6. The annual forecast of target market demand will be the basis for your annual marketing plan and the annual plans of production/operations, personnel, finance and the like. Consequently, the annual forecast should be more precise than the long-range forecast.

7. Follow the A-B-C-D (Always be collecting data) Rule in forecasting. Gather information throughout the year.

8. After you have forecasted industry conditions and target market demand, forecast your sales and profits (under a no-change strategy on your part).

9. Gain acceptance of your forecasts through involvement.

LOOKING AHEAD

During the forecasting process you've projected changes for your target market, distribution channel, direct competitors, and other external market forces, given your long- and short-range environmental forecasts and industry product/service-target market demand.

The long-range view should provide you with a better idea of future opportunities and threats. The annual forecast should then give you a fairly accurate view of the environmental conditions affecting your target market and its demands for the next year. The knowledge will help you forecast company sales, expenses, and profits, given the new environmental conditions, under a no-change strategy on your part.

The next step: estimate the planning gaps that you may be facing.

THE EIGHT PLANNING STEPS

Step 1. SWOTs: Present. Gain an Overall Perspective by Historical Analysis of Total Sales, Expenses and Profits, and of Sales and Profits by Products/Services

Step 2. SWOTs: Present (cont.). To Help Decide Where to Concentrate Planning Efforts, List Target Markets Currently Served with Present Products/Services and Analyze by Sales and Profits

Step 3. SWOTs: Present (cont.). Develop Performance Profiles for Each Product/Service-Target Market

Step 4. SWOTs: Future. For Each Product/Service-Target Market, Forecast Market Environment, Target Market's Demand, and Your Sales and Profits (Assuming You Continue Your Present Strategy)

 Step 5. Gap Analysis

Step 6. Examination of Strategic Options and Strategy Selection

Step 7. Strategy Documentation and Evaluation

Step 8. Fleshing Out, Documenting, and Formatting the Annual Marketing Plan

Step 5: Gap Analysis

GAP ANALYSIS DEFINED

Gap analysis is the process of comparing management's performance goals (usually sales and some measure of profit) with your own sales and profit forecasts (given a no-change strategy).

Performance goals stem from an understanding, either explicit or implicit, of what management would like accomplished. Put another way, performance goals are management's vision path for the product/service-target market.

WHY GAP ANALYSIS?

Gap analysis is practically always performed, even if it's merely done intuitively. But formal analysis is infinitely better. It avoids misunderstanding. And, gap analysis answers the perpetual question, "Why change?" Some people will always insist on continuing the current marketing program. Gap analysis will point out the practicality–or impracticality–of a status quo strategy.

Gap analysis, then, points out the degree of change required to reach performance goals. Small gaps may suggest fine tuning, whereas large gaps may require a new approach. It's important that you know if minor changes will be good enough, or if you have to think about redoing your entire strategy.

If a change needs to be made, gap analysis continually focuses everyone's attention on the most critical issue–the gap. Every proposed action can be and should be related to how it will help close the gap.

GAP ANALYSIS: THE PROCESS

Understand (or Determine) Performance Goals

In some organizations the performance goals are set by management and passed down to the persons responsible for preparing the marketing plans. No communication problem here.

But in many cases the person developing the marketing plan, especially if it's for only one product/service-target market, will have to get management to articulate its vision path. Otherwise, he/she will have to estimate what is expected.

It's best if you can get management to state performance goals for at least two reasons. First, management has some idea, although not always clearly articulated, what performance goals should be. If you develop plans they perceive as being too low in sales and/or profit, the plan (and perhaps you!) will be dismissed as lacking vision.

Second, persons in management may not be in agreement as to what these goals should be. In that case, you should try to get consensus.

Forecast Results (Under a No-Change Company Strategy)

Sales and profit forecasts, of course, would have been developed during SWOTs: Future. If there are other performance goals besides sales and profit, forecast company results for these areas, also given a no-change company strategy.

Adjust for Inflation

If your forecasts do not include an inflation factor, and management's performance goals do, make appropriate adjustments.

Format Gap Analysis Results

Use a chart which highlights the gaps. The chart in Figure 2.49 illustrates Micron's sales and profit planning gaps. Management's sales performance goal was a 20 percent increase over five years. The planning gap was almost $800,000. It's easy to see that to bridge this gap, corrective and/or new strategies would have to be far-reaching.

FIGURE 2.49

Gap Analysis–Under a No-Change Strategy (in $1,000 dollars 1992)		
	1993	1997
Sales Planning Targets	2,496	2,880
Projected Sales	2,300	2,100
Projected Gap	(196)	(780)
Contribution to Corporate Planning Targets	676	780
Projected Contribution to Corporate	600	490
Projected Gap	(76)	(290)

Management's profit performance goal was also a 20 percent increase for the next five years. Innovative plans would be essential to bridge the profit planning gap (almost $300,000).

What If Performance Goals Seem Unreachable?

You're prejudging the solution. First, try to bridge the planning gap ("how to" suggestions will be given in Step 6). Give it your best shot. Then if your performance goals still seem beyond your reach, talk to management. More will be said about this later (Step 7).

What If There Is No Planning Gap?

Consider yourself one of the fortunate few. You may opt to keep planning targets where they are and use this opportunity to tighten up your organization. Or, you may decide to raise performance goals to create "stretch." Your best choice is probably the latter, as will be explained shortly.

GUIDELINES FOR SETTING PERFORMANCE GOALS

Some people differentiate between performance goals, goals, objectives, and planning targets. Here the terms are used interchangeably. Trying to differentiate between them usually creates more misunderstanding than it is worth. As one company's planning manual admitted: "The previous edition [of this manual] made a distinction between *objective* and *goal* which has been abandoned because of the resulting confusion."[1]

If it's up to you to set performance goals, here are some principles to follow. Even if your performance goals are mandated by management, these guidelines will help you in setting objectives yourself when you develop action plans (Step 8).

Performance Goals Must Be Exciting, Yet Believable

> Where there is no vision, the people perish . . .
>
> –Proverbs 19:28

Everybody likes to be with inspirational people. They put us at our best. Why? They're excited about their lives and their work because they're striving to achieve something which to them is *very* important. Their performance goals are so motivational that their lives seem significant and *exciting* to themselves–and consequently to others.

Uninspiring performance goals are no more interesting in business than in an individual, and the company that sets up uninspiring objectives invites a potentially fatal case of passivity in its employees. Highly creative and aggressive people gradually wilt if the atmosphere around them is dulled. The mediocre quickly become even more so. That's why, as already mentioned, it's often a good idea to raise your goals if no planning gap exists. Your present performance goals, if they can be reached without stretch, may not be inspirational.

Exciting performance goals help set a tone of urgency throughout the company, a sense of competitive spirit. As Roger Penske, president of Penske Corporation put it, "People don't wait for you when the green flag drops–and it's the same thing in business."[2]

On the other hand, absurdly high objectives are just as bad. It does little good to establish objectives so elevated that no one really believes they can be achieved. Only half-hearted efforts will go into developing plans and putting them into action.

Where, then, should performance goals be set? Perhaps this has been best summarized by the former chairman of AT&T, Frederick R. Kappel, who said: "Part of the talent or genius of the goal setter is the ability to distinguish between the possible and the impossible–but to be willing to get very close to the latter."[3] Note, however, that an attainable goal that nobody believes in is little better than one that really is impossible. Part of the "genius" of management is to convince everybody that they can rise to the challenge.

Performance Goals Must Be Set for Minimum Acceptable Levels

Given that performance goals should be demanding and exciting, where should one draw the line? For example, if sales for a product/ service are now $500,000, why not $5 million in five years? Then again, why not $20 million? Certainly you'd like to accomplish that. In fact, why not $50 million?

To establish the proper levels, determine the minimum acceptable amount (must goals) for each performance goal that will create *vitality* and *excitement*. These levels, then, become minimum acceptable performance goals. Any amounts beyond these levels (want goals) would be nice to obtain, of course. But they are not essential.[4]

To help you in the "mechanics" of setting growth rates, refer to Figure 2.50, a table of compound growth rates. It shows, for example, that if you wish to increase sales 10 percent annually, your present sales would have to increase by 161 percent in five years.

This table is useful in two ways: It lets you know how much you would have to increase sales or profits over a period of time in order to sustain a certain growth rate (the example above), and it also lets you work backwards. That is, if you want to double your sales in five years, what would be the approximate growth rate? Figure 2.50 points out that it is approximately 15 percent.

But don't get hung up on point values. Rather keep in mind that it's more important *not* to be grossly wrong in setting performance goals than it is to be exactly right.[5]

FIGURE 2.50

Year	1%	2%	3%	4%	5%
1	101%	102%	103%	104%	105%
2	102	104	106	108	110
3	103	106	109	113	116
4	104	108	113	117	122
5	105	110	116	122	128
6	106	113	119	127	134
7	107	115	123	132	141
8	108	117	127	137	148
9	109	120	131	142	155
10	111	122	134	148	163

Year	6%	7%	8%	9%	10%
1	106%	107%	108%	109%	110%
2	112	115	117	119	121
3	119	123	126	130	133
4	126	131	136	141	146
5	134	140	147	154	161
6	142	150	159	168	177
7	150	161	171	183	195
8	159	172	185	199	214
9	169	184	200	217	236
10	179	197	216	237	259

Year	15%	20%	30%	40%	50%
1	115%	120%	130%	140%	150%
2	132	144	169	196	225
3	152	173	219	274	338
4	175	207	286	384	506
5	201	249	371	538	759
6	231	299	483	753	1139
7	266	358	628	1054	1709
8	306	430	816	1476	2563
9	352	516	1060	2066	3844
10	405	619	1379	2893	5767

Performance Goals Must Be Feasible

Good enough. But you may feel like one manager who asked, "How can I be sure that performance goals I set are realistic? I'd hate to stick my neck out for performance goals that we possibly couldn't achieve." Take a look at your gap analysis charts. First, examine the trend lines of your past performance. This will show you how ambitious your performance goals are, given past performance. It's also helpful to have comparative data on what other firms in your industry have done to serve as a reference point. Possibly your association has data.

Concerning the feasibility of increased sales growth, market growth rate is often a key determinant. How much you can reasonably expect to gain depends heavily on whether your market is growing, static, or declining.

A Growing Market. Naturally, this is the most favorable environment for sales growth. Competitors may be struggling to meet demands; buyers will be looking for backup sources of supply; and new customers–who probably have no fixed product allegiance–are swelling the ranks of purchasers.

Figure 2.51 gives you an idea how much of a market growing at 20 percent per year you'll need to capture to meet your objectives. The figure points out a rather obvious fact: if the market growth rate is equal to your desired growth rate, all you need to do is to maintain your market share. And, if the market is growing faster than your desired growth rate, you don't even need to maintain your market share in order to meet your growth objectives. For example, if your market share is 10 percent, and the market is growing at the rate of 20 percent a year, in year one you need only 5 percent of the new growth in order to meet your objectives. By year five you only need to pick up 3.5 percent. (Please note: This example was used to show the advantages of being in a growing market. In most cases, a continued loss of market share is disastrous.)

But what happens when the market growth rate is slower than your desired rate? Look at Figure 2.52. If your market share is over 50 percent, right off, in year one, you are in an impossible situation–at least in trying to grow by capturing percentage of growth. Your desired growth rate, not only in rate but also in absolute

FIGURE 2.51

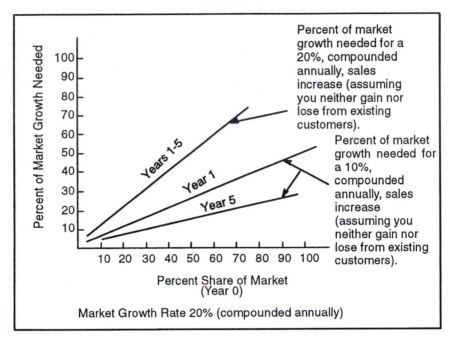

numbers, is greater than that of the total market. If you have a smaller share of the market–say 10 percent–during the first year you'll have to capture 20 percent of the growth. And this rate will have to increase annually because of the difference between the market's growth rate and yours. By the fifth year you'll have to get 28 percent of the new business because now your market share will have increased to 15.4 percent.

You may not have an accurate reading on the size of your market–or its growth rate–but it may be a good idea to make some subjective judgments and then construct a chart appropriate for your situation. Such analysis will help you keep your strategy within the bounds of realism. And it can be used to help make a point.

A Static Market. Growth is much harder to obtain in a static market. Your competition is also looking for growth, and since they probably have excess capacity (like you), you can expect them to be

FIGURE 2.52

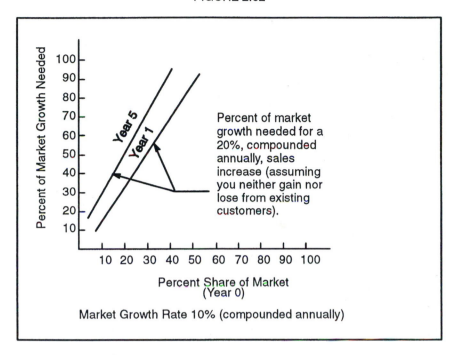

Percent of market growth needed for a 20%, compounded annually, sales increase (assuming you neither gain nor lose from existing customers).

Percent Share of Market
(Year 0)

Market Growth Rate 10% (compounded annually)

aggressive. In addition, buyer loyalties are probably well-set. Unless you really have competitive advantages over your competitors, don't look for much growth here.

A Declining Market. If you're operating in a declining market, some competitors will be getting out of the business. So you may be able to pick up some business in the short run. But remember that your competitors are leaving for a very good reason. The market is declining. You may find yourself getting more and more of less and less until you end up, finally, with all of nothing.

Of course, the size of the market and the size of your firm determine how attractive the market is to you. Market attractiveness is relative. Many smaller companies have found that what are decidedly declining markets (dogs) for a large firm are actually growth bonanzas (stars) for them. The vice-president of a small chemical company could hardly contain himself pointing out how they had picked up a "real steal" from a major chemical company. "We knew that they had classified this operation as a dog. The market was too small for them. We negotiated, keeping in mind their point of view–not ours. We got it at a very, very good price." He went on to say that the plant–the whole operation–had worked out exceedingly well, and was extremely profitable.

Of course, you just can't expect to grow without taking into consideration funds that you'll need to achieve that growth (or sustain present sales). Sometimes these funds can be generated internally, other times not.

Performance Goals Must Be Situational

Each product/service should have unique performance goals. Avoid the "global" approach. For example, one firm has over 200 products. The sales objective for each of these products was 6 percent, obviously an overall desired growth rate. But does this global performance goal make sense? Of course not.

Looking at your own situation, if you have more than one product/service-target market, you'll have differing market conditions for each (certainly the case in the above example of the firm with 200 products). It's only logical to set performance goals for each product/service-target market. If you have a number of products/ services-target markets, individual growth rates may very well vary from a plus 30 percent to a negative 10 percent.

Performance Goals Must Be Set for Every Key Area

Setting performance goals would be far simpler if there were only one major objective for a given product/service-target market. But most firms have several. Consequently, there must be performance goals for each key area. The common key areas are growth, profitability, and–where information is available–market share.

Performance Goals Must Be Within Somebody's Control

Performance goals must be stated in such a way that whoever is responsible for achieving them has the resources within his/her authority to accomplish them.

For example, if the person developing the marketing plan does not have authority over administrative expenses, the performance goal should be stated in such a way that this person will *not* be held accountable for these expenses. That's why using merchandising profit and/or contribution accounting (see Step 1) is often more desirable than a complete P&L, for instance, using allocated costs.

Performance Goals Must Not Impose Process Restrictions

Differentiate between performance goals and the means (process) for accomplishing them. For example, the president of a small electronics firm described his company's main performance goals as "to have the best product on the market." Discussion revealed, however, that the firm's real desire was to reach a certain level of sales and profits. Follow-up analysis suggested several strategies more financially promising than that of producing the best product. When the company acted upon one of these, its profits improved appreciably. In retrospect, the president realized that his goal was actually a strategy: several steps had been omitted in the planning process. Once the performance goal was clearly specified, the firm was no longer bound to the pseudo-goal of producing the "best product" on the market. It was free to consider other alternatives and, as it turned out, more rewarding strategies.

Performance Goals Must Be Specific

Make performance goals specific. It is always easier to agree on broad performance goals than on specific ones. But a broad goal, by definition, leaves much open to interpretation. By contrast, a specific goal promotes unity of purpose: everyone knows what must be accomplished. Knowing where you want to arrive also enables you to evaluate the various ways of getting there. Moreover, you're in a position to measure your progress en route and, if necessary, to make adjustments.

"Measure" is a key word, because a specific performance goal is concrete and measurable, whether in dollars, percentages, or proportions. For this reason, "increase sales" is not a specific performance goal, for what constitutes "increased sales?" One thousand dollars? Ten thousand dollars? One hundred thousand dollars? At best such a performance goal indicates your broad aim. Suppose, however, you determine that your performance goal for a specific product/service target market is to increase sales by 7 percent next year, 40 percent by the end of five years. These are specific performance goals because they describe exactly what you want to achieve; progress toward performance goals of this kind can be measured every step of the way. And when you get there, you'll know it.

Sometimes it's difficult to hammer performance goals into specificity. The following process is typical. You may think in terms of "increasing sales." You must then decide on what "increasing sales" actually means. A performance goal, subjected to intense scrutiny, its possible consequences weighed and balanced, can only emerge the better for it. Setting specific performance goals is often uncomfortable. There are so many uncertainties. No doubt this explains why there are so many vague goals.

Performance Goals Must Encompass Your Planning Horizon

First, determine your planning horizon–how far into the future you wish to plan. There is no right time span. The length of the planning horizon usually varies with turnaround time. Firms with heavy, fixed commitments usually plan further into the future than companies without such investments. However, as we've mentioned, many firms have found that five years is about right.

Then decide upon your planning targets for the end of your planning horizon. Next, determine your planning targets for the end of the first year. If you're experienced in planning, you may wish to set targets for the interim periods as well. But if you're just starting, settle for planning targets for the first year and the end of your planning horizon. Keep the process as simple as possible.

Performance Goals Must Be Subject to Revision

While working through the planning process, you might find that there is no way you can reach the predetermined performance goals. Or you may find that they are too low and need to be revised upward. If either situation happens, and you're the person who sets the performance goals, then change them.

Some companies are willing to change yearly performance goals, but are very sticky on the long-range ones. For example, a manufacturing company that uses a seven-year planning horizon makes adjustments in its short-range goals (one year) in the event of an economic downturn. Its planning-horizon goals, however, usually remain the same. The company's reasoning is as follows: In the short run, management may be able, for example, to do little to counter a recession. But over a long period of time, commitments to predetermined courses of action are not fixed the way they are in the short run, so managers have more leeway and should be able to adapt.

Performance goals are also subject to revision in another way. Since you'll roll over your plan every year, you'll have more than one chance to reassess your planning horizon performance goals.

Performance Goals Must Be in Writing

The very act of transferring an idea to paper is a test of its worth. It is alarming how many flashes of inspiration fail this initial test. Commitment to paper also serves to focus debate. Of course it is fine to hash out performance goals verbally, but before final acceptance, write them down.

There is another reason why goals should be in writing. Through time, we tend to forget. Having them in writing and in a prominent place, such as in a fact book, tends to remind you and to reinforce your original commitment throughout the planning process and in following years.

POINTS LEARNED

1. Gap analysis is the process of comparing management's performance goals (usually sales and some measure of profit) with your own sales and profit forecasts (given a no-change strategy).
2. Gap analysis points out the degree of change required to reach performance goals.

3. If it's up to you to set performance goals, follow these 11 guidelines.
   • Performance goals must be exciting, yet believable
   • Performance goals must be set for minimum acceptable levels
   • Performance goals must be feasible
   • Performance goals must be situational
   • Performance goals must be established for key areas
   • Performance goals must be within somebody's control
   • Performance goals must not impose process restrictions
   • Performance goals must be specific
   • Performance goals must encompass your planning horizon
   • Performance goals must be subject to revision
   • Performance goals must be in writing

LOOKING AHEAD

Once you complete Steps 1-5 you'll be in an enviable position. Because of a thorough, strategy-directed analysis, you'll probably know more about the present and future marketing conditions for your product/service-target market than anyone else in the organization. Furthermore, you'll understand the planning gaps you may be facing, and recognize the magnitude of change required.

Your next step is to put together a winning strategy.

THE EIGHT PLANNING STEPS

Step 1. SWOTs: Present. Gain an Overall Perspective by Historical Analysis of Total Sales, Expenses and Profits, and of Sales and Profits by Products/ Services

Step 2. SWOTs: Present (cont.). To Help Decide Where to Concentrate Planning Efforts, List Target Markets Currently Served with Present Products/ Services and Analyze by Sales and Profits

Step 3. SWOTs: Present (cont.). Develop Performance Profiles for Each Product/Service-Target Market

Step 4. SWOTs: Future. For Each Product/Service-Target Market, Forecast Market Environment, Target Market's Demand, and Your Sales and Profits (Assuming You Continue Your Present Strategy)

Step 5. Gap Analysis

Step 6. Examination of Strategic Options and Strategy Selection

Step 7. Strategy Documentation and Evaluation

Step 8. Fleshing Out, Documenting, and Formatting the Annual Marketing Plan

Step 6:
Examination of Strategic Options and Strategy Selection

No company can do everything it wants. There are always limitations of some sort. Not enough people. Or money. Or facilities. So strategy selection represents making practical choices and putting forth effort where it will do the most good.

Developing winning strategies has always been important. But today it is even more critical. A hundred years ago a product/service possibly would have lasted one, two, or even more generations. But now, because of rapidly improving technology and greater competitive pressures, the rate of obsolescence for products/services is greatly accelerating. This means that the rate of obsolescence of strategies is also greatly accelerating.

Charles H. Travel emphasizes the increased need for strategic management in his book, *The Third Industrial Age*. From the beginning of the industrial revolution he recognizes the following three eras (dates approximate):

1860-1950	"The age of the entrepreneur"
1950-1970	"The age of the professional manager"
1970-??	"The age of the strategist"[1]

If Travel were writing today, he no doubt would have included another era:

1990-??	"The age of the total quality driven strategy"

All of this underlines the need to continually review your present strategy and, when necessary, make changes.

Unfortunately, the process isn't easy. As Rothchild put it:

> [Formulating strategies] is complicated, difficult, and even frightening: complicated because it takes considerable time and effort to develop options; difficult because it requires new insights and a willingness to look at the problem from a variety of angles instead of from the same perspective; and frightening because it requires admitting your past and current strategy won't work in the future and because it may require a personal change, more risk, or even a recognition that a new management is necessary.[2]

Step 6 will give you pointers on how to examine strategy options. We've included a case example showing how Micron developed its strategy following the principles covered in this step.

During the SWOTs analyses, you examined:

- The target market
- Distribution channels
- Direct competition
- Other forces, such as indirect competition, technological, economic, and government influences
- Internal factors

As a result, the present and future strengths, weaknesses, opportunities, and threats concerning your products/services-target markets–given your present strategy–were brought to light.

Gap analysis pointed out your present strategy's effectiveness in the future. More than likely you'll have to develop a new one.

The greater your knowledge of various strategies and the conditions under which they're most effective, the more likely you'll be able to develop the best strategy for your situation. Although there are many things to consider while reviewing or developing a strategy, the correct answers for these three questions are critical:

Question 1. Are you considering the right market segment(s)?
Question 2. Are you capitalizing on opportunities for product/ service differentiation and/or reduced costs?
Question 3. Are you optimizing competitive advantages (while minimizing competitive restraints)?

Guidelines for answering these questions follow. These guidelines, however, are offered with three common sense caveats. First, some of them may not apply to your situation. You may be a product manager charged with developing a marketing program for a given product/service. In that case, your scope of responsibility will probably *not* include changing the core product/service.

Second, the applicability of the guidelines is situational. For example, one competitive guideline is: do not meet a competitor who has numerically superior resources head-on. This makes sense unless you happen to know that your competitor is likely to misplay its hand. Be sure your SWOTs findings justify applying a particular guideline.

Third, if your marketing plans involve multiproducts/services-target markets, you must plan to ensure coordination of activities in order to gain the potential benefits of sharing. For example, marketing a product/service to a given target market by itself might not be profitable. However, when combined with other products/services-target markets, it might make sense. A possible benefit could be economies of capacity utilization generated by the sharing of distribution facilities. More will be said about this later.

QUESTION 1. ARE YOU CONSIDERING THE RIGHT MARKET SEGMENT(S)?*

Background

The Importance of the Right Target Markets

Selecting target markets is possibly the most important decision you will make in the marketing planning process. Once you've selected your target market, you've decided on what business you will be in as well as who your competitors will be, and the broad parameters for your marketing program, such as specifications for your product/service, your promotion, your pricing policy, and the

---

*Some of the discussion under "Question 1" appeared in Robert E. Linneman and John L. Stanton, *Making Niche Marketing Work (How to Get Bigger by Acting Smaller)* (New York: McGraw-Hill, 1991). Reprinted by permission.

requirements for your distribution channels. So don't take this step lightly. This section provides insights for looking at the market–what segments to consider.

A Broadly Focused Marketing Strategy Often Leads to "Getting Stuck in the Middle"

There is the story about a person who went out quail hunting for the first time and kicked up a covey. The hunter thought he didn't need to aim because the sky was full of quail. Furthermore, with #8 shot, he would fill the sky with shot. He began to speculate how he would carry all the quail home.

You probably know how many he got. Zero. Just because there are a lot of targets and you've got a lot of shot doesn't mean that you don't have to take aim.

Similarly, broadly focused marketing usually leads you to "get stuck in the middle" and wind up with an empty game pouch. Let's look at a situation that happened several years ago.

A diversified company, consisting of 11 business units, was experiencing declining sales and a resulting drop in profitability. A consultant was called in. It took the consultant only a short time to realize that all of the business units' products and services were stuck in the middle.

You see, the company had been following a broadly focused approach in each of its divisions. These broadly focused approaches worked, in a limited way, when the economy was good. There was enough business to go around. The company had eked out a minimal existence.

Then a recession hit. It became a real buyers' market. Buyers could, and did, become more selective. They chose either the lowest-cost products and services or those that were differentiated in some specific way. To fend off bankruptcy, the company merged with another firm.

What causes us to become stuck in the middle? Trying to be all things to all people–offering a little bit of something for everybody (Figure 2.53).

On the other hand, a firm that practices what has been termed "precision target marketing" views the overall marketplace as consisting of a number of discrete markets. Such a firm designs marketing programs for each of a selected number of these market segments.

Figure 2.54 shows how a market could be divided into a number of market segments. A firm would choose which market segments it wishes to serve (target markets), and would then design appropriate marketing programs for each of these target markets.

The Need for More Highly Focused Strategies

A number of years ago, *Fortune* described how the mass market in the United States was becoming a myth: markets today are far

FIGURE 2.53

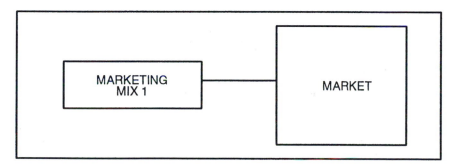

FIGURE 2.54

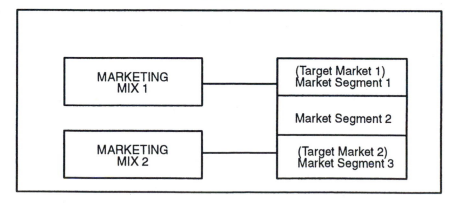

less homogeneous than in the past. The broad middle class which used to offer such a large target market no longer exists due to the polarization of middle-class incomes.[3] Then, more recently, *The Wall Street Journal* ran a series of articles entitled "The Shattered Middle Class." These articles pointed out that, "There is no longer one set of values that broadly fits the bulk of the middle class. There are fewer things that everybody wants and fewer things that everybody feels compelled to do. . . . the traditional middle class consumer is an endangered species. No longer is there such a large group of buyers that can easily be identified by their common goals, motivations and values."[4]

The growing diversity in U.S. markets may be highlighted by noting some of the new trends: unrelated persons of opposite (or same) sex sharing living quarters, single-person households, working mothers, career women, single-parent families, the graying of the U.S. market, the increasing importance of minorities, male child-caring, male narcissism, and, of course, the aging yuppies.

Acronyms abound. DINKS (Double Income, No Kids), MOBYs (Mommy Older, Baby Younger), DOBYs (their daddies), BUPPIES (Black Urban Professionals), PUPPIES (Poor Urban Professionals), DUMPIES (Downwardly Mobile Professionals) or D-DUMPIES (Deliberately Downwardly Mobile Professionals), WOOFs (Well-Off Older Folks), OPCU (One Person Consumer Units), SKIPPIES (School Kids with Income and Purchasing Power), TOBYs (To Old to be a Yuppy), and SINCOMs (Single Income Outrageous Mortgages).

And some splinters defy acronyms (hard to believe). Like latchkey kids (children of working parents who must spend part of the day at home unsupervised), sandwichers (adults who care for both their children and their aging parents), and, fast-track kids (children who are attending the right schools, classes, etc., to make sure they'll be on the right –translated "fast"– track). And the list could go on and on.

So we've become what has been called a "Baskin and Robbins society." Everything must be in 35 flavors. Furthermore, there is now a widespread tolerance of these new nontraditional lifestyles–a remarkable change in itself.

The result? There are no longer markets for products/services that everyone likes a little. There are only markets for products/services that somebody likes a lot.

Competition Is Forcing Most Companies to More Narrowly Focus Their Marketing Strategies

Today, more and more companies are designing marketing programs for increasingly smaller target markets. In 1989 we surveyed the *Fortune* 500 industrials and the *Fortune* 500 nonindustrials. About 75 percent said that they were, for at least some of their products and services, focusing in on smaller market segments. Of the remaining 25 percent, one-half said that they planned to start doing so within the next two years.

Reflecting this trend, terms such as "narrowly focused," "narrow casting," "microspecialization," "micromarketing," "micromerchandising," "precision target marketing," "customized marketing," "multi-imaging," "regionalized marketing," and "localized marketing" are becoming more prevalent.

We like "precision target marketing." It's more descriptive of what's happening. As one executive stated, "We previously looked for orders anywhere and everywhere. We now select specific markets in which we believe we can increase share at predetermined margins and then target customers within these markets whom we believe can deliver share."[5]

Using precision target marketing enabled Chubb Corporation to win in a land of losers. Other property and casualty insurers commoditized their products and, while doing so, took a hit on their return on shareholders' equity (an annual return of less than 5 percent). Chubb, on the other hand, concentrated on a few narrowly focused markets. Among these markets were expensive houses and directors' and officers' liability and fidelity insurance. For these segments Chubb provided outstanding service. The result? Chubb's annual return on shareholder equity averaged 29 percent over a 5-year period.[6]

Campbell Soup Company has moved away from a "blanket" approach. Its 22 regional offices no longer are merely extensions of its corporate headquarters. Each of these regional offices now develops its own marketing programs and gets an advertising and trade promotion budget. Some 10 percent to 15 percent of Campbell's $181 million advertising budget supports such regional spending.[7]

Barnett Banks' rapid growth in Florida is at least partially due to the attention it has given fragmented markets. It approaches the market as a number of different marketing segments and designs marketing programs accordingly. For example, Barnett put in a small 500-square-foot branch costing $45,000 in Moorings Park. This office was designed especially for a private life-care facility located in affluent Naples. Within a short time it captured $12 million in deposits.[8]

The benefits of precision target marketing are clear. Look at the retailing industry. In the last decade or so, the fastest growing retailers were those which targeted their products/services toward differentiated image-oriented merchandise. For example, between 1975-85, specialty retailers, such as The Limited and The Gap, experienced annual growth rates of 50.7 percent and 20.6 percent. On the other hand, general retailers experienced a much slower growth rate: JC Penney, 6.0 percent; Sears, 5.2 percent.[9]

On the other hand, firms that try to reach out to too many market segments with one product/service run into trouble. For example, General Motors (everybody's "whipping boy") designed smaller, more fuel-efficient E/K cars. These were compromise models designed for two quite different segments: (1) its traditional customers; and (2) the affluent young buyers who had rejected Detroit's luxury cars. But General Motors came up short: the cars were "focused on a non-existent market." The new line was viewed as being too small for the traditionals, and too lacking in pizzazz for the yuppies.[10]

That was in 1988. But Detroit doesn't learn easily. Later that same year, General Motors' Oldsmobile division unveiled a new marketing campaign to attract young, upscale families while still appealing to the division's traditional buyers.

The result? According to *Adweek*, the campaign didn't appeal to the younger buyers as much as it drove off the older ones. "Turning off middle-aged males was perhaps one of the biggest [advertising] gaffes of the '80s."[11]

But the lesson was still to be learned. At the Japanese Auto Show in 1991, new models revealed that Japan's car makers seemed intent on filling scores of small market segments. How did Detroit respond? Said a vice president of General Motors, "I don't think these are cars built with the bulk of American users in mind."[12]

Technological Advances Make Precision Target Marketing Feasible

The ability to serve more focused markets is already available to you and your competitors. Consider computer-aided design (CAD), computer-aided manufacturing (CAM), flexible manufacturing, just-in-time inventory, offshore sourcing, computer-linked purchasing, more targeted media (such as cable TV and, through the use of selective binding, even *personalized* magazine editions), point-of-sale scanning services, single-source data, and more sophisticated methods of data tracking, analysis, storage, and retrieval.

Advances in management information and communication systems are well understood. But perhaps less known is the ability of manufacturers to vary product configurations at a minimal cost. The Japanese provide an excellent example.

Japan's manufacturing emphasis began right after World War II. There have been four stages to date (with Japan now well into the fifth–high technology).

Stage 1. Low price/low labor costs. Devastated by the war, Japan concentrated on industries requiring low labor costs and little capital.

Stage 2. Low price/large scale, efficient production. The next focus, starting around 1950, was in industries such as steel and ship building, using modern, cost-effective plants.

Stage 3. Focused production. The next step was moving to fill certain niches, perhaps best illustrated by small cars.

Stage 4. Flexible production. Using the *kanban* system, the Japanese produced many models instead of one at very little extra cost.[13]

The *kanban* system of flexible production deserves a closer look. Widely misunderstood in the United States, *kanban* means something more than "just in time" inventory. Although having inventory arrive at the moment needed is an extremely important ingredient, it is only part of the process which makes the *kanban* system highly effective. One of the other key ingredients is the reduction in changeover times.

A reason many companies cannot produce a wide range of products is that it takes too long to change over from one model to another. The costs are just too high. The Japanese have been able to greatly reduce changeover times. For example, note how Toyota was able to reduce the initial set-up time for a bolt maker from eight hours to one minute. Mazda reduced set-up time for a ring gear cutter from 6.5 hours to 15 minutes. Yanmar has changed the set-up time for a cylinder block line from 9.3 hours to nine minutes.[14]

Such improvements have enabled the Japanese to design many different models to suit the needs of diverse markets at little extra cost. Witness what happened at Yanmar Diesel. In the recession of 1975, Yanmar faced a doubtful future. The demand for diesel engines and farm machinery had plummeted. Yet the company emerged victorious from this crisis as a result of adopting the Toyota production system.

The results were astonishing. Between 1975 and 1981 factory productivity almost doubled. At the same time, costs of some parts were reduced by 72 percent. Furthermore, work-in-process inventories were cut by as much as 80 percent. Required break-even production volume dropped from 80 percent to 50 percent of capacity.

For Yanmar to have achieved these improvements using conventional methods, its production volume would probably have had to be increased three times and its product variety reduced by at least 75 percent. Although Yanmar did increase its volume, it increased it by much less than three times. And, instead of reducing product variety, it increased the number of different engine models from 250 in 1976 to over 900 in 1981. Of course Yanmar's competitive advantage was strengthened significantly. Furthermore, Yanmar did not have to invest in larger volume manufacturing facilities. These achievements are especially noteworthy since prior to these changes Yammar was considered a well-run company![15]

Flexible production enables Japanese companies to target small market segments, making them very formidable competitors. Companies in other countries, if they hope to compete in today's marketplace, can be expected to adopt Japan's flexible production technologies.

Precision Target Marketing: The Wave of the Future

The increasing diversity of needs, coupled with the new technology necessary to serve this diversity economically, points to a trend that will have increasing impact on marketers: the need to continually become more precise in the targeting of markets. As you, then, think about market segments that seem appropriate for your situation, continually ask, "Have I segmented this market finely enough?"

Selecting Target Market(s):
Where to Look First

In a speech, called "Acres of Diamonds," Russell Conwell told a story about Ali Hafed, a wealthy Persian farmer.

> One day Ali Hafed heard of the fabulous wealth he could possess if only he owned a diamond mine. That night he went to bed a poor man. Not because he had lost anything, but because he realized he was not as rich as he could be. He knew he must have a diamond mine.
> So he sold his fruitful farmlands and began his search. Far and wide he roamed. Youth and wealth dwindled. Ali Hafed, aged, destitute, and brokenhearted, cast himself into the ocean, never to be seen again. However, not long after Ali Hafed had sold his farm, the most magnificent diamond mines in all of history–the Golconda mines–were discovered on Ali Hafed's old farm.

Of course you're interested in increasing sales and profits. But before you go off into "foreign" lands, focus on your current customer base. Here lie your greatest strengths.

For the Internal Analysis in Step 3, you reviewed your present segmenting strategy for a given product or service. You examined your present customer base to see if you had heavy users, light users, users who were expanding their purchases, users who were decreasing their purchases, as well as nine other classifications.

Now review these 13 classifications, along with examples of how some companies have retargeted their markets. While going through these classifications, continually ask yourself, "Have I segmented this market finely enough? Or, am I trying to be all things to all people?"

1. Who Are Your Heavy Users?

The 80-20 rule probably applies to your product/service-target market. But are you taking care of this 80 percent?

Perhaps you're in the same situation as a small job shop manufacturing company. Demand had outstripped its production capabilities. The president was considering expanding the plant. However, an analysis of the customer base revealed that over one-fourth of the firm's customers accounted for less than 2 percent of its sales. These customers were highly unprofitable because of set-up times required and short production runs. (Research had shown that any run less than $5,000 was not profitable.) Further examination revealed that almost none of these customers had the volume potential to become profitable customers. Nor was there any strategic reason for keeping these customers.

The low-volume, low-potential firms (those having a potential of less than $5,000 per run) were dropped. In effect, the company had segmented the market and redefined its target market as firms that had the potential of purchasing at least $5,000 a year.

This retargeting helped the company greatly increase profits. The sales force redirected its efforts toward profitable (or potentially) profitable accounts, thereby increasing sales. Manufacturing capacity was increased because of the elimination of numerous jig set-up and take-down times. In fact, plant expansion was no longer necessary. Furthermore, order processing time was cut by discontinuing service to these unprofitable, low-potential customers. Make sure you're taking care of your 80 percent.

2. Who Are Your Heavy, Heavy Users?

Okay. So you know who your heavy users are, and you're concentrating your efforts here. That makes sense. You're spending most of your time (and budget) on the 20 percent of your customers who account for 80 percent of your business. Following the old 80-20 principle. So far, so good.

But what about your really heavy users? You may have a small percentage of customers who purchase a very large percentage of your product or service. For example, the airlines found out that 4.1 percent of adults made 70.4 percent of all airline trips.[16] These were the heavy users. So, to court their favor, frequent flier programs were rolled out.

But among this 4.1 percent–the heavy users–there was a group of really heavy users, i.e., those who took trips to Hong Kong, Calcutta, Marrakech, and the like, once a month or more. To make sure they didn't lose these customers to other airlines–and to gain some heavy, heavy fliers from other airlines–programs like United's Executive Premier (for those who fly 75,000 miles or more a year) were developed.

At Chase Manhattan, once you've arrived (with a heavy, heavy account), you don't have to wait in line. Instead, you'll get your own personal banker. Need a lot of money, but the bank is closed? No need to worry. You can get a cashier's check delivered to your apartment. You'll be invited to special dinner parties at Chase Manhattan's posh Madison Avenue branch. Amid Persian rugs, marble halls, and crystal chandeliers, you'll get to know some of the bank's wealthiest clients–like yourself.

3. Who Are Your Light Users?

Following the 80-20 rule, one national beverage processor targeted the heavy users of milk in an advertising campaign. However, because these heavy users already drank a lot of the beverage, it was difficult to increase their consumption.

At the same time, the other 80 percent of the market was neglected. The many submarkets that have very low per capita consumption were prime material for niche marketing programs. It makes sense to treat your 20 percent with respect. But often it makes no sense to ignore your other 80 percent.

Industry leaders often neglect the minor purchasers who are (or might become) the fastest-growing market segments. Witness what happened to General Motors, Ford, and Chrysler when they ignored the consumers who wanted small cars. Or Xerox when it disregarded the market segments that wanted small copiers.

Sometimes the light users can lead to new and potentially profitable market segments. So check out your light users.

That's what Hillside Coffee did. It found light coffee usage among teens and adults in their early twenties, groups made up of individuals known for having a sweet tooth. The solution was sweet-flavored coffee blends like Vanilla Nut, Swiss Chocolate Almond, and Chocolate Macadamia.

It's true that in many cases your light users may never become tomorrow's 20 percent. Still, you might be able to convince them to spend more. For instance, Foster's ad campaign, "Diet for Two," shows an ice bucket with a 22-ounce bottle of beer. Although Foster is trying to persuade women to drink more beer, it's doubtful they are trying to get women to match the quaffing of the steelworkers of Pennsylvania.

You can be sure of one thing—people change. They grow older. They become more sophisticated. They take up new hobbies. They pursue the latest fads. Or they just don't have a reason for buying much of your product or service. But you'll never convince those light users to buy more by ignoring them. Look for the diamonds in your own backyard.

4. Which Customers Are Expanding Their Purchases?

If some customers are suddenly buying more, they may point to new markets. Joseph McQuade, manager of worldwide business development for Convatec, told us how Convatec noticed its sales for Stomahesive, an adhesive dressing used to attach colostomy devices, were far greater than was expected. Research revealed that doctors and nurses liked the adhesive qualities of Stomahesive. They were cutting up the dressings and using them for other purposes. So Convatec came out with Duoderm. It was essentially the same product, but it was cut into strips that made it easy for doctors and nurses to use. A success? You bet!

So don't just sit back and grin when one of your products or services shows unexpected gains. Find out who's buying and why. The answers may help you turn casual admirers into first-rate suitors.

5. Which Customers Are Decreasing Their Purchases?

Milk companies noticed that as their customers grew older, they drank less milk. One of the reasons? Milk is too hard to digest for many elderly people who have a deficiency of lactase. The solution: put an enzyme in milk that makes it more digestible.

Some supermarkets were not happy with their sales growth rates. They knew customers should be spending more in their stores. They discovered that some customers were stopping at delis after buying their groceries to pick up something for their evening meals at home. To cater to this segment, in came salad bars and supermarket delis containing prepared foods. And the food is not cooked by amateurs either. For instance, Kings, a New Jersey supermarket chain, hires experienced chefs.

When good customers begin to spend less, you owe it to yourself, and to them, to find out why. You may not miss them at first, particularly if stable overall sales mask the decline in their spending. But you will miss them eventually. Perhaps a small change in your product or service will bring them back. Perhaps you'll need to make a big change. But think twice before you close your eyes to customers who begin to close their wallets. It costs less to keep a customer than to gain a new one.

6. Where Are Your Customers Located?

Sometimes overlooked are the geographic differences within a country. For instance, in the United States, geographic differences may be greater than you think. Look at what an automobile manufacturer faces. People on the East and West Coasts like small cars. Per capita sales of small cars are twice as high in these regions as they are in the middle states.

In the Southeast, people want compact pickups. But in the Southwest, buyers prefer full-size pickups. Compare Miami with Houston. Miami households have fewer children, and the city is geographically more compact than Houston. Guess where more station wagons are sold? Small wonder that automobile manufacturers are splitting up the mass market and trying to grow bigger by acting smaller.

Campbell Soup Company found out that, on the average, its soups were "just right." But the "just right" was based on averages. The soups were too spicy for Midwesterners and too bland for people in the Southwest. The solution: Campbell adapted their soup recipes to regional tastes.

So take a close look at your customer base by region. By urban neighborhood versus rural neighborhood. By city. By zip code. Or possibly even by block.

7. Which Customers Can You Serve Most Profitably?

What are two of the most profitable sections in the supermarket? The salad bar and prepared foods. Astute supermarket managers noticed that many of the noontime customers were shopping at the salad bar and prepared food sections just to buy lunch. In response to this observation, supermarkets developed promotional programs, such as sending fliers to nearby office complexes, to increase sales to this profitable market segment.

Wawa, a convenience food chain, noticed that many of its customers were buying sandwich fixings at lunch time. They did the logical thing: they introduced in-store sandwich preparation.

Produce growers thrive on consumer pick-your-own programs. They shift the cost of picking, warehousing, and transportation (often the lion's share of costs) to the consumer. Then, too, the consumer's quality standards dramatically change. They accept produce in a pick-your-own situation that they would never accept in a retail environment. (Ever try filling up a five-gallon pail with perfect strawberries? After the first pint, anything that's close to red looks good. Mighty good.)

The end results are larger profits for the producers, and for the consumer, cheaper produce, besides the thrill of eating it fresh-picked! Everybody wins.

8. Do Your Customers Have Different Price Sensitivities?

Quite frequently there's a rather wide range of price sensitivity within a company's customer base. Airlines and hotels found that pleasure travelers were far more price-sensitive than people on business.

Credit card companies discovered that some customers wanted all kinds of services regardless of price. Not so with others.

Office supply companies felt they were insulated from price cutters. After all, they offered their bread-and-butter clients, the corporate accounts, service (and they really did). Furthermore, the corporate accounts were believed to be rather price-insensitive. But office supply companies were shocked when many of their corporate customers, both large and small, flocked to discount office supply houses such as Staples. Customers abandoned the extra service in exchange for 50 to 70 percent discounts. As the old saw goes, "Every man has his price."

So look at your customers. Examine their price sensitivities. These might reveal a number of segments.

9. What Do Customers Really Value?

You've examined your customer base (Step 3). Let's assume you notice wide variances in key buying motives among your customers. You've hit pay dirt. You've found hidden market segments.

That's what they did at Du Pont. Its discrete clinical analyzer is a highly sophisticated, automated laboratory instrument used in the health-care industry. The analyzer is expensive, costing tens of thousands of dollars, and that's just for starters. Operating supplies sometimes cost as much as the analyzer.

After ten years the market was saturated. However, one segment of the target market was largely untapped: small hospitals and clinics. This segment had different key buying motives than the larger hospitals. They could not afford the high-priced model. They needed additional training on how to use the discrete clinical analyzer. They also needed reliable servicing.

To meet this segment's needs, Du Pont put together a special program. First, they came out with a new model for the large hospitals, giving liberal trade-in allowances. Then Du Pont reconditioned the trade-ins. The reconditioned instruments were sold, along with on-site training and service guarantees, to the small hospitals and clinics. Sales to this segment increased threefold.[17]

This successful marketing program was developed because Du Pont noticed wide variations in key buying motives among its customers.

10. Do Your Customers Have the Same Frequency of Purchase?

You probably have a group of customers who purchase your product only infrequently. How can you make people who sporadically buy your product or service become frequent purchasers? Let's see how some companies have tackled this problem.

Some have used clubs: the "Book-of-the-Month" Club, record clubs, videotape clubs. You name it, there's a club for it. Clubs make it easy–and cheap–for consumers to get started. And then every month customers can pick from an outstanding collection, converting infrequent purchasers into those who buy once a month. This is especially true for subscribers who must let the company know when they don't want next month's selection.

A variation of the club idea is the Fruit-of-the-Month offered by members of the Florida Gift Fruit Shippers Association. People like to give fancy boxed fruit as gifts, but they only come to Florida once a year. So the gift-fruit retailers sell subscriptions for monthly (or any frequency) shipments. Another win-win situation. The customer gets fancy fruit all year long, and the retailer sells more fruit. Simple but profitable.

There are only just so many birthdays and holidays each year. So with general card sales growth of only 0.6 percent, greeting card companies turned to untapped segments. People who would just like to send a card of thanks, to thank a child for cleaning his or her room (part of Hallmark's To Kids With Love line), or to thank a person for a great evening. Or to send a card just to express an emotion, such as missing someone, or love, or joy.[18]

Thanksgiving and Christmas are big holidays for turkeys. But then, after these occasions, sales drop off. After all, who wants to wrestle with a 20-pounder week after week? So many companies, such as Perdue and Louis Rich, came out with all kinds and sizes of turkey parts, from fresh to microwaveable to precooked. Did it work? Just look at turkey sales.

Companies are using the same strategy with chickens. Tyson Foods slices up more than 57 varieties of chicken products, from parts to gourmet dinners, and has had outstanding success. Tyson's value-added sales (versus basic poultry) increased by over $1 billion between 1980 and 1988.[19]

Usually you've got to play a proactive role. For example, in the 1950s and 1960s a summer vacation was the norm. Only a few went to the Caribbean in the winter. And what about now? Do you think millions of Americans coincidentally decided to go to Jamaica, St. Croix, and the British Virgin Islands for a second vacation? Or, could it have been the airlines, the cruise ship companies, and destination marketing at work?

Maybe your product or service is by definition the type that customers need only infrequently, such as catering for a wedding. (Let's face it–most people get married only twice.) Or tombstones. (Again let's face it–most people get buried only once.).But if you have some frequent purchasers, you usually can find more.

11. What Promotion Best Appeals to Your Various Customers?

Do some of your customers prefer a person-to-person sales approach? Would another method of sales promotion, such as a direct mail sweepstakes, be more effective for others?

When different customers have different key buying motives, you often have to vary your promotional efforts. For example, Du Pont produces Kevlar, a fiber that's stronger yet lighter than steel. Some of the market segments that Du Pont identified were aircraft designers, plant engineers, and commercial fishing boat owners. Each of these segments had different key buying motives. For aircraft designers, the high strength-to-weight ratio of Kevlar was appealing. Plant engineers were interested in using Kevlar in asbestos-free pumps. For commercial fishing boat owners, Kevlar could be used in the construction of boats that would carry more fish and travel at increased speed.

So advertising to each of these segments was different, although the product was the same. To the aircraft designers, Du Pont said, "The L-1011 is 807 pounds lighter because of Kevlar 49." To the industrial plant managers, Du Pont said, "Now, a better answer to your toughest packing problems: asbestos-free Kevlar." To the commercial fishing boat owners, Du Pont said, "The boat hull made of Kevlar saves fuel, gets there faster, and can carry more fish."[20]

12. Who Makes the Purchasing Decisions?

Who makes the purchasing decisions at a supermarket? Only one type of individual? You'd have to be a Rip Van Winkle to say yes to that one. Now, besides homemakers who shop, there are women who work outside the home, husbands, latchkey kids, and so on. Each represents a number of different segments, and each has different key buying motives.

One of the segments Cascade dishwasher detergent has targeted is single men. As a result, some of Cascade's ads speak about the problems of single males.

But sometimes the people who make the purchasing decisions are not the ones who actually buy the products or services. They're the influencers: the kid screaming in the grocery cart.

Kid Cuisine, a new, prepared dinner targeted to kids, is a success. It treats kids as if they're the target market even though Kid Cuisine dinners are purchased by their parents. What kind of TV shows do you suppose Kid Cuisine is advertised on? You got it. On kids' shows, not shows watched by their parents, the purchasers.

Guess who's driving men to drink? Women. That's right. But fortunately, they're steering them away from the hard stuff. Women, who are more likely to experiment with different kinds of drinks, have moved toward the lighter, more flavorful ones. They have introduced men to coolers and schnapps. The marketing response? Among others, ads that include women in social-drinking situations. The result? Lightness dominates the alcohol industry.

13. Do All Your Customers Buy Your Whole Line of Products or Services?

Do you have some customers who buy your complete line of products and services? Do you have others who buy only one or two items–real cherry pickers? If so, you've got different segments with differing key buying motives.

In the personal computer industry, some computer buyers want a working system and do not want to worry about putting all the components together. On the other hand, there are the computer techies who prefer to assemble their own computing systems. They select components from various suppliers' product lines.

Bell of Pennsylvania found that the number of special services (call-waiting, call-forwarding, three-way calling, and speed calling) wanted by its customer base varied. So they offered a package of the four services for only $8.03 a month, a savings of 25 percent. Purchased separately, the services would cost $10.70. Some buyers still preferred to purchase only parts of the package at the full cost. By serving both segments, the company comes out ahead.

Answer these questions, and you'll know how your present market can be segmented. In the process of determining market segments, it's usually a back-and-forth process. For example, you may have decided that there are regional differences. But, when you looked closely at key buying motives of these regional segment classifications, you may have found that some of the customers within these segment classifications valued immediate service while price was the main concern of others. This finding would lead to the splitting apart of the regional market segments.

But such a process has value. As Mitchel Scott of Armstrong World Industries said: "For us segmentation is used not so much to increase or decrease market targets as to more clearly understand and serve customer expectations within the customer base we currently have. By selling more to these resegmented markets, the end result is the same–increased sales and profits."

The best place to probe for new segments is in your present customer base. But sometimes the grass is greener. . . .

Selecting Target Market(s):
Where to Look Next

Your best bet for finding those hidden market segments is, of course, in your own backyard–with your familiar product and service target markets.

But your best bet can't be your *only* bet. If you don't look beyond your well-studied customer base, you can forget about new customers. And without new customers, no business can survive.

Consider the fate of the American big-city department store. Throughout the prosperous 1980s, one after another succumbed to financial decline and bankruptcy. Did they fail to meet their old customers' needs? Not really. By and large that segment remained steadfast. Rather, the department stores' troubles arose from ignoring all those other customers in the market, such as the prosperous and savvy two-earner families, shopping together in the evening and demanding top value and service. Without these (and other) new customers, the department stores' customer base was bound to shrink.

Ahead are seven potential veins of new market segments along with examples of how they've been mined by imaginative firms. Use these as a starting point, but don't let them limit your imagination.

1. Look at Those Who Use the Product or Service Category but Not Your Brand

There are people out there who use your competitors' products or services but not yours. Why? More than likely, your competitors are serving the heart of the market and there's room for precision target marketers. Like you. This is true in almost every market.

Consider toothpaste. Who would ever think there was room in the market for more toothpaste? After all, how many ways can you brush your teeth? You might believe that all the market segments have been covered. Not so!

For example, as kids become a more important part of household decision making, they offer new marketing opportunities. Oral-B, a new toothpaste on the market, is strictly for kids. Does it taste like adult toothpaste? No. But did you ever hear 7-year-olds ask for spearmint? No. They ask for bubble gum, and that's what the toothpaste tastes like.

Will adults buy it for their own use? Not likely. But are kids buying it (or are parents buying it for the kids)? You bet. Of course, before this product came out, parents were buying kids toothpaste that was already on the market. But only because they lacked a better alternative. Bubble-gum-flavored toothpaste became a successful product because insightful marketers discovered there were needs not being met by existing brands.

Notice that we're not talking about increasing your share of a mass-marketed product or service from 22 percent to 24 percent. Rather, we're talking about developing new products and services for people who already use the same type of product or service. We're talking about finding weak points in the mass market and then positioning products and services for subsegments.

Look again at your product or service category (or categories). Are there customers buying your competitor's products or services simply because there are no alternatives? Because no one has recognized their unique needs? If so, you're halfway there. You already know the territory.

2. Look at Those Who Don't Use the Product or Service Category but Could

Perhaps there are a number of potential customers who could be buying your competitor's or your product or service but don't. Find out why.

Look at what happened with snacks for dogs. For many years the primary dog snack was a grain-based biscuit such as Milk-Bone. This category occupied a couple of shelf facings in the supermarket. But a good percentage of dog owners didn't buy these dog treats.

To get greater penetration, the grain-based dog-treat manufacturers lowered prices. But many dog owners still walked right by the displays. They wanted treats for their dogs, and they didn't think that grain was a treat. After all, when was the last time you saw your dog attacking a wheat field?

But when more expensive dog snacks, such as jerky or beef, were put on the market, the nonusers flocked to buy them. So at a time when dog ownership is going down, revenue from premium snacks is going up. Today one aisle at the supermarket is usually devoted to pet food, and a large percentage of it to premium dog snacks.

There may be potential customers out there that you've never seen, and, what's more, neither have your competitors. Find them. The present products and services just may not be–or may not be perceived to be–tasty enough, healthy enough, or easy enough to use. Solve these problems, and both you and the customers win.

3. Look at Creating New Products or Services in an Old Category

While some businesses are trying to make improvements in existing products and services, others are taking a new look. They're trying to find new solutions to old problems. These marketers believe there is no such thing as a mature market, only tired products and services.

For example, for years people have been running off athletic fields with incredible thirsts. Some companies offered new flavors, new sizes, and new packages for the same old drinks The result: the same old sales. Then Gatorade offered a new choice–not only a refreshing drink but one that replenishes body electrolytes lost during exercise.

When the product was created by scientists at the University of Florida, none of the big companies would touch it. Why? Because it was targeted to a small market segment. But eventually, Stokely-Van Camp (later acquired by Quaker Oats) realized the potential and bought Gatorade. Now Quaker Oats dominates the market (it turned out to be a very big segment) and everyone is trying to enter. Small wonder. Gatorade is Quaker Oats' largest profit contributor.

How long have people been using cloth diapers? So long that no one thought there was much of an opportunity here. That is, until Procter & Gamble noticed that it wasn't easy to care for cloth diapers when traveling. Or, for that matter, anywhere away from home. So, Pampers was targeted for this market segment.

Notice how sometimes you get a nice surprise when you create a new product in an old category? Who would have thought that Gatorade would have garnered such a share of the market? Or that disposable diapers would almost replace cloth diapers?

Today there are categories of me-too products and services that have been around for years. But someone, sometime, is going to make a breakthrough. How? By recognizing some need that the category is not satisfying.

4. Look at Technology Within Your Company

You probably already have the technology to serve new market segments, but you may not recognize it. Not so at 3M, which is well-known for its use of technology to develop new products. While most of us think of Post-it notes, that's only one product out of a multitude. For example, 3M has highly developed technology in films, adhesives, and plastics. The company used this technology to make decals to replace paint used on airplanes, thereby creating a new market segment. The product was a natural, because airlines wanted to do everything possible to keep weight and fuel costs down. The use of plastic decals, which are much lighter than paint, is an excellent example of using a firm's technology to satisfy a market segment's key buying motives.

Who is the largest producer of unbranded photography film sold by Kmart and other mass merchandisers under their private labels? Again, 3M, using its technology to serve a segment neglected (intentionally) by Kodak.

Or take Reflectone, a producer of flight simulators targeted primarily at the government. Reflectone realized that parts of this technology, such as interactive video and computer-aided instruction, could be used in other situations. Why not, they thought, devise a totally electronic center for film deposits and pick-ups?

Using the technology developed for flight simulators, they produced a fully automated kiosk for film deposits and pick-ups. Drive up and, by means of interactive video and automation, you'll be greeted and given instructions, have your questions answered, and get a receipt and delivery date.

A warning. Although you will be familiar with your new products or services (after all, they are part of your existing technology), you probably won't be as knowledgeable about your new target market. While we have urged you to focus on your present customers, it's equally essential (more so, if that's possible) to focus on your potential customers.

Misunderstanding your target market spells failure. For example, have you ever seen a Reflectone film kiosk? Probably not. They're no longer produced. Why? Reflectone's management was oriented toward selling to the military. Marketing activity was primarily directed toward top generals and toward fulfilling the government's extensive contract requirements. Government contracts have well-specified minimum standards. If you meet these, you have a good chance of getting the contract. Uncovering consumers' key buying motives, so vital to consumer marketing, were skills never mastered by Reflectone's management. And so the automated kiosks became just another good idea.

Make sure that your technology is used so that it will respond to users' key buying motives.

5. Look at Marketing Skills Within Your Company

Perhaps one of your company's strengths is marketing. If it is, then you should utilize these skills to serve new market segments. Let's see how some companies are following this principle.

For years Midas very successfully specialized in mufflers. But, with its well-known name, why not offer other services? And so today you can pull into a Midas center and get new brakes, shock absorbers, springs, a front-end alignment–as well as a muffler.

At Sears, not only can you buy kitchen cabinets, storm windows, roofs, and gutters, but you can also have Sears install them. Of course, the installations are not done by Sears. Sears doesn't have the expertise. Installation is done by independent subcontractors hired by Sears. But by utilizing its skill in marketing, Sears provides a valuable service to its customers while taking some off the top from installers.

Hallmark Cards, having a well-recognized and respected trade name plus a distribution system of 6000 independent dealers, capitalized on these market strengths. Hallmark expanded its product line into noncard items that could be sold through its distribution system. New products included crystal, pewter, and jewelry.

But a word of caution. Just because customers value your name for one product does not necessarily mean they will hold your other products in high regard. Years ago, Sears had no trouble selling appliances to the middle and upper-middle classes. It decided it could sell clothes to this clientele as well. The customers were already in the store, after all, and had demonstrated considerable loyalty to the brand name.

Sears consequently upgraded the quality and price of its clothing, only to find that the better-heeled customers continued to pass through these departments (en route to the appliances) without buying anything. They still purchased their refrigerators from Sears, but they bought their clothes from department stores and specialty shops. The Sears name on a man's suit was simply not the same, at least in the minds of customers, as the Sears label on a washing machine. It was a costly mistake in strategy, and the direct result of Sears' failure to gauge the attitudes and values of its customers. After all, the customer determines the market, not the seller.

6. Look at Conglomerate Diversification

Do you see attractive markets but lack the technology *and* marketing skills to capitalize on them? Then think about diversification. But we really urge you to think twice–in fact, ten times–about it. Be careful! The list of those who have tried and failed at conglomerate diversification is miles longer than the list of those who have reaped big profits. You don't have to look far to find failures.

For example, take food manufacturing companies. It's no news that about 50 percent of all food dollars is spent in restaurants, fast food outlets, and other similar businesses. So what do you suppose many of the big food manufacturers did? Why, they went out and bought restaurants. How are they doing? Just ask Campbell Soup. After several years of floundering with Hanover Trail Steak House, they sold it.

Company after company has found that the market segments that will realize the most profits and growth are those product and service markets that they know the best. And so they're shedding unrelated businesses. "Back to basics" and "stick to your knitting" are today's watchwords.

Just as the Sirens lured Ulysses to the rocky coast, the siren call of conglomerate diversification can lead you into rocky territory. Often it's better to stuff cotton in your ears.

7. Look at Emerging Markets

Do you want another place to look? Look at emerging markets. The possibilities are almost limitless. Look at the segments–the growth markets of the 1990s–*American Demographics* came up with after they examined the marketplace.[21]

Parents. There were more than 4 million births in [1989], the highest number since 1964. About 90 percent of Americans have children at some time during their lives. For a huge segment of society, that time is now.

Children. The baby boomlet started in 1977, but it's peaking right now–making children a hot market for the 1990s.

Teenagers. The oldest members of the baby boomlet became teenagers in 1990 when they celebrated their thirteenth birthdays. After a decade of steep decline, the teenage population will grow again.

Fathers. As the baby boomlet begins to walk, talk, and do homework, fathers will become more important.

Empty Nesters. The family nest is most likely to empty when people are in their fifties. The baby boomers will begin to turn 50 in 1996. You can bank on healthy growth in the number of empty nesters toward the end of the decade.

Grandparents. In just ten years, one-third of all grandparents with grandchildren under the age of 18 will be baby boomers.

The Very Old. The number of people aged 85 and older will continue to grow rapidly in the 1990s, making it the only growth segment among the elderly population.

Individuals. In the 1980s we moved from the family to the household as the primary unit of consumption. In the 1990s, we'll move from the household to the individual.

Stepfamilies. Families are not a hot market for the 1990s, but stepfamilies are. They now account for 20 percent of married couples with children.

The Fit. Millions of baby boomers will join in a passionate battle against time, doing everything from running marathons to undergoing plastic surgery.

The Unfit. Beyond age 40, serious health problems become much more common. The number of people with chronic diseases should increase sharply with the aging of the baby boomers in the 1990s.

Asians. Asians are the fastest growing minority group in America today, a market over 8 million strong.

Hispanics. Hispanics will become this country's largest minority group by 2010, when the U.S. Census Bureau projects that they will outnumber blacks.

Activists. As the baby boomers become middle-aged, the nation's activists will take center stage. If your business is not prepared for attack, the activists could severely damage your company's image.

Savers. As college costs loom on the horizon, the baby boomers will try desperately to save money. This makes the boomers hot prospects for saving instruments in the 1990s.

Downscale. The pendulum of public concern is swinging back in favor of helping poor and near-poor people. We may even see a redefinition of poverty which increases–not decreases–the size of the downscale segment.

Upscale. With the baby-boom generation entering its peak earning years, the number of affluent households will grow.

The Middle Class. Americans continue to identify themselves as middle-class, no matter how upscale their income. To get your message across, don't talk to the elite or you'll miss your market.

Women in Charge. As career-minded baby-boom women gain in job experience, the number of women who control the bottom line will grow rapidly.

Workers. The share of the population in the paid labor force is greater today, at 66 percent, than ever before in our history.

Students. During this decade, the number of students aged 18 or older will approach, and might even pass, the number of students under age 18 for the first time in history.

Entrepreneurs. There are too many boomers for the few top spots in America's businesses. The consequence will be a lot of new businesses started by frustrated employees.

Vacation-Home Owners. The baby-boom generation is about to become prime customers for vacation homes. Look for vacation-home ownership to take off in the next few years.

Fun Seekers. Americans now spend more money on entertainment than on clothing. Expect the fun-seeking to continue in the 1990s, especially for entertainment experiences like Disney World.

Housewives. Markets may have fragmented, but traditional markets still exist–they've become markets just like all the rest. We've come full circle: from housewives as the mass market of the 1950s to housewives as an important market of the 1990s.

What products and services could you offer to these emerging markets? Of course, the *American Demographics* list is just a beginning.

Common-Sense Guidelines

To what extent should you segment the market? Let's take a look at four fundamental guidelines:[22]

- The closer your product/service is to a commodity-like product/service, the more likely it is that you should utilize a less-focused marketing approach.
- The more that buyers have similar key buying motives, buy in the same quantities, and react to similar marketing programs, the more likely you should utilize a less-focused marketing approach.
- If your product/service is in the introductory stage, the more likely you should follow a less-focused marketing approach. As the product/service moves toward maturity, precision target marketing is the preferred method.
- The more your competitors follow target marketing and serve smaller and smaller market segments, the more likely you'll have to do the same. Blocking competitors by serving multi-segments can be a very competitive weapon. Take a lesson from Heublein. Several years ago Wolfschmidt, a new brand of vodka, attacked Smirnoff on price, charging $1 less while claiming to be of the same quality.

  Heublein (Smirnoff) decided against matching the price of Wolfschmidt. Instead, they raised the price of Smirnoff by $1 and came out with a fighting brand, Relska. Relska was priced the same as Wolfschmidt. Heublein also came out with another brand, Popov, that sold at a price lower than Wolfschmidt. So Heublein outmaneuvered Wolfschmidt by encirclement. They had a premium brand (Smirnoff), a fighting brand (Relska), and a cheaper brand (Popov).[23]

In addition, to make sure that the market segments you have isolated could become viable target markets, ask these questions:

- For a given product/service, will segment members respond similarly to a given marketing program? That is, will all segment members be reached by and/or react similarly to a given promotional program? Channel of distribution? Pricing policy?
- Does your product/service offer a significant benefit to the target market? You may be going "a segment too far." (See Figure 2.55)

Always ask, "What does the target market really value?" Often segment strategies fail because the products/services are not sufficiently differentiated from other products/services serving different and/or broader market segments. It's not enough to be different. You must offer a product/service that has a unique characteristic that buyers value. It's reported that Campbell Soup Company, although an advocate of precision target marketing, is retrenching a bit, acknowledging that in many instances it may have gone a "segment too far." It is now pulling back somewhat from customized marketing and is spending more money on its base businesses.[24]

QUESTION 2. ARE YOU CAPITALIZING ON OPPORTUNITIES FOR PRODUCT/SERVICE DIFFERENTIATION AND/OR REDUCED COSTS?

Okay. So you've decided that you should further subdivide your present target market, or you think you should consider new target markets. But you lack insights as to how you could develop differential advantage for this new target market. Or, it may be that you want to increase differential advantage for an existing target market.

Gain valuable pointers for product/service differentiation by analyzing value chains.[25] Value chains will also help you spot how you can reduce your own costs.

FIGURE 2.55

The Generic Value Chain. Examine the value chain (Figure 2.56). Note that there are five primary activities: inbound logistics; operations; outbound logistics; marketing and sales; and service. The support activities are divided into four classifications: infrastructure (general management, finance, accounting, and the like); human resource management; technology development; and procurement.

The hazards of viewing these activities in isolation are obvious. Narrow examination may lead to suboptimization. For example, a company may reduce manufacturing costs, only to find its service costs skyrocketing because of a higher frequency of repair rate. Then, too, making incremental changes in a given activity can reach a point of diminishing returns.

FIGURE 2.56

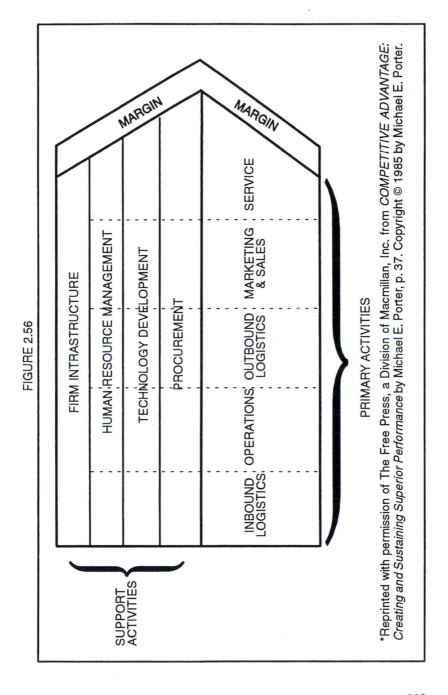

235

One of the key benefits of the value chain is that it highlights the linkages between activities. It serves as an analysis tool to help you better view the firm as a system. This is extremely helpful, especially in a total quality environment.

Note that the value chain highlights the relationship between direct activities and support activities. In some industries human resource management may be a source of competitive advantage. For instance, Arthur Anderson, the leading accounting firm, gains considerable competitive advantage from its superior method of college recruiting and training.[26]

Even a firm's infrastructure, as part of the value chain, should be viewed as something more than fixed costs. In fact, the firm's infrastructure can be a source of competitive advantage. For example, a firm's president may be an invaluable source for top management contacts. Likewise, the firm's management information system may be able to help improve its cost position.

Far greater benefits may even be realized by reconfiguring the value chain. Iowa Beef Packers, for example, built processing plants in close proximity to the cattle supply. This reconfiguration allowed the firm to use nonunion labor, and it also reduced transportation and weight-loss costs.[27]

Exploiting linkages within the value chain can be a valuable source for cost reduction and differentiation. The Japanese excel at this. For example, they achieve product quality and reduction of manufacturing costs through their much publicized *kanban* system involving, among other linkages, just-in-time inventory.

The Distribution Channel Value Chain. Besides understanding your value chain, it's also necessary to understand your firm as a part of the overall channel value chain. Each channel member has its own value chain.

Through an understanding of channel members' value chains, it is sometimes feasible to reconfigure the product/service and/or the amenities surrounding the product/service, so that all parties gain. A manufacturer of chocolate might deliver chocolate to a confectioner in tank cars, rather than in molded bricks. This could reduce manufacturing costs on the part of the manufacturer, as well as shipping, handling, and melting costs for the confectioner. Thus, both parties would benefit.[28]

QUESTION 3. ARE YOU OPTIMIZING COMPETITIVE ADVANTAGES (WHILE MINIMIZING COMPETITIVE RESTRAINTS)?

Background

While it has always been important, competitive strategy is even more critical today. During the 1960s and early 1970s (in the United States), mediocre companies were able to grow right along with their more efficient competitors. However, with the relatively slow growth of the mid- to late-1970s and 1980s, the party ended. Those companies that survived often did so solely at the expense of their competitors.

But, perhaps the major cause of this intensified competition is the "new" competitors from abroad, such as Canada, Germany, and, most notably, Japan and the "little dragons"–Korea, Taiwan, Hong Kong, and Singapore. And on their heels, soon to launch major attacks, is the gang of six: China, Indonesia, the Philippines, Thailand, Malaysia, and Burma.

Several years ago a consulting firm, after studying a number of marketing plans, concluded that the lack of competitive assessment (and subsequently, effective competitive strategies) was a major fault with most of these plans. And this was before the brunt of the new competition was being felt. It seems that many companies' plans implied that their competitors were going to "roll over and play dead." Or, at best, that their competitors were going to continue doing what they had in the past.

Knowing what the consumer/user wants isn't sufficient, after all, if a dozen other companies (perhaps with far greater resources) are already serving the same consumer/user wants. Even if you should discover a unique "want" (or market segment), what good will it do you if a larger, more powerful competitor notes your success and then takes over this market? AMC didn't fold because it failed to understand the consumer. It folded because of General Motors, Ford, and Chrysler–not to mention Toyota, Nissan, Honda, Volkswagen, Hyundai, and other imports.[29]

In addition to understanding consumer wants, then, design a strategy that considers your competitors' and their likely actions. As the Chinese strategist Sun Tzu observed, circa 500 BC:

> Know the enemy and know yourself; in a hundred battles you will never be in a peril. When you are ignorant of the enemy but know yourself, your chances of winning or losing are equal. If ignorant of both your enemy and yourself, you are certain in every battle to be in peril.

Many marketers have borrowed concepts from the military to help design competitive strategies. These strategies have been termed "marketing warfare."

Benefit from studying military concepts. You'll get fresh insights to help you think strategically. Then, too, since many firms are utilizing these concepts in developing their marketing strategies, you've got to know them, too. They'll help you figure out what strategies your competitors plan to use against you.

Selecting your optimum competitive strategy from among one or more of the following 14 strategies depends on how you stack up against your competitors, both now and in the future, in terms of:

- Key success factors
- Management's current major emphasis
- Market share
- Target market's ratings of augmented products/services
- Relative financial strength
- Commitment: aggressive/holding/divestment

Your SWOTs analysis will have given you the answers.

Fourteen Key Competitive Strategies

First, two universal guidelines: comparative advantage and competitive focus. If you have a *major* comparative advantage, use it. Then you can ignore the 14 competitive strategies. But the word *major* is the key. The advantage must be something more than a slightly better product/service, manufacturing/operations or sales force. It must be of *major* significance.

Look at a military example. Suppose, for instance, that in 1939 Hitler had had the atomic bomb and a method of delivery. Given that scenario, even though the Allies had larger and superior resources, it wouldn't have mattered. The Germans would have won the war.

In the business world, however, cases of major comparative advantage are rare. Most companies offer essentially me-too products/services, or their products/services can be closely copied. Consequently, competitive strategies must be a considered in developing most marketing plans.

The second universal guideline: competitive focus. You'll probably remember the story about the two men on safari and the lion (Step 3), illustrating the benefits of viewing competitors as separate entities. A monograph by a consulting firm, Hays-Hill (now Cresap Management Consultants), points out that unfortunately many businesses develop strategies considering all competitors as one group: "them." But each of your competitors will have a unique strategy, usually at odds with one another. You can miss out on profitable opportunities if you don't take advantage of your competitors' differences. The water buffalo wishes it could (see Figure 2.57).

Competitive Strategy #1: Offense

One of the most noted military historians was the Prussian general, Carl von Clausewitz. He studied hundreds of battles, arriving at a number of principles of warfare which were published in *Vom Kreig* (*On War*) in 1832. One of these was the principle of force. Clausewitz found that in open-field battles, where neither side has a comparative or defensive advantage, there were only two instances among all those he studied where the numerically inferior forces (as defined by having one-half or fewer troops than the opponents) defeated the numerically superior forces. Even the brilliant strategist General Lee, with 30,000 troops, was no match against General Grant's 125,000; and so Appomattox.

The principle of force boils down to this: possess superior resources at the point of attack, or don't engage in a head-to-head, open-field battle with a competitor.

Reis and Trout point out that there are two fallacies to guard against. The first is the "better people" fallacy. The quality of your

FIGURE 2.57

Companies tend to behave as if their competitors were a homogeneous entity. As a result, their strategies and tactics are undifferentiated. Any company with less than a 50 percent share of market that behaves this way puts itself in the position of a defender and sacrifices enormous latitude. In the animal world a pack of hyena, perhaps 20 strong, will overcome a water buffalo many times the size of each hyena. They do it instinctively by surrounding the water buffalo and making repeated half-attacks, causing it to whirl about constantly using up its defensive energy. The hyena's behavior is a form of social order which allows them, as a group, to confront on equal terms the more massive water buffalo. If this ordering did not exist the water buffalo could take on its attackers in sequence overcoming each one, and ultimately the pack, with ease. Companies, by behaving as if competition were a homogeneous entity, put themselves at a disadvantage. There is no such social order among participants in a business. In fact it is expressly illegal. Companies of all sizes are missing the opportunity to exploit the differences and lack of alliances among competition. The water buffalo would not.

Competitive Analysis (Chicago: Cresap, Management Consultants), p. 31. Reprinted by permission.

personnel won't make a difference against a numerically superior competitor. For example, pit the best team in the NBA against the worst. If the worst team can field nine players against only five of the best team's players, there is no question who would win. Of course you should try to improve your personnel through recruiting and training. But don't lead your personnel on a foolish charge. Most of the members of the English Light Brigade were the finest, best-trained men in the world. Even though the Russians had less training, they had an overwhelming numerical superiority. They won.

The second fallacy is the "better product" fallacy. Many marketers think that if you have a slightly better product/service and conduct a good promotion campaign, the consumer/user will soon know about it and then switch to your product. But it just doesn't work that way for colas, or for margarines, or for most other products/services.[30]

Principles of Attack

If after an assessment of the competition, you decide that your resources are superior enough to warrant an open-field engagement, keep two principles in mind:

Principle 1. Make Your Attack at Your Competitor's Most Vulnerable Position. But make sure that it's a true weakness. Ask yourself, "Can my competition match my attack without undermining its own position?" When Datril was introduced (positioned directly against Tylenol), it was decided that the new product would attack Tylenol on price. Tylenol was retailing for $2.85; Datril was introduced for $1.85. So what did Tylenol do? It immediately matched Datril's price. Tylenol was an extremely profitable product and could easily afford to counter an attack in price. Datril's expected price advantage never materialized. Datril has never been a factor in the marketplace.[31]

On the other hand, let's look back a few years ago at a marketing battle between Burger King and McDonald's. Burger King decided to increase its market share by attacking McDonald's. One of McDonald's strengths was its finely-tuned assembly line system. Burger King decided to launch the campaign, "Have it your way." McDonald's did not want to change its finely tuned system to match

Burger King's customization. Even though Burger King was attacking a foe that was numerically superior, the campaign was successful.[32] But the gains were only temporary. Burger King inexplicably changed from this strategy to "Herb the Nerd," and quickly lost all the ground it had previously taken.

Principle 2. Launch Your Attack on as Narrow a Front as Possible. The key to success is having numerically superior resources, not necessarily in general, but at the point of battle. If you attack your competitor with too many products/services in too many territories, your efforts will be dissipated. As a result, the numbers so important for victory may be shifted to your opponent.

When You Can Take On Mr. Big

Principles 1 and 2 apply when the numbers are on your side. But what if they're not? This is when the strategist earns his or her salary. If you are outnumbered, figuring out how to succeed in that marketplace means using more brains than brawn.

Look for the leader's Achilles' heel. Signals include blindness to market shifts, changes in technology, rigid game plans, changes in financial objectives, high reaction costs, portfolio restraints, and governmental regulatory pressure.[33]

Blind Spots. In the 1960s there used to be a joke heard around Detroit.

> Question: Do you know what the three most overrated things in America are?
>
> Answer: Home cooking. Sex. And Japanese cars.

"Invincible" leaders have a tendency to see themselves that way–invincible. It happens all the time in a number of ways.

Some overlook consumer demand (Xerox ignored–or underestimated–the demand for small copiers). Some don't respond to changes in technology (Zenith stayed with handcrafted TV sets while great changes were taking place in design and automated production). Some don't take account of changes in channels of distribution (Sears stayed pat, but people went to specialty stores like Circuit City and discounters like the Price Club).

Changes in Technology. The leader's strength may be in technology, but new advances can wipe out this advantage. Electromechanical cash registers were replaced by electronic cash registers, and typewriters by dedicated word processors. Dedicated word processors were replaced by microcomputers, and so on.

Of course, if you're Mr. Big in the market, you should view these examples as symbols of your own vulnerability. If you rise above others by developing better technology, you're probably in an industry in which your competition can easily surpass you with even better technology. Present technology is never a protection for market position. Sometimes your competitors may even develop a technology impossible for you to match. Then it might be best to throw in the towel and look for another arena.

Rigid Game Plans. A competitor might be reluctant to meet an attack if it has to change the strategy that has served it so well in the past. McDonald's didn't want to change its finely tuned assembly-line method of making hamburgers to meet Burger King's "Have It Your Way" campaign. This was a successful battle (but not a victory) for Burger King.

Crippling Financial Objectives. A leader might be after short-term profits and, therefore, choose not to come out with niche products and services to meet the competition. As General Motors did with small cars and the Japanese.

If one of your competitors becomes a leveraged buyout, watch for shifts in financial priorities. For example, the buyout of one service company caused the firm to focus on very short-term profits. As a result, the company eliminated a number of services that didn't have immediate payoffs. It became vulnerable–and lost business–to competing firms that were not subject to such short-term pressures. The same thing happened to R.J. Reynolds. Mired in debt, it lost market share while Philip Morris jabbed away.

Even the threat of a corporate buyout can be a sign of vulnerability. When top management is trying to deal with corporate raiders, attention to the marketplace often wanes. For instance, while trying to decide who should own the company, United Air Lines lost significant market share.

High Reaction Costs. A leader may resist cutting prices to meet the competition's invasion of the fringes of its market because it would require across-the-board cuts. Such price cuts might spell lower profits, lower dividends, or lower share prices for the leader.

Or it might mean that the leader would have to use another channel of distribution, thus disrupting its present channel relationships.

GTE Sprint had only a small percentage of total land lines for long-distance calling in the United States. But its lines were 100 percent optical fiber. They knew that AT&T could never match their advertising claim ("100 percent optical fiber"). For AT&T to replace all its land lines with optical fiber would cost billions of dollars! This made Sprint's attack very effective since AT&T's response costs were too high.

Portfolio Restraints. The leader might be a division charged with generating cash. Or it might be a weak performer. In either case, this division might find it impossible–or imprudent–to ask for funds to engage in a marketing war.

Regulatory Pressures. Firms can lose their competitive edge if they are subject to unusual regulatory pressures from the federal or local government. A company might be under government surveillance because of an antitrust suit, or predatory pricing, or other infringements of regulations that might restrict aggressive retaliation.

The leader may even be reluctant to retaliate in the marketplace because of false beliefs about regulatory pressures. New marketing employees of the Bell regional operating companies frequently were miffed by old-timers who insisted that certain marketing activities were ruled out by regulations. Yet nowhere could these regulations be found!

Or perhaps the leader is used to behaving in a certain way. AT&T had many executives accustomed to reducing price to please regulators rather than focusing on customers' needs. When first deregulated, AT&T was a lamb ready for slaughter by competitors with finely honed marketing skills. In fact, its market share slid from 100 percent to 65 percent in seven years.

Competitive Strategy #2: Defense

Another Clausewitz principle: the superiority of defense. The rationale goes like this. The defending army is protected in some manner: trenches, bunkers, foxholes, or the like. Because of this protection, the attacking force is at a disadvantage.

Clausewitz found that, as a general rule of thumb, the attacking force should have a numerical advantage at the point of attack of at least three to one. Otherwise, the results will be similar to the Confederate general Pickett's charge at Gettysburg.

This principle holds in business situations, too, although the required ratio may differ. Unfortunately, too many companies with insufficient resources are willing to take on a market leader. Look at Exxon's move against IBM in office automation. At the time Exxon made its bid to move into office automation, it was a larger company than IBM. But at the point of attack, Exxon's resources were only a fraction of IBM's. The outcome: similar to that of Pickett's Charge.

Here's an axiom you should cut out and place on your desk–where you can see it every day: It's not how many resources your firm has, but how many resources your firm will commit at the point of attack.

But now let's suppose you are the defender. Here are five rules to follow in defense of your market:

Make Sure the Numbers Are on Your Side. Your defense might result in higher costs (in absolute terms) for your attacking competitor than for yourself. But if the end result for you is bankruptcy, then what's the point?

The Best Defense Is a Good Offense. Continually improve your product/service. Make it difficult for your competitors to catch up. IBM managed to dominate the mainframe computer market for years by continually coming out with new models–models that offered greater performance at a lower price.

Deny Your Competitors a Base. The usual way to respond to a new entrant is to wait and see. Will the competitor be able to gain a toehold? Or will it withdraw? The best defense, however, is not to take chances. What if your competitor's product/service succeeds? Then you'll have a costly battle on your hands. Stop your competitor's launch before it gains a beachhead. (For more specifics, see "Competitive Strategy #3: Preemptive").

Always Block Strong Competitive Moves. A classic and very successful example is Honda's defense against Yamaha. Yamaha made a public announcement that it was going to replace Honda as the number one manufacturer of motorcycles in Japan. As reported by Abegglen and Stalk, the president of Honda issued a battle cry: "Yamaha has not only stepped on the tail of a tiger, it has ground it into the earth! Yamaha wo tsubusu!" This has a number of meanings, including "we will crush (break, smash, squash, butcher, slaughter, or destroy) Yamaha." And that's exactly what Honda did.

Honda used product variety and pricing to defeat Yamaha. In a year and a half, Honda brought out 81 new models to Yamaha's 34. Both firms cut prices drastically. Yet Honda's price to dealers was still lower than Yamaha's. Dealers were able to realize 10 percent larger profits from handling Honda motorcycles than from handling Yamaha's. As a result of this "war," Honda increased its share of the domestic market from 38 percent to 43 percent, while Yamaha's declined from 37 percent to 23 percent.[34]

Be Swift and Consistent in Your Defense. If one of your competitors (or potential competitors) makes an aggressive move, always—and immediately—retaliate against it. Ideally, you'll be able to direct your "disciplining" solely at the aggressor. These retaliatory actions will let other potential aggressors know that you'll always rise to your own defense.

But a warning. Don't count on defensive strategies as a cure-all. They are best used to hold a position (neither gaining or losing ground) in the short term. To gain ground, at some point you must do something in addition to playing defense.

Competitive Strategy #3: Preemptive

Preemptive strategies forestall or limit competitors' effectiveness. Ideally, they can discourage your competitor(s) from taking aggressive action. Consider the advice of Sun Tzu:

> The supreme excellence of war is not to win a hundred victories in a hundred battles, but to subdue the armies of your enemies without even having to fight them.

Deterrence is the ultimate business strategy. It lets the firm win without costly "fratricidal battles with competitors."[35] Your competitors will usually have target dates for achieving market and profit goals. They may forego the battle if the dates don't seem attainable.

A number of strategic actions can be effective in raising barriers, making it more difficult for a competitor to take aggressive action. Among these are:[36]

Fill the Product Line. Consider model/service proliferation. Seiko, with worldwide marketing of 2,300 models of watches, left very little uncovered territory–and thus few opportunities–for competitors.[37]

Block Channel Access. Deny your competitor entry to the market by exclusive agreements. Or, by filling up your customers' inventories through the use of sales promotions and volume discounts.

Raise Buyers' Switching Costs. Train buyers in the use of your product/service. Making it difficult for customers to switch to competitors' unfamiliar products/services.

Keep Prices Low. In price/volume industries, a low-price policy often acts as a deterrent to would-be competitors. The cost of catching up on the cost curve, coupled with a continuing low-price policy by you, might keep them out of the market.

Raise the Cost of Gaining Trial. Make it difficult for your competitors to entice buyers to sample their products/services. Keep your prices low on products/services that are faced with competing brands so that your customers are not tempted to stray.

Increase Capital Requirements. Don't let your competitors enter the market on a low-cost, experimentation basis. Finance your buyers, or, institute liberal return and/or warranty policies.

Create the Specter of Overcapacity. Be the first to build a plant which would meet all future industry growth demands. This could discourage other firms from adding capacity. And, it just might deter potential competitors from entering the market.

Foreclose Alternative Technologies. Buy up patents that potentially could make your product/service obsolete.

While the rewards of using preemptive strategies can be great, don't underestimate the risks. You don't want to wind up facing antitrust action.

Competitive Strategy #4: Psychological

Like preemptive strategies, psychological strategies are meant to deter a competitor from taking certain actions. Psychological strategies differ from preemptive strategies in that your actions are meant solely as signals to competitors.

Threaten Retaliation. Indicate to your competitor that it will face severe competitive retaliation unless it changes its approach. For example, if you learn of a competitor who is going to initiate a significant price reduction, threaten to lower your price even more. The other firm, fearing a price war, may then decide not to lower its price.

Use Legal Actions. If you're a small firm, consider a lawsuit to let a larger competitor know that you're not going to give up without a costly fight. The threat of legal action may result in the larger firm being more cautious, for example, in terms of pricing policies. Conversely, if you're a larger firm, you could use the threat of lawsuit as a method of warning a smaller competitor to back off from trying to gain market share. A long, expensive lawsuit could be debilitating for the smaller firm, consuming energy and resources needed for the marketing campaign.

Make Announcements. For example, two years before bringing out its 370 computer, IBM made announcements about the superior performance capabilities of this model. The announcements let competitors know that lower-price "knock-offs" of IBM's present computer would not be successful in the marketplace. In addition, these announcements were enough to cause prospective buyers to wait for the 370, instead of buying a competing model already in existence.

Bluff. A firm may announce new product lines, new plant expansions, new acquisitions, etc., when actually it has no such plans. Its aim is to throw competitors off balance. Of course, to be successful, the bluffing firm must possess credibility, and its stock is rapidly depleted where bluffs are never carried out. If psychological strategies are to work and be legal, you've got to be skillful in market signaling.[38]

Competitive Strategy #5: Niche

Almost all markets are divided into segments. A niche marketing strategy of precision target marketing usually refers to serving smaller segments of the market. Following a niche strategy means staying away from what might be termed the "heart of the market."

The heart of the market is where the volume sales are, and this market segment is usually dominated by large firms. Conversely, "market specialists" or "market nichers" seek small market segments that the dominant firms are likely to ignore or overlook.

The aim of niche strategic marketing is to find a segment of the market (1) small enough that it can be defended, yet (2) large enough to offer desired growth and profit opportunities. You've probably heard of General Electric's silicon bathtub caulking. But have you ever heard of a caulking company called Polymeric Systems, Inc.? Well, they're bigger than General Electric . . . in silicon caulking used in the manufacturing of women's hosiery (in thigh-high hosiery, an elastic band contains a small bead of especially blended silicon caulking to help keep the stockings in place). This is a market too small for General Electric to consider. Yet Polymeric Systems, a small company, prospers in this niche.

For obvious reasons, a small company usually follows niche strategies. However, larger companies may also do so. Instead of following niche strategies for only one or several markets, however, large companies usually follow niche marketing in many different markets. Furthermore, they will usually try to sell to larger niches (like silicon bathtub caulking, instead of silicon caulking used in the manufacture of women's hosiery).

Sources of potential market niches are almost endless. For example, a niche may be isolated by concentrating on one or more of the following:

Product/service features

Custom products/services
High end–loaded with features
Low end
Ancillary products/services
Bundled products/services (turnkey service)
Unbundled products/services

Customer

Size
Specific customer
Location

Service

  Time of day
  Ancillary service
  Quick service
  Technical advice/training
  Billing procedure/credit terms
  After sale back-up
  Repair/maintenance availability
  Availability of replacement parts

Careful analysis of the market is likely to reveal a number of possible niches. Take another look at the 13 questions under Question 1. For example, who are your light users? Who are the non-users? Also examine the Buying Motive Check Sheets (Figures 2.25-2.27) for additional insights.

Rules to Follow in Niche Marketing

Choose a Niche You Can Defend. Niche marketing does not change the principle of force. The company with the larger force still wins. But in niche marketing you are staking out a small segment, thereby reducing the size of the market so you will have the superior force. Quite simply, you are trying to be a "big fish in a small pond." A niche marketer must always keep in mind one of Napoleon's principles: "The art of war with a numerically inferior army consists in always having larger forces than the enemy at the point which is to be attacked or defended."[39]

In any industry, there's usually one segment that is larger than all the others. It's surrounded by a number of niches of varying sizes (see Figure 2.58). The heart of the market has a mesmerizing effect. Most firms tend to gravitate toward it. But here is where competition is most intense.

Make sure you direct your efforts to a segment you can defend. In general, it's easier for you to defend a product/service based on features rather than price. And the most defensible segment of all usually is a commodity-like product/service that is turned into a specialty product/service designed for a given target market.

Other defensible niche markets are the smaller, "less profitable" segments ignored by larger companies. The Japanese automakers

FIGURE 2.58

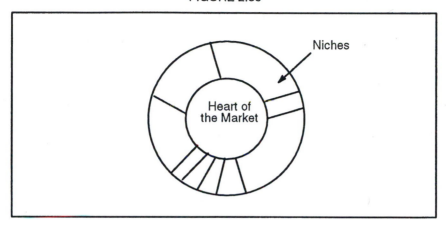

were able to gain an entry into the U.S. automotive market because they went after the low-end customer. Although this was a niche that was served by the "Big Four," they served it only half-heartedly because of the niche's relatively low profit potential. They were willing to let the Japanese become the dominant players in this segment.

Don't Invite Competition When You Can Avoid Doing So. It may boost your ego to brag about success stories at trade conventions and in the press, but such publicity may awaken sleeping giants.

Make "low profile" your watchword, like one fresh chicken supplier specializing in serving Chinese restaurants. To keep competition from knowing the size of his business, he didn't have logos on his delivery vans. Furthermore, the vans weren't even painted the same color.

Be Prepared to Withdraw When You're "Outgunned." Perhaps you've staked out a market segment that large competitors neglected until now. But it may have grown to the point where they now find it attractive. Regardless of why they attack, retreat unless you have a competitive advantage in the field. It's only in the movies that the outgunned small-time rancher beats the monied interests that are stacked against him. And it takes a sentimental script to help him do it.

React Quickly. A niche marketer has to be able to respond swiftly to opportunities in the market. Keep your organization flexible.

Management should be prepared to capitalize on market developments as they occur. And, conversely, be ready to shed quickly any products or services that are no longer profitable.

If you're losing a battle, don't hesitate to discontinue the losing product/service. Don't waste resources. Look for other marketing opportunities. This is the advantage of having a lean and flexible organization. You can react more quickly to market opportunities because you're not hampered by bureaucracy.

Consider Serving More Than One Niche. A single-market niche strategy can easily become ineffective. Your product/service may become obsolete. Or, your target market may dry up. Or, a company with greater resources may enter into your target market. Or management may be asking for more growth than can be expected. For these reasons many market nichers follow a practice of serving several niches, called "multiple niching." This provides all the benefits initially derived from the niche strategy while minimizing the dangers of serving a single niche.

Competitive Strategy #6: Flanking

Flanking strategies involve moving into unserved market segments and becoming a dominant force there. Although similar to niche strategies, they differ in one major aspect. The aim of niche strategies is to find market segments where a company can meet sales and profit performance goals–period. On the other hand, flanking strategies are part of an overall strategy against one or more competitors.

A classic example of a flanking strategy is Miller's Lite beer. Miller's incursion into the light beer market was part of an overall strategy to increase marketing and production efficiencies, thus making the company more competitive with Anheuser Busch and others.

A successful flanking strategy should encompass the following:[40]

Uncontested Segments. The flanking attack must be launched in uncontested market segments. Otherwise, an attack is simply an offensive move. When Miller launched its flanking attack with its Lite beer, for example, it was focusing on what was essentially an unserved segment. Although there had been a number of breweries selling to this market segment, their penetration was almost zero.

Surprise. A flanking move depends on taking your opponents by surprise. Suppose you plan a flanking attack by opening a certain market. What if your competitors find out about your plans? If they also believe the segment is worthy of cultivation, then they might beat you to the marketplace. Or, if they should choose *not* to enter into this segment, they might make pure defensive moves by adjusting their marketing programs to make sure that your new product/service won't succeed.

Because of this, test marketing is often a no-win proposition for a flanking move. If the test market indicates a "no-go" situation, then there's no sense in pursuing it any further. On the other hand, if the product/service test market points to success, it probably will alert competitors who may beat you to the market.

Rapid Penetration. Clausewitz stated, "Without pursuit no victory can have great achievement." For a flanking strategy to be successful, the rollout should be immediately reinforced. The best time to build a commanding market position is at the beginning of a campaign when the competition is disorganized or nonexistent. And the best campaigns are well financed. Successful flanking campaigns, such as Lite Beer (another good example is Close-Up toothpaste), were accomplished by intensive financial commitments before they became successful. Not afterwards.

Competitive Strategy #7: Buy Out/Sell Out

Buy Out Strategy. Another option is to buy out a competitor. This lessens competition. Then, too, you might gain competitive advantages from the sharing of such business areas as research and development, advertising, channels, sales, order processing, manufacturing/operations, and logistics.

Sell Out Strategy. Competition–as well as internal factors–may dictate that the wisest strategy is to take your stake and look for another game.

Competitive Strategy #8: Counteroffensive

Some companies will use certain products/services to foil aggressive competition. Take an example of two competitors, called here A and B, in the consumer paper products industry. Both companies produced similar products. These generic products are labeled here as X and Y.

The matrix in Figure 2.59 illustrates the situation. Company B was spending large sums for advertising and store promotions for its product X, challenging A's leadership. Company A believed that B was getting its funding for its product X largely from the cash flow of its product Y.

Company A's strategy was as follows: it used its product Y, which had but a small volume, to start a price war in product Y. It was A's intention, as A's executives put it in a strategy meeting, "to shake B's money tree." Since B had a large market share in its product Y, a price war here would be very costly to B. As a result, B would have less funds to support its offensive strategy for its product X. On the other hand, because of A's small volume in its product Y, the cost to A would be minimal.

FIGURE 2.59

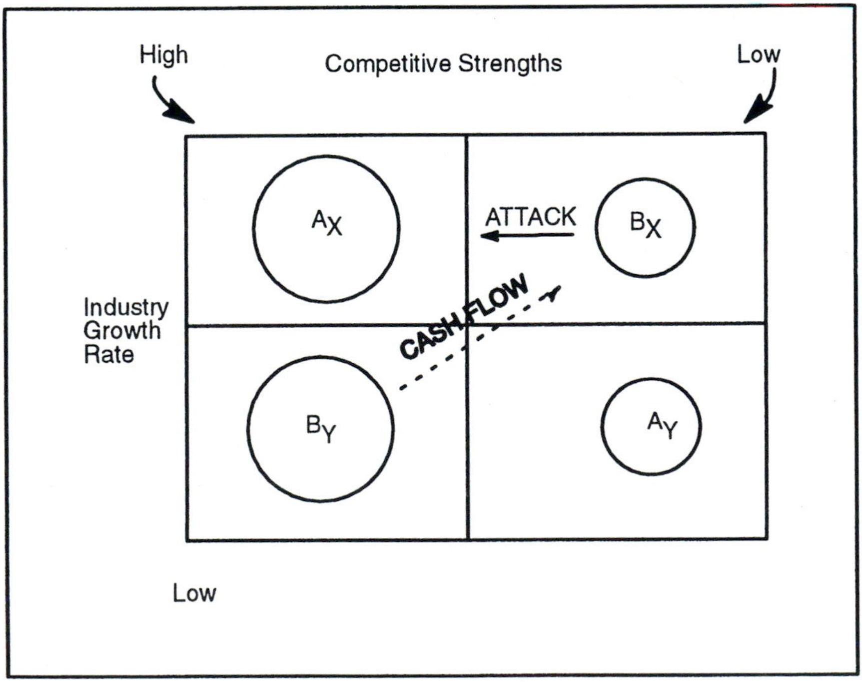

If you decide to use counteroffensive strategies, remember, you have to wait for the competition to throw the first punch. Be sure you can take it.

Additionally, a speedy response is an absolute necessity with this strategy. Once a competitor makes a move on your market, you must act quickly. So if you're relying on a counteroffensive strategy, make sure that your decks are clear for action (translation: you've taken care of potential administrative logjams).

A final caution. Don't confuse counteroffensive strategies with complacency. Many executives have called their "strategy" counteroffensive when in fact they were just caught with their pants down.

Competitive Strategy #9: Bypass

To avoid having to make a frontal attack on a powerful competitor whose resources outweigh yours, consider using bypass strategies. Bypassing can be accomplished through product diversification, technological innovation, and expansion into new territories.

When David Foster took over as Colgate's CEO, he realized that a frontal attack on Procter & Gamble, the company that dominated the marketplace, would be foolish. So he used a two-pronged bypass attack. On one side, he expanded Colgate's foreign markets. On the domestic front, he made several acquisitions which allowed him to market products in areas where P&G offered no competition. Within ten years he more than tripled Colgate's sales, and had moved the company into a strong competitive position against P&G. "The outcome: In 1971 Colgate was underdog to P&G in about half of its business. By 1976, in three-fourths of its business, it was comfortably placed either against P&G or didn't face it at all."[41]

In high-tech industries, companies often use the bypass strategy by leapfrogging into new technologies instead of imitating the competitor's product/service. In the video game market, Intellevision used technological bypassing to best Atari, and Nintendo used that same strategy to bypass Intellevision.

Competitive Strategy #10: Encirclement

Snip away at your competitor's market share until your competitor is weakened. Then launch a frontal attack. For example, Procter

& Gamble sometimes pursues this strategy. Instead of meeting an established competitor head-on, Procter & Gamble will further segment the market. It will then come out with products for these smaller segments, thus siphoning off sales from the established competitor. When its competitor's overall position is sufficiently weakened, Procter & Gamble then makes a frontal attack on its competitor with a me-too version of its competitor's product.[42]

Competitive Strategy #11: Diversionary

A common military strategy is to make a decoy thrust. Its purpose is to get the enemy to think that it is facing a major attack. So deceived, the enemy then will mount a full defensive or counteroffensive effort against this decoy. This effort will spread the enemy's forces so it will not have adequate resources available to meet the major attack which is then mounted in another area. For example, in World War II the Germans failed to meet the Normandy landing with full force. The Allied forces had led the Germans to believe that General Patton was going to strike further north.

Similarly, a number of years ago, one of the USAF's tactics was to send aircraft ahead of the major strike force. The decoy aircraft would head toward a target in a different locality from that of the major strike force. These decoys would drop chaff, giving the appearance on the enemy's radar screen of a major strike force. The enemy would then scramble fighters. By the time the major strike force of bombers appeared on its radar screens, the enemy would have fewer fighters left for interception.

In a like manner, diversionary strategies may help you gain advantage over your competition. This strategy, to be successful, requires intimate knowledge of your competitors and how they would react under given conditions.

Suppose that you wanted to increase your market share in your existing market territories. Further suppose that your main competitor had as one of its goals, "To be dominant in all marketing territories." Following a diversionary strategy, you would signal that you were going to open up new marketing territories (even though your research had indicated these territories would not be profitable). The purpose of your move would be to entice your competitor to mount a major marketing campaign in these new territories. If your diversionary strategy was successful, your competitor would spend considerable resources in these new markets. You would then wage your major campaign in the existing market territories, meeting less resistance from your weakened competitor who would now have fewer resources.

Other situations offering opportunities for diversionary strategies occur wherever your competitors pride themselves on technological advancement, service facilities, complete product line, and so forth.

One pet food manufacturer was ready to launch a new product. As a diversionary strategy, it produced bogus advertising and collateral material. These promotional materials featured product benefits that were meaningless to its target market. This promotional campaign would be doomed to failure. And, as a result, so would the new product.

It then leaked details of this proposed (bogus) campaign to its main competitor. The competitor took the bait. It underestimated the impact the product would have on the market, and made no counter-offensive moves.

Meanwhile, the pet food manufacturer launched the product, using its real promotion program (the new product was very successful). The diversionary strategy was believed to have delayed the competitor's counteroffensive attack by four months.

Competitive Strategy #12: Commando

A company might make small intermittent attacks to harass a competitor. The intent of these raids would be to keep the competitor off balance and weakened. Thus, physically drained and demoralized, the competitor would be less able to mount an offensive campaign, block flanking moves, and/or defend its existing markets. Naturally, the commando raids should cause greater expenditure of resources, proportionally, for your competition.

Tactics to carry out commando marketing strategies might include lawsuits, raiding of employees, selective price cuts, extensive promotional bursts, and so forth. Legal action has become a very popular tactic. In fact, many companies now budget for such legal actions.

Competitive Strategy #13: Guerrilla

Similar to commando strategies, guerrilla strategies utilize small intermittent attacks to harass competitors (tactics are also similar). However, guerrilla strategies differ from commando strategies in intent. Guerrilla strategies' ultimate aim is to demoralize the competition so that it will eventually decide that remaining in the market is not worth the costs. To use military analogies, the American colonies' War of Independence was won not because the British were defeated, but because the British perceived the resource drain of continuing the war not worth the price. For the same reason the United States withdrew from Vietnam.

It's easy to see why guerrilla strategies will best work against a competitor's fringe businesses, rather than its core business. Ideally, the fringe businesses would be those that the competitor views as marginal businesses; i.e., the fringe business is a cash flow drain, and the competitor needs cash to expand its base business. Or, perhaps the fringe business is outside the competitor's core business area. Or possibly the competitor views the opportunities in other markets to be far greater than those to be found by staying with the fringe business.

Ideally, guerrilla marketing warfare would consist of attacks in the remote corners of an adversary's market, which will not be as strongly defended as major market areas. It is best to wage a series of small attacks rather than a few large ones. By this method, the competitor suffers greater disorganization.

The key to successful guerilla strategies is never to "stand and fight." You start a fight. When the competitor responds, you leave. You can still win the war. When the Americans finally sat down and negotiated the withdrawal from Vietnam, an American general leaned across the table and said to his Vietnamese counterpart, "You may have won the war, but you never beat us in a single battle."

Competitive Strategy #14: Lull to Sleep

Put a frog in a pan of boiling water. It will make every effort to jump out of the pan. However, if you put a frog in a pan of cold water on top of a stove, the frog will swim around and possibly not even try to jump out. Now gradually turn up the heat. As the water gets hotter, the frog will probably swim around slower and slower until it eventually croaks (pun intended!), without even trying to jump out of the water.

Mask, as much as possible, your offensive strategies. If your competitors find out about them, they may kick up quite a fuss. This is especially true if your strategy is perceived as threatening, as Yamaha's pronounced strategy was viewed to be by Honda.

In other words, it's ideal to have your strategy in place and to have part of your objectives achieved before your competitor is aware of what has happened. For example, the Japanese captured 17 percent of the U.S. dry soup market before a leading U.S. soup manufacturer caught on.

Put Your Competitive Strategies to a Test

Many companies are setting up "adversary councils" to ensure that their strategies are effective. These groups (or individuals) are charged with developing likely strategies that competition will follow, and then anticipating how competitors might react to the company's proposed strategy.

More specifically, the adversary councils are given:

- The company's past strategy
- The competitors' past strategies, and to the extent that they are known, growth and profit objectives

Then they are charged with answering the following questions:

- Given the above, what will our competitors do next year?
- What will our competitors do if we follow a certain (proposed) strategy?

Use an outside person(s) in the adversary council. You'll get more objectivity. But make sure the adversary council is extremely familiar with your industry.

STRATEGY FORMULATION
IN A TOTAL QUALITY ENVIRONMENT

First and foremost, it's got to be a cross-functional effort. Of course, in some areas, marketing might take the lead. In others, it's operations. In others, it's finance. And so on.

But start with the customers. Answer these questions:

Who are our customers?
What is quality to our customers?
What are we offering to these customers?
What are the gaps that must be filled (considering existing and potential competition)?

Next, develop product/service features that respond to targeted customers' needs and developing the processes to produce these features.

You've got to work closely–and right from the start–with other functional areas. Make sure that what you want delivered (the augmented product or service) to your target market can be done at a desirable cost and within a desirable time frame. In this way, you eliminate the "hot potato" phenomenon, where the engineering department (hopefully with input from marketing) designs the product, then tosses the blueprints to manufacturing. Manufacturing checks them out and decides the product is too expensive and/or difficult to make, and tosses the blueprints back to engineering for redesign. Engineering reworks them, throws them back to manufacturing, and so on.

So, in total quality planning, strategy development is not just the purview of the marketing department (or any other functional area), who develops the strategy and then tries to sell it to the rest of the company. Strategy development is the result of a team effort; an effort where all functional department inputs are made before and during strategy development, and not just as an afterthought.

Total quality planning saves a lot of time, money, frustration, and ill-feelings, and as a consequence, makes the firm more competitive in the marketplace.

But what if you don't operate in a total quality environment? Can you still develop a marketing strategy while gaining some of the benefits from total quality planning?

Changes in the marketing strategy will cause reverberations, ranging from high seas to tidal waves throughout your company. So try to involve other functional area managers while developing the marketing strategy.

How to make these efforts for involvement will be company-situational. What makes sense in some companies would be ridiculous in others. Here are a few ideas. We've talked about these techniques before in other planning situations (SWOTs: Present and Future), but they apply here as well:

- Formal meetings ranging from one hour to weekend working sessions
- Informal conversations
- Printed information, from internal or external sources, with appropriate sections highlighted

You may or may not succeed completely, but you might be able to make some positive movements toward total quality planning.

Do Comprehensive Planning While Developing Your Strategy

As a practical matter, if you make a major strategy change, its implementation probably will be gradual. It takes time, for instance, to develop needed expertise, production/operations facilities, and/or necessary logistics. Few companies can switch to different products/services and/or target markets overnight. Plan on a transition that will optimize your present opportunities while you gradually phase in a new strategy.

So, make sure that the strategy you select will enable you to meet performance goals in *both* the long and the short range. Consciously think about your annual plan while you're developing/evaluating your overall strategy. Of course, there's no need, at this time, for the annual plan to be completed in detail. That will be done later (Step 8). All you want to do is to make sure that the annual plan has a reasonable chance of meeting your performance goals.

Strategy Formulation
in a Total Quality Environment:
A Case Example

Let's see how strategy development might have taken place at Micron in a total quality environment. Micron's planning team realized that it had to bridge huge sales and profit planning gaps (see Figure 2.60). And, the company was limited in resources. Practical choices would have to be made.

The planning team closely examined its SWOTs: Present and Future. After much discussion, in a number of formal and informal meetings, team members believed that they could close the short- and long-run sales and profit gaps. Their strategy, when implemented, would stop and reverse the momentum of IMPRO, and to a lesser extent, that of Moltec. Moltec, because of its financial condition, did not pose much of a threat.

The strategy chosen was a combination of defense and offense. The defensive element of the strategy was to improve Micron's strengths: product features and reliability. The offensive element was to correct its sales-force and service shortcomings.

There were six prongs to this strategy. The first was to adjust price to be consistent with Micron's superior product quality image. At the time, Micron's selling price was below IMPRO's and Mol-

FIGURE 2.60

Gap Analysis–Under a No-Change Strategy (in $1,000, dollars 1992)		
	1993	1997
Sales Planning Targets	2,496	2,880
Projected Sales	2,300	2,100
Projected Gap	(196)	(780)
Contribution to Corporate Planning Targets	676	780
Projected Contribution to Corporate	600	490
Projected Gap	(76)	(290)

tec's, even though the target market viewed Micron's product as superior to both competitors' products. Further, customer analysis indicated that low price was not a critical factor in the purchase decision. Further proof of this finding was found in the fact that both IMPRO and Moltec had gained share even though their prices were higher than Micron's.

The specifics of the pricing plan were as follows: during the first year, price was to be raised to industry parity. It was to remain at this level also during year two (1994) to prevent possible "price shock" by frequent price increases. In the third year (1995), however, price would be increased to 5 percent above that currently charged by IMPRO and Moltec. It was believed that IMPRO and Moltec would hold the line on prices (except for inflationary adjustments).

The second prong was to maintain product superiority through an increase in R&D expenditures. Forecasts had predicted that rapidly changing applications would constantly require new accessories and some instrument redesign. Therefore, R&D expenditures were to be increased to $250,000 in 1993 and eventually raised to $400,000 in the last year of the five-year plan.

In examining the value chains of both Micron and its target market, it became obvious to the planning team that there should be better contact between Micron and its customers. Although Micron had always worked closely with customers on an informal basis, why wasn't this also done formally? The planning team decided to set up a customer panel. This panel would meet periodically, at least quarterly. All members of the planning team would interact with the panel, but administering the panel would be the responsibility of design and engineering.

A portion of the R&D expenditures was to be spent on process improvement to help reduce production costs and process defects. The plan reflected the reduction in the cost of goods sold in years four and five to 40.7 percent of sales (based also on Micron's raise in selling price) from 43.5 percent for years one and two.

The third prong of the strategy was to increase salesperson contact with potential customers. In the first year, one additional salesperson, experienced in the sale of high-end oscilloscopes, would be hired.

Industry contacts had led Micron's executives to believe that it would be possible to hire one of Moltec's or IMPRO's salespersons. The planning team felt that overtures had to be made to these salespersons as soon as possible. (There had been some discussion about Micron acquiring Moltec, but the idea was quashed. The only thing that Micron could gain by acquiring Moltec would be its sales force. Furthermore, the planning team believed that if IMPRO acquired Moltec, it too would gain little.)

Micron's management had to face the fact that both of these sources for a salesperson might come up dry. A contingency plan would have to be in place. Their plan was to use a headhunter to locate a salesperson with a background that would make him/her quickly adaptable to selling high-end research oscilloscopes. Since the planning team wanted to get the salesperson on stream as soon as possible, it was decided that, as part of the contingency plan, the search should start for the headhunter immediately. If the candidates from IMPRO and Moltec should turn down Micron, then there would be little time lost.

A second salesperson would be added in the second year (1994). In year five (1997), a sales associate would be added. This person would be an inside salesperson. His/her primary responsibility would be to make the outside salespersons more efficient by, among other things, qualifying sales leads. (Note: The adding of a sales associate five years out seems to be planning at a ridiculously minute level. Yet it was done for a purpose. Micron's planning team hoped to hire a sales associate much sooner. Suppose Micron's sales and profit results were better than projections in years two or three. Then the planning team felt that their parent company would be more likely to approve the addition. After all, it was part of the strategic plan.)

The fourth prong of the strategy was to provide worldwide customer service with a 24-hour service hot line. This hot line would put the customer in immediate touch with one of Micron's experienced engineers. He/she would be able to give advice and instructions on how to correct operating problems. For more serious problems, the engineer would be authorized to have the oscilloscope returned to Micron. Forty-eight hour service (maximum) turnaround would be mandated. All shipments would arrive by overnight express at Micron's expense. If the product could not be serviced within the required time constraints, a loaner would be sent to the customer.

Given the trouble-free history of its oscilloscopes, Micron did not foresee significant use of the hot line. An additional engineer would not need to be added. One engineer would be on call each night. A hot line call would be forwarded to the engineer's pager for immediate callback. The engineers would receive compensation for being on call.

Costs of the hot line would be greatest in year one. This would be due to installation costs. In years two through five costs would significantly decrease.

Micron's planning team did not believe that a service hot line would be a sustainable competitive advantage in the long run. Still it was felt that the loaner aspect of the strategy would be more difficult for the competitors to match, since both competitors (especially Moltec) were financially weak.

To make potential customers aware of the hot line, advertising expenses would also be significantly increased. In year one, expenses would increase only slightly, by $15,000, to $75,000. However, after the first year, when the system had been debugged, advertising would increase to $125,000 per year for the remaining four years.

The implementation of the hot line was linked to a contingency plan. Implementation would not begin until midyear of 1993. If sales were disappointing, the hot line would not start until the following year, unless corporate gave Micron the go-ahead. Although the planning team did not like the idea of postponing the hot line, it felt that this would be the expenditure that could be delayed with the least cost to sales. If the hot line was postponed, the increases in advertising expenditures would also be postponed.

The fifth prong was to evaluate its target marketing practice. Currently, Micron was serving customers in the industrial, educational, and governmental markets. But were sales equal in all of these markets? Then, too, were some types (size, areas of specialization) of companies/institutions more likely to purchase Micron's oscilloscopes? And so on.

Although it was generally understood who had purchased the units, no formal analysis had been made. Examining its customer base would be no big deal. Micron had sold fewer than 100 units since its inception. And yet the rewards could be great. It might show the sales force how to better spend its time. And, possibly it might reveal that Micron should further segment its current market.

The sixth prong was that of continuous improvement. This would be company-wide. As part of their annual plans, each functional area would identify processes that needed improvement. During the course of the year, then, each functional area would determine how these improvements would be made.

Think about some of the benefits Micron reaped by applying the total quality approach to strategy development. By using a cross-functional team approach in strategy planning, each functional department was involved in every phase of strategy development, and not just informed after the fact.

Do you think engineering would have agreed to wear pagers at night if it was a marketing department directive, rather than a suggestion by the manager of engineering? Or, what do you think manufacturing's reaction would have been if marketing had suggested that manufacturing plan to reduce production costs and defects?

Getting functional area buy-in on Micron's new strategy may have only been possible because of company-wide total quality planning.

POINTS LEARNED

1. Selecting target markets is possibly the most important decision you'll make in the marketing planning process.
2. A broadly focused marketing strategy often leads to "getting stuck in the middle." Practice precision target marketing.
3. In your search for new target markets, first look within your present customer base.
4. Use value-chain analysis to help make sure that you are capitalizing on opportunities for product/service differentiation and/or reduced costs.

5. Make focusing on your customers primary. But in the process, don't get blindsided by competition. While competitive strategy has always been important, it is even more critical today. Consider the 14 key competitive strategies to help you optimize competitive advantages (while minimizing competitive restraints).
6. Put your competitive strategies to a test. Use adversary councils.
7. Strategy formulation in a total quality environment demands a cross-functional effort. Strategy development is not just the purview of the marketing department (or any other functional area).
8. Do comprehensive planning while developing your strategy. Make sure that the strategy you select will enable you to meet performance goals in both the long and the short range.

LOOKING AHEAD

You've developed a strategy. Now it's time to document and evaluate that strategy.

THE EIGHT PLANNING STEPS

Step 1. SWOTs: Present. Gain an Overall Perspective by Historical Analysis of Total Sales, Expenses and Profits, and of Sales and Profits by Products/Services

Step 2. SWOTs: Present (cont.). To Help Decide Where to Concentrate Planning Efforts, List Target Markets Currently Served with Present Products/Services and Analyze by Sales and Profits

Step 3. SWOTs: Present (cont.). Develop Performance Profiles for Each Product/Service-Target Market

Step 4. SWOTs: Future. For Each Product/Service-Target Market, Forecast Market Environment, Target Market's Demand, and Your Sales and Profits (Assuming You Continue Your Present Strategy)

Step 5. Gap Analysis

Step 6. Examination of Strategic Options and Strategy Selection

 Step 7. Strategy Documentation and Evaluation

Step 8. Fleshing Out, Documenting, and Formatting the Annual Marketing Plan

Step 7:
Strategy Documentation
and Evaluation

Let's suppose that you've been operating in a total quality environment for a year or two, and that you've followed this procedure (Steps 1-8) in previous planning cycles. Furthermore, suppose that after going through Steps 1-6 in this planning cycle, the consensus of the planning team is that strategy changes are not needed. Then is Step 7 necessary? No. Not for this cycle. But check with management. Explain that you're not going to make strategy changes. Get their approval before putting together the annual plan. It just might save you a lot of time and embarrassment.

But now let's assume that strategy changes will have to be made. Further, let's assume that you now have a tentative strategy which you believe will enable you to meet your performance goals. Your next step is to carefully spell out (document) and evaluate this strategy. You'll go through four major phases:

1. Strategy Documentation/Evaluation for a Single Product/Service-Target Market
2. Strategy Documentation/Evaluation for Multiple Products/Services-Target Markets
3. Major Change Analysis: Strategic Activities, Expenses, and Revenues
4. Management Review

STRATEGY DOCUMENTATION/EVALUATION FOR SINGLE PRODUCT/SERVICE-TARGET MARKET

To help explain the process, we're continuing to use the Micron case as an example.

Write Out Your Proposed Strategy

Explicitly state the product/service to be offered, the target market, key buying motives, key success factors, competitive focus, and major elements of the marketing mix. (See Figure 2.61.)

Check the Competitive Viability of Your Proposed Strategy

During the SWOTs analyses, you predicted what your competitors would do (assuming no change on your part). Now estimate how they will react to your tentative strategy, given their market objectives and resources. Will existing competition ignore these changes? Copy them? Outdo them? Will your strategy attract new competitors, either direct or indirect? If so, what will be the nature of this new competition? Given these potential competitive responses, does your proposed strategy make sense? Can your strategy be adjusted to minimize likely competitive responses?

You'll probably go through a hammering/fitting process. When you're satisfied that your strategy is sound, given likely competitive reactions, make necessary changes on the strategy description form (Figure 2.61). Then, fill out the form in Figure 2.62. There is nothing sophisticated or complicated about the form. But, assessing how you think your competitors will react to your strategy will force you to be more rigorous in your thinking.

Assess Internal Feasibility/Capability

Most plans fail because of overcommitment of personnel and overcommitment of money. It's nice to talk about serving a number of target markets, but there are costs involved. A director of the New York-based consulting firm, McKinsey & Co., put it this way, "Breadth of choice equals complexity; complexity equals increasing cost."[1]

It takes highly qualified personnel to develop marketing programs. Clearly, this is no job for the inexperienced. Then, too, product/service tinkering can create production/operations problems. Although Campbell Soup Company is a believer in micromarketing, it does limit the extent of its product variation. Larry

FIGURE 2.61

STRATEGY DESCRIPTION

Product/Service
Research Oscilloscope -- high end

Target Market
Highly specialized research scientists at universities, government and industrial research labs

Key Buying Motives
Extensive applications, high performance and reliability, immediate service

Key Success Factors
R+D, production quality control, highly specialized sales engineers, immediate service capability

Competitive Focus
Defensive -- improve product features and reliability. Offensive -- correct salesforce and service shortcomings (focusing chiefly at IMPRO)

Major Elements of the Marketing Mix

Product/Service Changes
Increase product R+D to improve product features (Design + Engineering)

Set up customer panel (Design + Engineering)

Promotion
Add salesperson in Year 1, another salesperson in Year 2, a sales associate in Year 5

Price
Increase advertising expenditures to promote hotline
Raise to industry parity in Years 1+2;
5% above industry prices in Years 3, 4+5

Place
Increase process R+D to lower production costs

Add 24-hour hotline and provide immediate service

Other
Examine customer mix (profiles)

FIGURE 2.62

ASSESSMENT OF COMPETITORS' REACTION TO PROPOSED STRATEGY		
Reaction by Specific Competitors (or groups)		
Competitor IMPRO	Competitor MOLTEC	Indirect Competition The "Majors" who produce Low-end oscilloscopes
Reaction to Strategy	Reaction to Strategy	Reaction to Strategy
Impro will probably try to acquire Moltec. Even if this acquisition is successful, Impro will not achieve substantial competitive advantages, especially if we are successful in hiring one of Impro's or Moltec's salespersons. With or without Moltec, Impro will not be able to aggressively counter-act our strategy because of limited financial resources. Impro may, however, slightly increase its advertising expenditures. It is not expected that Impro will lower (or raise) its prices.	Moltec will probably be acquired by Impro. If not, because of Moltec's weak financial condition, it will not be able to respond to our strategy. It is not expected that Moltec will lower (or raise) its prices.	It's not likely that the "majors" will enter the high-end market because of the rapid growth in the low-end market and the small size and the relatively slow growth in the high-end market.

Carpenter, senior marketing manager for soups at Campbell, said that they limit the number of nacho cheese soups. "Beyond two it gets a little complex. You run into production problems and something goes wrong."[2]

You also stand to lose marketing efficiency. When General Foods Corporation sponsored regional promotional events, such as a show at New York's Radio City Music Hall and a rodeo in Dallas, these regional efforts cost two to three times more than a national promotion program.[3]

Determine the actions required (if any) to develop the necessary strengths in the key success areas. You might find it helpful to use a check sheet similar to Figure 2.63. You'll note that other functional areas, besides marketing, are evaluated. After all, if your strategy is going to work, it's going to require a coordinated effort of all functional areas within the firm. Consequently, the capabilities of these functional areas have to be assessed, especially if you're making any changes in strategy. Because of this need for coordinated efforts, get other functional area managers involved during strategy development.

If you find yourself on the short side of required resources, consider scaling back your strategy. For example, consider concentrating on one market segment. Since you are likely to find that 80 percent of your sales come from one segment and the remaining 20 percent is scattered among a number of others, given limited resources, your best alternative may be to direct your energies to serving the 80 percent. By so doing, you'll probably increase sales to this market segment. You may not even lose customers. Sales to the other segments may continue through sheer serendipity.

In a total quality environment, assessment of internal feasibility/capability should be hardly necessary. Since the various functions are involved from the beginning of the planning cycle, capabilities will have been considered by all functional areas while the strategy is being developed.

For example, take the Micron case. If the manager of design and engineering felt his/her staff didn't have time to staff the hot line, he/she never would have permitted a hot line to be part of the strategy. Unless, of course, additional resources were forthcoming.

FIGURE 2.63

INTERNAL FEASIBILITY/CAPABILITY

Proposed Strategy <u>Defensive / Offensive   (YEAR 1)</u>

Functional Area	Key Success Requirements	Evaluation of Current Abilities	Corrective Action Required
<u>Marketing</u> Sales	hire sales person, Assimilate into Company, supervise	More time required of marketing mgr., will reduce number of sales calls by marketing mgr.	Must free-up more time of marketing mgr.
Customer service	Set up hot line (in cooperation with engineering)	" "	" "
<u>Design & Engineering</u>	Must spend more time with customers	No serious discrepancies	None
	Set up hot line (in cooperation with marketing)	" "	" "
	Set up customer panel	" "	" "
<u>Manufacturing</u>	Improve process R+D	No serious discrepancies	None
<u>Finance</u>	No additional requirements (major)	No discrepancies	None

<u>Feasibility Assessment</u> OK, except for time requirements of the marketing manager. The marketing manager will have less time for making sales calls. Recruitment of new salesperson is critical.

*Modified from:
William E. Rochschild. *Strategic Alternatives*. AMACCM. New York, 1979. See pages 197, 198.

This highlights again a benefit of total quality planning: reduced planning time. And this means faster reaction time, making the firm more competitive.

Have You Thought About How Your Strategy Would Fare in Other Than the Most-Probable-Case?

Plan approval does not release you from responsibility should the plan fail. You know you'll be judged according to results–not according to how good the plan looked on paper. One way to ensure that your plan will succeed is to make certain that you have developed a strategy with flexibility. After all, no plan is executed without a single hitch. It pays to expect the unexpected.

Specifically, your flexible plan should allow for:

Change Through Incrementalism. If your strategy involves major changes, can these changes be made gradually? Remember, you have to allow time to educate people. And, also, remember that anything new is bound to have "glitches." Of course, the smaller the scale of operation, the less difficulty you'll have in making corrections.

Try to start out small, even though you may have large-scale plans. For example, a major food company started with three restaurants on the West Coast, although its intention was to build a chain of over 600. This firm knew that a number of modifications would have to be made, and it recognized that it would be far easier to make these modifications on a very small scale.

A Short Chain of Command. A short chain of command will enable you to make adjustments more quickly and easily. Decisions won't get lost in an unwieldy bureaucracy.

Optimum Delay of Capital Expenditures. If your strategy involves major changes and capital expenditures, try to delay these capital expenditures as long as you can. Environmental shifts may make some, or perhaps all, of your capital expenditures obsolete. Consider, for example, subcontracting manufacturing, renting warehouse space, and/or leasing retail space instead of making capital expenditures in those areas which may have little adaptability.

Of course, in some instances you may have to "go for it." As one executive put it, "You either build a refinery or you don't." But always analyze the situation to see whether you really need to make all planned capital expenditures in the short term. Greater flexibility often comes as a result of such delays.

Adaptability of Capital Expenditures. Again, if your strategy calls for capital expenditures, is there any way you can allow for multi-purpose uses? For example, one bank was concerned that electronic banking might make its present network of branches obsolete. Consequently, it located and designed all of its new branches so they could be used for other purposes, should electronic banking take over. The cost was minimal, and there was little loss in aesthetics and functional practicality.

Develop Contingency Plans

There is one constant: the future is unpredictable. And Murphy's Law points out which way things are likely to go. (O'Leary's Corollary: "Murphy was an optimist.") The "law" touches on an unpleasant truth. A gambler once approached this point in a different way. "Don't prepare just for average bad luck," he said, "but for outrageously bad luck." If such luck comes your way, will you have an adequate supply of critical resources? Money? Manpower? Physical facilities? Raw materials? Energy?

Max Gunther, in *The Luck Factor*,[4] analyzed the characteristics of lucky people (not those who win the Irish Sweepstakes once and then that's it, but rather those who seem to be lucky throughout their lives). He found these lucky people to be possessed of what he terms "The Pessimism Paradox."

Lucky people are extremely pessimistic. They are happy–but pessimistic. They always seem to be planning what they will do in event of disaster. For example, J. Paul Getty, who was one of the richest men on earth, said, "When I go into any business deal, my chief thoughts are how I'm going to save myself when things go wrong."

Indeed the results of a study of bus drivers revealed that those who have the fewest accidents were those who were always thinking of what they would do if some problem arose. The drivers who were in the most accidents invariably depended upon luck.

In the same book, Gunther introduces "Mitchell's Law," named after Martha Mitchell. He relates how he visited Martha Mitchell in

1975 to try to get her to write her autobiography. He had expected to see a haughty individual. Instead he found a rather meek woman. Here was a person who had risen from a poor background to become a highly paid model, who had married a very successful Wall Street bond lawyer, and who later had become the social leader in Washington, D.C. During their conversation she volunteered what Gunther later named Mitchell's Law: "Life is slippery like a piece of soap. If you think you have a grip on it, you're wrong."

Murphy's Law says that things are likely to go wrong, while Mitchell's Law says that we have very little control over things. These laws suggest that regardless of how sound your tentative strategy may seem, it's advisable to have a flexible strategy.

Look at your strategy again. Can you adapt it both to most-probable *and* to pessimistic futures? Or does its effectiveness depend solely on a most-probable or an optimistic future? As a result of this check you may wish to discard the tentative strategy entirely and design a completely new one. Or you may decide the risk is worth taking and that no change is necessary. Or you may decide to develop contingency actions.

Let's assume that you've decided to develop contingency actions. Here are two basic approaches you can follow: (1) build the contingency actions into the strategy itself, called developing a "straddle strategy;" or (2) develop specific contingency plans.

Straddle Strategies

A straddle strategy is a game plan which has enough flexibility to allow for adjustments, should conditions other than the most-probable occur. For example, in the early 1980s a very successful real estate developer was continually concerned about possible fluctuations in interest rates (and rightfully so!). So on building a new condominium development, or buying an apartment complex for conversion to sell as individual units, he made sure that the development could also be rented. Thus, in case of poor sales caused by high interest rates, he could generate income by leasing the units. This rental income would cover carrying costs. When interest rates dropped, the units could be sold. The potential impact of high interest rates was neutralized.

Contingency Plans

The second approach to building plan flexibility is to develop specific contingency plans. These contingency plans remain "on the shelf" and are used only if some condition other than the most-probable case should occur. Contingency plans helped the Federal Reserve Board chairman, Alan Greenspan, avoid a "meltdown" during the October 19, 1987 stockmarket collapse. Long before the crash, Greenspan formed a crisis management team to examine contingency problems, and to put together options to follow in the event of a dramatic drop in stock prices. Officials of the Federal Reserve Board claimed that these contingency plans enabled swift reaction when the actual crash occurred.[5]

There are three basic steps involved in contingency planning: determining key contingency events, specifying trigger points, and developing contingency actions.

1. Determining Key Contingency Events. Begin with contingency plans for no more than one or two contingent events. To help isolate the most important, closely examine the most-probable case future you developed. Are there any forecasts you believe could go either way? Would such fluctuations greatly jeopardize your plan? If so, these would be key contingent events.

Contingency events may be positive as well as negative. In keeping with the policy of simplicity, you may wish to consider only negative events your first time through. As one executive stated: "If we have contingency plans for the worst that's good enough. Somehow we'll be able to figure out how to handle the best." While that may not be true in every case, simplicity does have a virtue. And it's probably better to have your flank protected, by looking at the worst-case scenario.

However, should you decide that there are no specific contingencies that are real issues, don't bother with contingency planning–it will only be perceived as an unnecessary chore.

2. Specifying Trigger Points. A trigger point indicates when a contingency event has developed to the extent of negatively affecting plan performance. For example, your strategy may be dependent upon a maximum annual inflation rate of 5 percent. Thus, your contingency plan would be "triggered" when the annual rate exceeds 5 percent for one quarter.

Make sure that you have a trigger point that is specific. Trigger points such as "high inflation," "increased competitive activity," or "economic slowdown" are meaningless. They give no specific indication as to when action should be taken. Result: you'll procrastinate. Your contingency plans will never be put into action.

Select a trigger point for each key contingent event. Use commonly reported events, such as GDP, rate of inflation, retail sales, money supply, or company sales to simplify monitoring.

3. Developing Contingency Actions. In developing contingency actions, follow these guidelines:

- Keep the plans simple, particularly when developing contingency plans for the first time. Avoiding complex plans will make preparation easier. Limit contingency actions to one page.
- Consider positive as well as negative reactions. To illustrate: in the event of a contingent downturn, a negative reaction would be to discharge personnel. A positive reaction would be to expand to unaffected markets. Positive actions usually help morale. Furthermore, they're more likely to improve your profits and competitive position.
- Estimate the funding necessary for implementing the contingency action. Make sure funding requirements are realistic and available; recognize that what is "realistic and available" usually varies with psychological perspectives. While business is on the upswing, management is usually optimistic, and funds are approved in this perspective. When profits are threatened, however, management may change its stance and reject what it had previously viewed as reasonable.

For an example of a key contingent event, trigger point, contingency plan, and format, see Figure 2.64.

If you're developing contingency plans for the first time, and if your planning team does not have a great deal of planning experience, be sure to keep the process simple. As one executive cautioned, "Contingencies tend to be downside, and people do not like to anticipate negative situations. If people do not like to plan in

FIGURE 2.64

CONTINGENCY PLANS		
Key Contingent Events (What is the event?)	Trigger Points (When the event occurs)	Contingency Plans (What we will do when the event occurs)
11.0 Sales fall below projections	11.0 Firm orders for less than six units by 6/1/92	11.0 See if corporate is willing to accept a lower contribution to corporate. If not, 11.1 Postpone hotline until year 2 11.2 Cap advertising expenditures at 60 K

general, contingency planning becomes an even more difficult task." So accept the fact that the contingency plans will not be comprehensive. But keep in mind that even very crude contingency plans can have great benefits. The process of thinking through "what-ifs" increases one's adaptability even if the unexpected–an event for which there are no contingency plans–should occur.

In preparing your contingency plans, refer back to the work you did under SWOTs: Future. This information will give you excellent guidance in determining what likely events might have a dramatic impact on your future plans.

Additional Questions to Consider*

Will Top Management Be Comfortable with the New Product or Service?

Consider top management's predisposition toward certain product and service lines. You know your management's inclinations. If not, find them out. Then consider if top management will stick to the plan. Some product and service target market strategies require long-term funding to give them a chance to develop. Others do not. If your company suffers from "quarteritis," consider the short-term payoff markets.

Here's why. Suppose that you've got two alternative products/services-target markets under consideration. One has a very promising long-range payout, but it's going to require considerable funding in the short run. The other product or service-target market is just the opposite. Short-term results are likely to be very good, but in the long term not so good. Under these conditions, you'll probably decide on the short-term alternative. (A sad commentary on U.S. business decision making. But sometimes it makes no sense to tilt at windmills.)

There's another reason for making sure payouts are compatible with management's thinking. "No manager who has a longer [planning] time horizon than his or her superiors can expect to survive."

---

*Some of the following discussion appeared in Robert E. Linneman and John L. Stanton, *Making Niche Marketing Work (How to Get Bigger by Acting Smaller)*. (New York: McGraw-Hill, 1991). Reprinted by permission.

Of course, there's a corollary that states, "But neither can the business survive if the time horizon is inadequate to encompass the actions required today in order to protect the business in the future."[6] But that's another story.

Is the Market Structurally Attractive?

Warren Buffett, the multibillionaire manager of Berkshire Hathaway, claimed, "I've said many times that when a management with a reputation for brilliance tackles a business with a reputation for bad economics, it is [only] the reputation of the business that remains intact."[7] An approach used for industry analysis can help marketers.[8]

Key determinants of a market's desirability are the size of the market, competition, bargaining power of the customers, bargaining power of the suppliers, threat of substitute products and services, and governmental control.

Size of the Market. The market must be big enough to make it worthwhile. As an executive of a trucking firm put it, "We look at the size of the market. We don't want to have our salespeople chasing something not that great."

But don't dismiss low-volume new products and services too quickly. New markets are not easily forecasted. Sometimes a product geared toward a seemingly small niche turns out to be a large market. Like Gatorade.

Competition. What about competitive intensity? Who will be your competitors? Small firms with limited resources? Or companies with deep pockets and commitment to the market? Is there a threat of new competitors? If so, what are their characteristics?

Can you be the market leader? Better think twice if you're going to play second fiddle. In many markets there's only room for number one.

Bargaining Power of Customers. Some markets aren't attractive because buyers have too much control over price. Or, when there are only a few buyers, the loss of one or two of them can change the balance.

Markets can also be unattractive when your product or service represents a significant portion of the buyer's overall costs, and when the buyer serves a highly price-competitive market. These buyers are willing to spend time looking for the best price, making you vulnerable to competition.

Bargaining Power of Suppliers. Is the product or service dependent on specific technology, materials, or parts from suppliers? If so, will the suppliers exact a toll and keep you from reaching your profit objectives?

Threat of Substitute Products and Services. How unique is your product or service? Do you need to worry about substitutes? If not now, how about in the future?

Governmental Control. Is this market in a highly regulated industry where the government will specify your profit level? For example, a pharmaceutical company found that it couldn't do business in Brazil. High inflation rates demanded frequent price increases. Yet the government refused to let the company make the necessary price increases. The reason: people needed the drugs and couldn't afford higher prices. A company executive told us, "We couldn't make a profit, so we shut down the plant." And then he gave us this bit of advice: "Avoid sob sister industries in countries with high inflation."

Value Added. As a rule, target those industries with high potential value added. There should be a relatively large spread between what you pay for raw materials, semifabricated materials, and parts, and what you sell your product for.

For example, see Figure 2.65, which shows the value added for two imaginary companies. In Company A there is $0.65 value added, and in Company B only $0.20. If the price of materials increased by 10 percent, Company B would like to pass these costs on to the purchaser. Yet, what if competitors can offer substitute products that are unaffected by the cost increases?

Company A is in a safer position. Because of the high value added, the firm, through increased efficiency, has a shot at absorbing the cost increases. A great advantage, especially in inflationary times.

Is the Market Accessible?

Identifying a market segment is useless unless you can reach it. For example, you may wish to serve a segment consisting of men who have the psychographic personality traits of high achievers.

FIGURE 2.65

High and Low Value Added		
	Company A	Company B
Selling price	$1.00	$1.00
Cost of raw materials, semifabricated materials, parts	0.35	0.80
Value added		
Expenses (selling, administrative, labor)	0.60	0.15
Profit	0.05	0.05

What media would you use to tap this segment? What channel of distribution? You need attributes that point to specific people by occupation, education, or high-income zip codes.

Is the Market Measurable?

You should be able to determine the overall potential of the market in quantitative terms. What is the market's potential?

If you're selling the same product or service to several markets, can you measure the purchases of each market? If you can't, you'll never know if your marketing efforts are paying off.

A tip-off on measurability: the clearer your answer to the question of market accessibility, the more likely it is that you can measure sales to this market.

Are the Payoffs Commensurate with the Risks?

What amount of your company's resources are you committing to this strategy? Is the payoff really worth it? Remember that the more distant the payoff, the more risky the venture. Government has a way of changing regulations. Tastes change. Technology has a way of advancing in unforeseeable ways.

*Does the Strategy Have Favorable Payoffs
in the Most-Probable-Case Future?*

Sometimes we tend to hedge our bets so we come up with a "no hit, no run, no error strategy." Of course you should think of the downside, but always remember that you're being paid to evaluate risks and develop successful strategies; not to avoid risks entirely. Sometimes very successful products/services are brought to the marketplace in spite of seemingly high risk factors. For example, the general consensus of many Sony executives was that the Sony Walkman would fail. But the chairman, Morita, took the gamble.

Is the Strategy Attractive in the Near Future?

The further out you go, the less predictable the future becomes. As Drucker points out in *Innovation and Entrepreneurship*, "It's not good enough to be able to say, 'In twenty-five years there will be so many very old people that they will need this.' One has to be able to say, 'There are enough old people around today for this to make a difference to them . . . [and] in twenty-five years there will be many more.'"[9]

Does the Strategy Allow Ample Time for Implementation?

The First Law of Aerial Wing-Walking states, "Never let go of what you are holding until you have a firm grasp on something else." The same is true with implementing strategies. Grant sufficient time for your strategy to take hold. If possible, don't abandon a not-too-successful, but profitable, strategy for a more promising one until the newer strategy is in place.

Are You Making Hockey-Stick Projections?

Make sure you're not making unreasonable forecasts. You should question estimates that take you from "way down here today," to "way up here" tomorrow, without any real explanation as to how this marvelous transformation is going to take place. A good check to prevent hockey-stick projections is to ask, "Which competitor(s) are we going to take sales away from?" And then, "What is there about our strategy that will enable us to gain these sales?"

STRATEGY DOCUMENTATION/EVALUATION FOR MULTIPLE PRODUCTS/SERVICES-TARGET MARKETS

Now let's take a case where you have multiple products/services-target markets.* You have tentative strategies for each but you want to be sure that they're more than just a collection of stand-alone products/services-target markets.

Stand-alone businesses are burdened by corporate overhead costs. They're vulnerable to competitors who don't have to bear such corporate dead weight. These competitors can invest more in R&D. Or in quality. Or in marketing. Or they can offer lower prices to the target market. Sooner or later these competitors will zap you.

To avoid this problem, products/services-target markets must be linked together into a cost-efficient network. This kind of strategy not only protects individual products/services from competitors, it may also give sister products and services competitive advantages. For instance, today Thompson Medical's original Slim-Fast is by no means a smashing sales success. Yet, this product receives continuing sales support. Why? Because it's a defensive flanker whose purpose is to raise the cost of market entry for a potential low-price competitor to its flagship Ultra Slim-Fast.

You need to have a strategic network of products/services-target markets. But strategic networks don't just happen; they must be planned. Here are guidelines to lead the way:

1. Classify market positions
2. Identify resource linkages
3. Look for additional markets
4. Set priorities

These guidelines just provide a starting point. It is inevitable that you will modify them to suit your purposes. For example, you may

---

*Since the Micron case only deals with one product/service-one target market, the Micron case cannot be used as an example for this phase.

find that for your purposes just reading through the guidelines will be all that you'll need to do. You'll pick up a few ideas on how to build the network and you can do so without paper and pencil. You'll never need to construct a chart. On the other hand, you may wish to follow them in a more formal written manner.

Classify Market Positions

One thing you know for sure: you're not going to drop everything you're doing today and start from scratch. You're going to continue, at least in the short run, serving target markets with your present products and services. So take a look at what you've got to work with. Start with the lowest level of product and service planning. Match each product and service to a specific target market (product or service target market). For each product or service target market, rate its growth potential and competitive position. Use a chart similar to the one shown in Figure 2.66.

Identify Resources Linkages

Some of your product and service target markets will be linked together by the use of common resources. A common linkage is production/operations and promotion. Other possible sources of sharing include brand name, technology, transportation, warehousing, channels of distribution, human resources, purchasing, and service facilities.

But it's not enough that various resources are shared. Real benefits must be achieved. For example, two products might use the same production facilities, but are there significant savings as a result of this sharing? Economies of scale? Leveling-off of production cycles? Or could these products or services be produced independently at or at about the same cost?

At this stage, concern yourself only with real drivers–linkages that provide significant cost benefits or, in some other way, offer substantial competitive advantages.

Using the same chart (Figure 2.66), map out significant activity and resource linkages between product and service target markets. The example in Figure 2.67 shows the relationship among five product or service target markets. In this case:

FIGURE 2.66

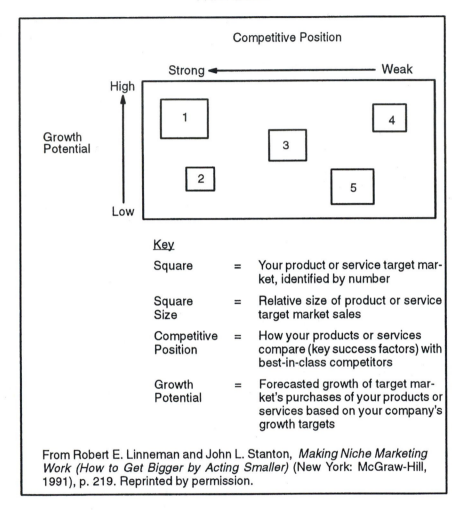

Key

Square	=	Your product or service target market, identified by number
Square Size	=	Relative size of product or service target market sales
Competitive Position	=	How your products or services compare (key success factors) with best-in-class competitors
Growth Potential	=	Forecasted growth of target market's purchases of your products or services based on your company's growth targets

From Robert E. Linneman and John L. Stanton, *Making Niche Marketing Work (How to Get Bigger by Acting Smaller)* (New York: McGraw-Hill, 1991), p. 219. Reprinted by permission.

- Product or Service Target Market No. 1 is sharing operations with No. 2 (both benefit)
- No. 3 is benefiting from No. 1's and 2's operations (but No. 1 and 2 are not benefiting from No. 3's operations)
- No. 4 is sharing logistics with No. 3 (but No. 3 is not receiving any logistics benefits from No. 4)

- No. 4 *could* aid No. 3 by sharing its sales force (but No. 4 would not benefit by sharing its sales force with No. 3)
- No. 5 stands alone–not sharing any major activity or resource with any other product or service target market

Look for Additional Niche Markets

You've identified the product or service target markets that share resources, which resources they share, and potential resource-sharing possibilities. But before you decide how to allocate your resources (devise a strategy), look at opportunities.

- Examine your present product or service target markets for new markets. Consider each one listed on your chart. Maybe linkages can be created (or enhanced) by further subdividing one or more of your present product or service target markets. Or perhaps subdividing a product or service target market will better capitalize on its potential. For example, it may be that you could add features to or subtract features from your basic products/services, thus opening up new market segments that you could profitably serve. For example, Zenith, Sony, and other producers of television sets now offer models that can double as security-monitoring systems. (Review Step 6 for suggestions on finding niches in your present markets.)
- Look beyond your present business for new product and service target markets. (Review Step 6 for suggestions on finding new markets.)

Identify resources linkages of potential product and service markets. You'll probably come up with a number of good prospects for inclusion in your marketing strategy. Select the best candidates. Number them and then position them in the chart. (See Figure 2.68.) In this case:

- No. 6 can share operations and R&D with No. 5, and both would benefit
- No. 7 can share advertising with No. 1, and both would benefit
- No. 8 stands alone

FIGURE 2.67

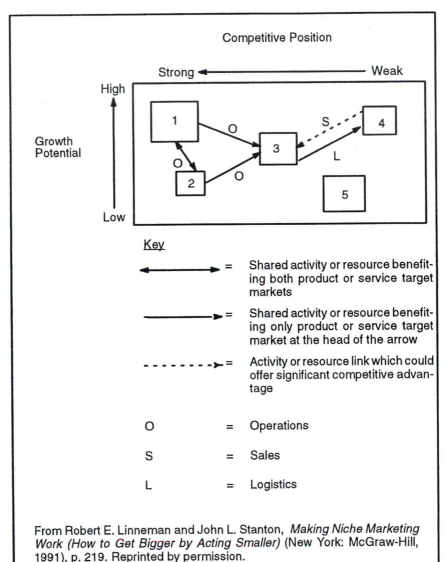

From Robert E. Linneman and John L. Stanton, *Making Niche Marketing Work (How to Get Bigger by Acting Smaller)* (New York: McGraw-Hill, 1991), p. 219. Reprinted by permission.

FIGURE 2.68

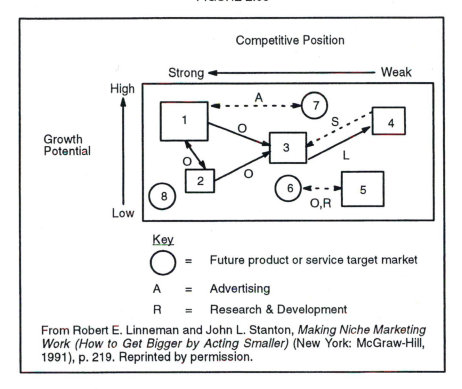

From Robert E. Linneman and John L. Stanton, *Making Niche Marketing Work (How to Get Bigger by Acting Smaller)* (New York: McGraw-Hill, 1991), p. 219. Reprinted by permission.

Set Priorities

Your diagram now includes those product and service target markets that are part of your present strategy, as well as new product and service target markets (those that passed the initial assay). Now put each of these product and service target markets through a four-question screening.

Why not follow a mini-midi-maxi approach? First, the mini-method. Just get cursory answers for all of the questions. If the product or service target market is an obvious misfit, eliminate it from further consideration. But if it seems feasible, then do a midi-analysis. If your product or service target market passes this test, then proceed with a detailed maxi-approach.

Will the Product or Service Target Market Help the Growth of Existing Business?

A new market might support a major component of your overall strategy. For example, a bank wanted to increase business in the upscale market. Because these kinds of customers begin using banking services early on, it's next to impossible to get them to switch once they've become upscale. So the bank went after a new, though unprofitable, segment–college students. When they become upscale and very profitable, they'll already be customers.

Will the Product or Service Lower Overall Costs?

Don't lose sight of the big picture. If a product or service target market shares costs with other product or service target markets, you stand to improve your overall competitive posture.

When cost-sharing benefits are very high, it may be possible to enter a market that appears unattractive when it is viewed in isolation. For example, management may have know-how that would give the firm a competitive advantage in new markets. Philip Morris was able to transfer its knowledge of consumer-goods marketing, especially cigarettes and beer, to other packaged goods such as yogurt, coffee, and ice cream. Philip Morris has been very successful in these markets.

Procter & Gamble's Attends (adult incontinence-protection pads) are made with similar production technologies as its baby diapers, Luvs and Pampers. Also, Attends uses the same distribution channels as the diapers. As a result, Attends is a profitable product. And, by sharing production and distribution costs, Attends helps increase the profitability of Luvs and Pampers.

A trucking firm had freight going in one direction and nothing in the other. Management looked to other markets (and found them) as a way to utilize this unused capacity.

However, be careful of just "filling holes in the factory." We found too many instances of companies being so mesmerized by using up excess capacity that they didn't properly evaluate the needs of the market. Always ask yourself, "Does the cost of linkages outweigh the benefits?" Sometimes the answer is "Yes." Often the costs of linkages are not obvious. With combined purchasing, for example, increased bargaining power may be a benefit. However, overall costs may be higher because of different ordering cycles or geographic distances between the processing units. The point is not to get too caught up with cost savings unless they're significant. Otherwise, you'll just be adding complexity to your business.

Will the Product or Service Improve Sales Stability?

A parts manufacturer for military jet engines was concerned about decreases in defense spending. Its solution: to seek markets to achieve sales stability. One of its finds was selling reconditioned parts to commercial airlines. Airlines, like everybody, are *always* interested in saving money.

Will the Product or Service Improve Your Competitive Position?

Perhaps a new product or service can serve as a flanker to keep out competition or check competitive inroads. Seiko, for example, produces different brands of watches, such as Lauris, Citizen, Pulsar, and Seiko. Heublein markets different brands of vodka, such as Smirnoff, Relska, and Popov. These are good strategic networks.

In some businesses the lack of related products and services places firms at a distinct disadvantage. Serving too few segments may allow competitive inroads. Look what happened to Harley-Davidson. The Japanese came in on the low end, and since Harley-Davidson didn't make much money with that part of the business anyway, the company retreated to selling only the larger, more profitable models, sometimes called "hogs." That was all right as long as the Japanese were following focused production. But when they started flexible production, and produced many different models, they too began to market the larger models. Soon they started seriously to erode Harley-Davidson's share in the "hog" market. Harley-Davidson demanded protection and got it. And, much to Harley-Davidson's credit, the company soon got its act together. But if it had not been for government intervention the outcome could have been different.

We're all familiar with how the Japanese came into the U.S. automobile market on the low end. However, once they got a foothold (established names, marketing know-how, distribution and servicing facilities), flexible production facilities enabled them to move into the high end. Which, of course, they did, thus eroding the high-margin markets formerly dominated by General Motors, Ford, and Chrysler. And now the Japanese are in the luxury markets.

Perhaps you need to take a careful look at your competition–both existing and potential–to see if you can find new ways to improve your competitive position. Figure 2.69 is a framework for thinking through this process.

Suppose that the chart in Figure 2.69 represents your position. You are competing with ABC Company, DEF Company, and XYZ Company in Product or Service Target Market 1 and with GHI Company and XYZ Company in Product or Service Target Market 4. Note that you have possibilities for cost sharing in two product or

FIGURE 2.69

Competitors	Product or Service Target Market			
	1	2	3	4
Your Firm	✔			✔
ABC Company	✔	✔	✔	
DEF Company	✔			
GHI Company				✔
XYZ Company	✔	✔		✔

From Robert E. Linneman and John L. Stanton, *Making Niche Marketing Work (How to Get Bigger by Acting Smaller)* (New York: McGraw-Hill, 1991), p. 219. Reprinted by permission.

service-target markets, 1 and 4. This may put you in a better cost position than DEF Company or GHI Company. On the other hand, ABC Company and XYZ Company may have cost advantages over you.

Your job, then, is to carefully assess the linkages that ABC and XYZ Companies possess. Do they offer enough cost savings to warrant your thinking about expanding into related markets, such as product or service target markets 2 and 3? Competitive analysis is a critical step in building a strategic network of product and service target markets.

Assess Internal Feasibility/Capability

Take a look at the charts (Figure 2.63) you completed for individual products/services-target markets. Perhaps make a master chart. Although internal feasibility/capability assessments may have made sense by themselves, when viewed all together they may indicate that too much change is demanded and/or overcommitment is likely.

Put Strategy (Resource Allocation) in Writing

By this time you've written out the strategy for each product/service-target market, including key buying motives, key success factors, competitive focus, and major elements of the marketing mix. But, no doubt, you'll also have resource limitations. So you'll have to make compromises. But even if you don't, probably some of the products/services-target markets will afford varying opportunities. For example, some may be able to provide cash flow (but offer little growth potential), whereas others may be a source of growth (but are cash users).

Decide (or state) your overall strategy (resource allocation) for your group of products/services-target markets. The chart in Figure 2.70 shows how a company might use a growth/strengths matrix to illustrate the strategic roles of its products (switches) for various target markets (greenhouses, awnings, roller shutters, and solar systems).

- Model 101-Greenhouse and Model 106-Awnings are products-target markets which are to provide growth (and profits).

These products will receive highest priority for investments (money and personnel) to develop markets and/or system modifications.

- Model 103-Roller Windows is considered to be a relatively stable product-target market. This product-target market must receive enough resources (money and personnel) to sustain sales and profitability. However, it will not receive funds for further market development.
- Model 106-Solar Systems is considered to be a question mark. Business strengths are weak. A small microswitch must be developed. Further research (currently being conducted) will determine if it should be considered as high-growth product-target market classification.

Investments (money, personnel) for this product-target market will receive a secondary priority to 101-Greenhouse and 106-Awnings.

MAJOR CHANGE ANALYSIS: STRATEGIC ACTIVITIES, EXPENSES, AND REVENUES

For product/service-target market strategies that are new or that require major changes, plan to further examine and document:

- Major activities and timing involved in implementing the strategies
- Sales forecasts and funding requirements
- Summary results and how they measure up against performance goals

When strategies are not complex, the listing of activities and funding requirements may be all that's necessary. But where strategies are complex and require a number of activities and expenditures, you'll find it useful to use worksheets for each product/service-target market strategy.

Noting major changes is not to be confused with detailed documentation of action plans necessary for the annual marketing plan. Such detailing will be carried out in "Fleshing Out, Documenting,

FIGURE 2.70

```
┌─────────────────────────────────────────────────────────────┐
│                                                             │
│         Strategic Roles for Products/Services-Target Markets │
│                                                             │
│                    Business Strengths                        │
│                                                             │
│                                                             │
│                    Strong              Weak                  │
│      High  ┌─────────────────────┬──────────────────────┐   │
│            │ GROWTH PROVIDERS     │ QUESTION MARKS       │   │
│            │                      │                      │   │
│            │ 101-Greenhouse       │ 106-Solar Systems    │   │
│            │ 106-Awnings          │                      │   │
│    Growth  │                      │                      │   │
│  Potential ├─────────────────────┼──────────────────────┤   │
│            │                      │                      │   │
│            │ CASH PRODUCERS       │                      │   │
│            │ 103-Roller Windows   │                      │   │
│      Low   └─────────────────────┴──────────────────────┘   │
│                                                             │
└─────────────────────────────────────────────────────────────┘
```

and Formatting the Annual Marketing Plan" (Step 8). For now, your primary concerns are to state major activities to see if you've got–or can get–the resources to carry out the strategy, and to forecast the results of your strategy to see if you're reasonably close to your performance goals.

Major Activities and Timing

List on a worksheet (see Figure 2.71) major activities that need to be performed and the required completion dates. This can be done separately for each functional area or for the entire business unit. (Here again we pick up the Micron case). This is a format for documenting decisions that you've already made.

Sales Forecasts and Funding Requirements

At this stage, the purpose of your sales and funding forecasts is to enable you to see if you are directionally correct. You want to find

FIGURE 2.71

STRATEGIC PLAN WORKSHEET *(Major Activity Requirements for the Marketing Department)*

Functional Area – Marketing	Year 1	Year 2	Year 3	Year 4	Year 5
New salesperson added	2/15				
Customer analysis completed	4/1				
Telephone hot line installed	7/1				
New salesperson added		2/15			
Inside salesperson added					2/15

out if your proposed strategy will give you a reasonable chance to meet your performance goals.

Approximations will usually suffice. In fact, you can't expect great precision. For example, your one-year forecasts will be tentative until you detail your annual marketing plan–which you'll do later on (Step 8).

Sales Forecasts. Forecast sales for time periods throughout your planning horizon. Some firms make sales forecasts only for year one and for the most-distant year. Of course, if you only make sales forecasts for these two years, you'll still make cursory forecasts for years two, three, and four. But, if for these years you can see no significant discontinuities and your new strategies do not call for any major budgetary and capital expenditures, it will not be necessary for you to make explicit forecasts for years two through four. (For appropriate sales forecasting techniques, see Appendix A.)

Expense Forecasts. Estimate those expenses necessary to support the strategy. At this stage approximations are all that is necessary. Expense forecasts will be refined when the plan is being detailed (Step 8).

While estimating expenses, consider the following:

- Marketing expenses should be estimated in conjunction with other marketing personnel.
- Other projections should be arrived at with personnel from other functional areas such as manufacturing, operations and R&D.
- At this step in the planning process, generally it's better *not* to allocate overhead. Simply concern yourself with additional direct costs.

As with sales forecasts, you may choose to make expense projections only for year one and the most distant year. Figure 2.72 provides an example of years 1 through 5.

Prepare **Pro Forma** *Statements*

In your discussions with management, you'll need to show projections of sales, expenses, and some measure of profitability. Your projections should appear in the same terms as your performance goals are stated (or implied).

If you're dealing only with one product/service-target market, then possibly your strategic plan worksheets will do. But for multiple products/services-target markets, in addition to showing sales, expenses, and profits for each product/service, target market, you should also have summary statements which show the overall results. Depending on your scope of responsibility and/or on how performance goals are stated (or implied), the form of these statements will vary from mere worksheet summations to statements of profit and loss, cash flow, and possibly even balance sheets. Figure 2.73 shows Micron's *pro forma* profit and loss statements for years 1 through 5.

Measurement Against Performance Goals

Next compare your projections against your performance goals. Figures 2.74 and 2.75 are charts illustrating Micron's performance goals, projections under a no change strategy, and projections under the proposed strategy.

What If Performance Goals Seem Unobtainable?

If your forecasts show that the gaps are insurmountable assuming your new strategies, search for other strategies. If the gap between your forecasts and the performance goals still cannot be bridged, talk with management. Management may respond by giving their reasons for believing the performance objectives can be attained. Or they may lower their expectations. Or management may authorize you to consider other products/services-target markets which previously would have been beyond your scope of authority.

Usually it is a give-and-take, back-and-forth process to determine which goals are genuinely reachable. The person developing the plan will first develop preliminary plans. If performance goals are felt to be unrealistic, he/she will report this to management at that time. Management may respond by giving reasons why it believes the performance objectives can be attained. The person developing the plan may give some counterreason. This process will continue until at some point agreement is reached. Management now believes that the best performance goals have been set and the

FIGURE 2.72

STRATEGIC PLAN WORKSHEET

FUNDING REQUIREMENTS (in 1992 dollars, in $1,000, for the business unit)

Functional Area	Year 1 Expense	Year 1 Capital	Year 2 Expense	Year 2 Capital	Year 3 Expense	Year 3 Capital	Year 4 Expense	Year 4 Capital	Year 5 Expense	Year 5 Capital
Salesperson (incl. expenses)	100		100		100		100		100	
Hotline	60		20		21		22		22	
Increased Advertising	15		65		65		65		65	
Salesperson (incl. expenses)			95		95		95		95	
Increased Sales Expense					45		55		75	
Inside Salesperson (incl. expense)									50	
Mfg, Design + Engineering increased R&D	70		120		195		195		220	
Increase in Unit sales ($)	400		800		1170		1170		1380	
(1) Increase in GP (per unit sales)	226		453		655		628		824	
(2) Increase in GP (for base sales)	59		59		116		133		133	
TOTAL INCREASE IN GP	285		512		771		821		952	
INCREASE / EXPENSE	245		400		521		532		627	
INCREASE IN CTC	40		112		250		299		330	
Capital Requirements		1		1		1		1		1

(1) Because of price increases, gross margin was 56.6% in 1993-94; 57% in 1995; and because of price increases and productivity, 57.7% in 1998-97.

(2) To reflect increased GP for base sales (1992 - $2,400,000) due to increased gross margin

FIGURE 2.73

Projected Profit and Loss Statements
(in 1992 dollars)

	1993	1994	1995	1996	1997
Sales Revenue	$2,800,000	$3,200,000	$3,570,000	$3,570,000	$3,780,000
Cost of Goods	$1,218,280	$1,392,320	$1,479,340	$1,453,500	$1,539,000
Gross Profit	$1,581,720	$1,807,680	$2,090,660	$2,116,500	$2,241,000
Expenses					
R&D	$250,000	$300,000	$375,000	$375,000	$400,000
Selling	$300,000	$395,000	$440,000	$450,000	$520,000
Advertising	$75,000	$125,000	$125,000	$125,000	$125,000
Administration	$210,000	$210,000	$210,000	$210,000	$210,000
Customer Service	$60,000	$20,000	$21,000	$22,000	$23,000
Total Expenses	$895,000	$1,050,000	$1,171,000	$1,182,000	$1,278,000
Contribution	$686,720	$757,680	$919,660	$934,500	$963,000

FIGURE 2.74

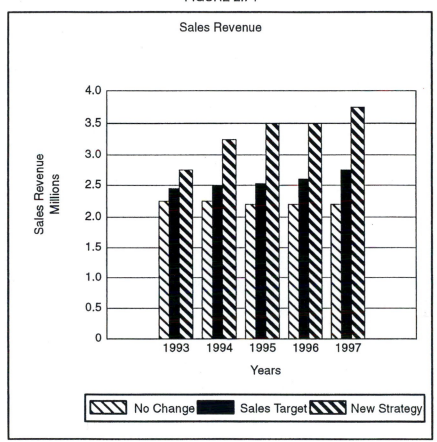

person developing the plans now believes that he/she can accomplish the performance goals.

What happens if, in your case, management is obstinate and clings to what you consider to be unrealistic performance goals? Do the best you can. At least your SWOTs analysis made you well prepared to defend your position.

FIGURE 2.75

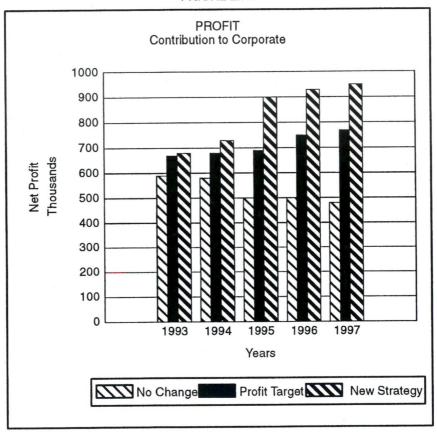

MANAGEMENT REVIEW

Now let's assume you've developed a strategy that you believe will enable you to reach your performance goals, and you're not operating in a total quality environment where a review would be automatic.

If your strategy is a continuation of your present strategy–and your charge is to develop an annual marketing plan to carry out that strategy–then usually a review with management, at this time, would not be necessary. But in some instances, such as when possible environmental shifts may pose a real threat, management may wish to review this strategy under these new conditions before you go on to develop an annual marketing plan.

Certainly you should discuss new strategies with management prior to developing detailed annual plans, budgets, and forecasts. In this way, you'll gain the following benefits:

- Management input concerning the broad direction of the business, while there is still time to change strategy.
- Increased probability that management will approve the completed plan, since it has been involved in the plan's preparation.
- Early consultation protects you from committing a major block of effort and time to the annual plan only to find that management disapproves of your strategy.

POINTS LEARNED

1. Write out your proposed strategy. Check its competitive feasibility. Assess your internal capability to carry out this strategy. Beware of overcommitment.
2. Think about how your strategy would fare in other than the most-probable-case future. Strive for flexibility. And develop contingency plans.
3. In addition, ask the following questions:

- Will top management be comfortable with the new product or service?
- Is the market structurally attractive?
- Is the market accessible?
- Is the market measurable?
- Are the payoffs commensurate with the risks?
- Does the strategy have favorable payoffs in the most-probable-case future?
- Is the strategy attractive in the near future?
- Does the strategy allow ample time for implementation?
- Are you making hockey-stick projections?

4. If you have multiple products/services-target markets, build a strategic network by classifying market positions, identifying resource linkages, looking for additional markets and setting priorities.
5. For product/service-target market strategies that are new or that require major changes, plan to examine and document: (1) major activities and timing involved in implementing the strategies; (2) sales forecasts and funding requirements; and (3) summary results measured against performance goals.
6. Be sure to discuss new strategies with management prior to developing detailed annual plans, budgets, and forecasts.

LOOKING AHEAD

Now that your strategy is set, your next step is to flesh out, document, and format your annual plan.

THE EIGHT PLANNING STEPS

Step 1. SWOTs: Present. Gain an Overall Perspective by Historical Analysis of Total Sales, Expenses and Profits, and of Sales and Profits by Products/ Services

Step 2. SWOTs: Present (cont.). To Help Decide Where to Concentrate Planning Efforts, List Target Markets Currently Served with Present Products/ Services and Analyze by Sales and Profits

Step 3. SWOTs: Present (cont.). Develop Performance Profiles for Each Product/Service-Target Market

Step 4. SWOTs: Future. For Each Product/Service-Target Market, Forecast Market Environment, Target Market's Demand, and Your Sales and Profits (Assuming You Continue Your Present Strategy)

Step 5. Gap Analysis

Step 6. Examination of Strategic Options and Strategy Selection

Step 7. Strategy Documentation and Evaluation

 Step 8. Fleshing Out, Documenting, and Formatting the Annual Marketing Plan

Step 8: Fleshing Out, Documenting, and Formatting the Annual Marketing Plan

INTRODUCTION

You've determined broad courses of action. And, in the process of deciding/reviewing your strategy, no doubt you have a pretty good idea of what to include in your annual plan. But that's not enough. You've got to be more specific. You have to set up detailed action plans, including timetables, responsibilities, and budgets. And they must be set up in a way that's easy to communicate. Furthermore, the plan must also serve as a control mechanism.

In many ways this step is the easiest part of the planning process. Yet, in other ways, it's the hardest. It's more dog work than creative effort. It's time-consuming.

And since you do have "rough" forecasts and some idea as to who is to do what, when, and at what cost, it's the part of the planning process that you're most likely to skip or give the once-over lightly.

The consequences: some things don't get done. Plans never really come off. You don't have adequate financial resources or time. Then, too, left to your own devices, you (like everyone else) tend to become more engrossed in the daily crises. These are urgent and very concrete. As a result, important projects that are critical for the overall plan, but whose payoffs are not immediate, tend to get put aside.

But even if properly implemented, things won't always go according to plan. Perhaps there's an economic downturn, or a wildcat strike which shuts down your customers' production. Or another firm acquires one of your key customers and this key customer now buys from its new parent. Or several of your key employees resign. Or all these things happen at once, plus a few more.

Consider the implications of the "Butter-Side-Down Law": "An object will fall so as to do the most damage." The corollary to this law serves as a painful emphasis: "You cannot successfully determine which side of the bread to butter."

So you must have checkpoints to continually monitor: (1) the starting and completion of individual projects (are they on schedule?); (2) the effectiveness of programs and budgets (are they doing what they're supposed to and within cost?); (3) sales and profits (are they according to plan?); and (4) the validity of your assumptions underlying your forecasts (has your environment changed?). But these checkpoints must not be passive. They must let you know when it's time to take action.

Since you'll probably have to change your plan during the year, it must be formatted so that it's easy to change. Following is a step-by-step procedure showing you how to flesh out, document, and format the annual marketing plan and how to get others involved.

INVOLVING OTHERS WHILE DEVELOPING A TOTAL QUALITY ANNUAL MARKETING PLAN

Throughout this book it has been emphasized that for total quality marketing planning to be successful, much depends upon support from others within your firm. So, let's talk about who should be involved and how you get their involvement while fleshing out and documenting the annual marketing plan.

Functional Area Managers

In a total quality environment, there has been an agreement on product/service features and processes needed to produce those features. Still, while you're developing the annual marketing plan you must coordinate with other functional areas (such as manufacturing/operations, finance, and R&D). For example:

- Manufacturing/operations must also prepare its plans. But, manufacturing/operations cannot make schedules until it has sales estimates.

- You may have to modify your plan in order to fit manufacturing/operations' schedules.
- Manufacturing/operations must consult with personnel about labor costs.

And in some companies, the marketing department may not follow the "classic" organizational structure. For example, in many industrial firms, the sales department is separate from marketing. If this is your situation, certainly you've got to coordinate with sales while fleshing out your plans.

These interchanges, besides being necessary, can have additional benefits. While working out detailed plans, unexpected opportunities as well as problems are exposed. Close coordination among the functional area managers makes it easier to take advantage of these opportunities, and better enables you to deal with the problems. Then, too, these interchanges will give everyone a chance to be exposed to tentative plans and problems of other functional areas, helping to ensure that the pieces will fit together.

Marketing Department Personnel

Involve others in the marketing department. If you have other managers reporting to you (called here department managers), a sizable part of the planning effort will be delegated. Ensuring a good fit will require extensive communication between you and department managers. Then, too, considerable interchange will have to take place among department managers, for example, between advertising and sales promotion sales and the department, to make sure that their plans mesh.

Besides having plans that are well-coordinated, there's a side benefit. This interchange helps them to better understand each other's problems, and to regard the marketing department as a system. As manager, it's your responsibility to challenge them to work together. Then it becomes their responsibility to make it work.

If your department managers will be required to develop plans for their own units, they should now develop tentative plans for their departments. This is necessary so that later on, when they submit formal plans and budgets, these plans will be in line with the overall marketing plan.

But there's no need for department heads to prepare "final" plans and budgets now. All you want is a general agreement. There's usually some last-moment negotiations involving "final" functional-area plans and budgets, and these will almost certainly require alternatives in departments' plans and budgets. Department managers should be conscious, however, of the importance of their estimates and that later on, when plans are finalized, they'll be expected to live up to their commitments.

On the other hand, what if you are not departmentalized? You should still involve the people reporting to you, even though they will not be developing their own plans. They'll be able to help you develop more realistic plans. At the minimum, they'll feel as if they have a stake in the plans. And they'll be more willing to walk the extra mile to make sure the plan is successful.

This is, of course, total quality planning. Remember, within your sphere, you're interested in internal customers (your own department heads and staff) as well as external ones. To be sure that your marketing plans work toward satisfying the needs of both of these groups, establish control points and programs for constant improvement–*kaizen*.

THE STEP-BY-STEP PROCEDURE

There are ten steps involved in fleshing out and documenting your marketing plan:

Step 8.1. Fully Describe Each Major Activity
Step 8.2. Develop Action Plans for Each Major Activity
Step 8.3. Assign Tasks
Step 8.4. Set Up Action-Plan Timetables
Step 8.5. Number Major Activities and Action Plans
Step 8.6. Consider Contingency Planning
Step 8.7. Forecast Sales
Step 8.8. Budget Expenditures
Step 8.9. Forecast Profitability
Step 8.10. Consider Factoring in Next Year's Inflation

For clarity, while going through the steps, we'll again use the Micron case as an example. (Keep in mind that the marketing department at Micron was quite small.)

Step 8.1. Fully Describe Each Major Activity

On the Strategic Plan Worksheet (Step 7, Figure 2.71) major activities were listed along with completion dates. This was suitable for the purpose of developing a strategy. Now each major activity–scheduled for the upcoming year–needs to be developed in greater detail for a marketing (operating) plan.

As an example, "New salesperson added" (Figure 2.71) should be expanded to describe the desired characteristics of the salesperson to be hired, such as experience and date salesperson would be on the job. (See Figure 2.76; the basic information is drawn from the Micron case.)

Note that these activities, like performance goals, should be as specific as possible. Major activities should be described in such a way that they are measurable. You should be able to tell when each activity has been accomplished. Ideally, activities should be in quantitative terms such as dollars, percentages, or proportions. Of course, there are many cases in which quantitative terms cannot fully describe what you may wish to accomplish. In these instances a compromise is necessary. You'll have to express what you want to achieve in the most concrete qualitative terms, such as quality and extent, that the situation permits. For example, looking again at the data from Figure 2.75, note the measurability:

Extent:

– One

Quality:

– Experienced salesperson, either from IMPRO or Moltec, now selling high-end research oscilloscopes to our target market.

Completion date:

– 2/15

FIGURE 2.76

ACTION PLAN	Responsi-bility	Budget (in $1,000)	Start Date	Comple-tion Date	Formal Review
2. Hire one experienced sales person, either from Impro or from Moltec. Salesperson to be on job no later than 2/15.					
2.1 Contingency plan 10.0. Locate headhunter	Pres		ASAP	Prior to 1/1	
2.2 Contact salesperson from Impro, Moltec to determine interest	Mkt mgr.	—	ASAP	Prior to 1/1	Pres.
2.3 Schedule interviews	Mkt mgr.		ASAP		
2.4 Interviews complete, selection made	Mkt mgr.	2	ASAP	ASAP (no later than 1/15)	Pres.
2.5 Salesperson on the job	Mkt mgr.			ASAP (no later than 2/15)	Pres.

As desirable as quantified objectives may be, don't force quantification just for its own sake. You're all too familiar with the bizarre, loophole-ridden results such situations can produce. Here's a minor, but typical, example: A number of years ago certain bomber squadrons had to meet gunnery standards periodically so that in the event of war they would be prepared. The measurable standard was to be able to fire, at 40,000 feet, 80 percent of their 20 millimeter cannon load into the ocean below. This standard is not exactly comparable with firing at jet fighters approaching at Mach 2. Actually, all they were measuring was the ability for the cannon to fire at 40,000 feet, where the guns often froze. But the sick tale does not end there. On at least several occasions, enterprising aircraft commanders dropped down to 2,000 feet, let their guns thaw out, and climbed back to 40,000 feet, where they resumed firing.

So use quantitative terms whenever possible. Fully describe each major activity that you listed on strategic plan worksheets. But supposing you're staying with your previous strategy and, consequently, did not fill out a strategic plan worksheet, then, using a form similar to Figure 2.75, fully describe major activities necessary for successful realization of your present strategy. In the same manner, specify those general activities not specifically associated with any particular strategy, such as ongoing training.

As for the number of activities you should include, most people err in establishing too few rather than too many. You should show major activities for each key area in the same way that you developed performance goals for each key area. Key areas, of course, are those which are essential to the successful completion of your plan.

If you feel you have too many major activities, use an adaptation of "must-want" criteria (see p. 191). Place these major activities in one of two groups: must activities and want activities. Must activities are absolutely essential to the completion of your marketing plan. Want activities would be nice to be accomplished, but are not absolutely essential. Concentrate–detail–the must activities. Handle the want activities on an *ad hoc* basis.

To help stimulate ideas as to what activities you should consider, Figure 2.77 gives a list of activities, grouped by marketing function. The list is extensive. Naturally, you'll only use a few of these for your marketing program.

FIGURE 2.77

Checklist of Ideas for Major Activities

Product Programs

1. Product development
   a. New product
   b. Product improvement
   c. Product change
2. Product introduction
3. Package development
4. Package introduction
5. Brand name selection
6. Phasing out products
7. Introduction or deletion of private brands manufacturing
8. Changes in warranty
9. Value analysis (to reduce product cost)
10. Searching out candidates for acquisition or merger

Pricing Programs

1. Change in price
   a. For the end customer
   b. Trade discounts
2. New product price
   a. Market skimming
   b. Market penetration
3. Change in price policy
4. Pricing to include or exclude services
5. Incremental pricing
6. Change in credit policies
   a. Discounts for quantity or prompt payment
   b. Extended terms to encourage early season shipment
7. Annual or longer-term pricing contracts including or excluding escalation clauses
8. Consignment (manufacturer retains title to product while in the channels and until the sale is made to end customer)
9. Rental or leasing

Distribution Programs

1. Change in channels used, for example:
   a. Adding or deleting classes of wholesalers or chains
   b. Adding or deleting classes of retailers
   c. Adding or deleting catalog
   d. Adding or deleting vending machine
   e. Adding or deleting direct-to-consumer (door-to-door)

    f. Adding or deleting direct mail

    g. Change from direct-to-user to going through wholesaler or vice versa

    h. Change from wholesaler to direct-to-retailer or vice versa

2. Change in distribution policies, for example:

    a. Manufacturer sells to some end customers or accounts direct, others through wholesalers

    b. Wholesaler takes on some customer service functions

    c. Shift from intensive, selective, or exclusive distribution to one of the others

    d. Shift from independent middlemen to company-owned outlets

    e. Shift from company-owned to franchised outlets

3. Improving quality of wholesale and retail representation
4. Adding company-owned or leased field warehouses to provide better service to trade channels
5. Adding or deleting company branch warehouses for shipping direct to end customers

Sales Programs

1. Redefine the sales job
2. Revise plan of sales organization
3. Revise territory layout
4. Revise compensation plan
5. Change number of sales personnel
6. Personnel improvement programs

    a. Qualifications sought   d. Training

    b. Recruiting   e. Promotion

    c. Selection   f. Incentives

7. Training programs for trade channel salespeople
8. Adding new accounts
9. Developing sales potential by market, county, or other control unit
10. Allocating or reallocating sales effort by account potential and location
11. Reporting competitive intelligence
12. Missionary sales effort

    a. With influencers (e.g., architects, doctors)

    b. In-store promotional effort

Advertising Programs

1. Advertising policies
2. Agency selection or change of agency

FIGURE 2.77 (continued)

3. Advertising campaigns
   a. Objectives
   b. Target market
   c. Product positioning
   d. Copy theme
   e. Media
   f. Reach and frequency
   g. Commercials and local co-op ads
   h. Testing commercials
4. Measurement of advertising performance
5. Special events programs (e.g., sponsored sports contests)
6. Corporate image advertising

Sales Promotion Programs

1. Programs for consumers
   a. Coupons
   b. Cents-off offers
   c. Sampling with product
   d. Contests
2. Programs for trade channels
   a. Point-of-sale materials
   b. Store demonstrations
   c. Store displays
   d. Dealer premiums
   e. Dealer mailings
   f. Dealer contests
3. Programs for sales force
   a. Product catalogs
   b. Sales presentation materials
   c. Samples
   d. Arrangements for trade shows
   e. Selling aids
   f. Price lists
   g. Mailings of advertising and promotional materials to buyers and buying influencers
   h. Sales contests

Publicity Programs

1. Announcements to the media
   a. New products
   b. Product improvements
   c. New ways to use product
   d. New business ventures
   e. Research findings
   f. Market expansion
   g. Customer success story
   h. Industry success story
   i. Financial news
   j. Corrective, explanatory stories to offset unfavorable news story

Service Programs

1. Customer service programs
   a. Installation
   b. Start up of new equipment
   c. Maintenance
   d. Repair
   e. Replacement
   f. Adjustment
   g. Technical service
   h. Warranty administration
   i. Field service stations
   j. Replacement parts inventories
2. Wholesaler and dealer service programs
   a. Service policies
   b. Training of trade service people
   c. Order fulfillment
      (1) Order acknowledgement
      (2) On-time deliveries
      (3) Controlling shipping errors
      (4) Controlling back orders
      (5) Providing information on delayed orders
      (6) Claims and allowances
      (7) Handling complaints
3. Internal services, assisting with production scheduling and inventory control
   a. Breaking down sales forecast by line item by week or month
   b. Notifying manufacturing of special sales promotions
   c. Recommending field inventory levels
   d. Recommending reorder points
   e. Coordinating field inventories with factory inventories

From Victor P. Buell, *Marketing Management: A Strategic Management Approach* (New York: McGraw-Hill, 1984). Reprinted by permission.

Step 8.2. Develop Action Plans for Each Major Activity

The reasons for developing action plans have already been covered. Although it's vital to develop action plans for major activities, it's also important to keep details to a minimum. Obviously, too much detail can obfuscate the important issues.

The following are guidelines which will help you determine the amount of detail necessary. Although each is presented separately below, all are interrelated and must be considered in context with the others.

Importance. How critical is the activity to the success of the plan? Obviously, critical activities need to be monitored more frequently.

Fast Reaction. If something should go wrong, how quickly do you need to take action? Necessity for fast reaction requires frequent checkpoints.

Timely, Accurate Measurement. Make sure that your reports give you an accurate picture of the "what is." For example, it might be advisable to check daily the number of sales calls made by salespersons. But, on the other hand, it might not be practical for you to check daily progress on a research project. Daily reports might serve little purpose. They would probably just get you–and others–upset over random walks.

Management's Expectations. How much detail does management want to see in your proposed plans? Then, how frequently does management want to be informed of your progress on a particular activity? The answer is probably quite frequently on action plans for critical activities, less frequently on other action plans. Possibly you will find that less critical activities can be reviewed only during informal discussions, or, if worse comes to worst, on a crisis basis.

Cost. Consider the cost, especially in manpower, to gather information needed for frequent monitoring.

Interface. At what point(s) does the activity need to mesh with other functional areas? Make sure that these are clearly specified.

Expertise. What is the level of expertise of the person assigned to the activity? (This will be discussed in greater detail in Step 8.3).

Step 8.3. Assign Tasks

Tasks left unassigned are usually not completed. Certainly the extent of detail involved in making these assignments depends both on who will be doing the task and on its importance to the overall plan.

Your situation might be such that you'll need to delegate. If so, consider the following guidelines.

Monitor Results, Not Methods. The action plans should specify what it is that you want accomplished, but should not go into the methods of achieving the goals (avoid imposing process restrictions). However, if there are certain ways of carrying out a task which are acceptable to you and others which are not, make those clear. Make sure the action plans include enough detail so that at a later date you and the person responsible for carrying out the plan will not cross swords because this person did not perform the activity the way you wanted it done.

Vary Performance Checks. Don't check the performance of all your personnel indiscriminately. Your really dependable people don't need frequent checks, and they will appreciate the confidence you show in them (don't overdo your confidence, of course).

It's wise to keep an eye on new activities–and personnel–whose behavior you don't know much about. Similarly, it's a good idea to monitor any activity–or person–whose performance has been inconsistent or not wholly dependable.

Strive for a Sense of Overall Operation. Accept the fact that even in the best of situations you can't monitor everything. It is important to choose monitoring points that give you a sense of the overall operation. That way you'll be aware when something starts to go wrong, even if you're not quite sure where.

Consider Monitoring "Range" Results. Recognize that demanding a single result point will seldom be practical; usually you're going to have to allow for upper and/or lower limits. For example, past experience may have shown that, for a given month, sales vary ± 10 percent. In such a case, any volume within these boundaries should be considered normal.

Make Sure Key Areas Are Really Key. Your people will inevitably direct their energies toward the key areas. Make sure that the areas you indicate to be key really are.

Step 8.4. Set Up Action Plan Timetables

For each action plan, decide on start and completion dates. The need for completion dates is well understood. But some people question the value of starting dates. Starting dates help in developing realistic plans in that you can better determine if you've overextended your resources. They also assist in plan implementation; they help you better schedule your activities. Then, too, knowing when certain tasks must be started provides monitoring points to let you know if you're on schedule. If you are behind, perhaps you can take some corrective measure to catch up. Better to find out that you missed a starting date than to fall short on a completion date.

Step 8.5. Number Major Activities and Action Plans

Examine Figure 2.75. Notice how the major activity is numbered (in this example, 2), and how each action plan is also numbered (2.1, 2.2, . . . 2.5). The numbering system has advantages. It facilitates cross-referencing between action plans, major activities, and strategies. Also, this type of system is very flexible. If, for example, you should wish to expand the action steps, you can simply add a sub-step between 2.1 and 2.2, making this action step 2.1.1.

Step 8.6. Consider Contingency Plans

As you did with strategy development, you should also consider developing contingency plans while putting together your annual marketing plan. There are two basic ways to do this. The first method is by handling contingencies in the same manner as recommended in Step 7: develop straddle strategies or set up contingency plans for specific contingent events. See Figure 2.78 for an example.

The second basic method is through variable budgeting. More will be said about this technique under budgeting (Step 8.8).

Step 8.7. Forecast Sales

You've already developed preliminary sales forecasts (Steps 4 and 7). Although you felt these forecasts were reasonably accurate, now that your marketing plan is more fully developed you can probably forecast even more accurately. And since this forecast will be a major cornerstone for annual planning throughout the firm, you want it to be as accurate as possible.

Use your salespeople in developing the sales forecast (check Appendix A for more about this forecasting procedure). If you don't use their input, make sure that you've got a very good reason for exclusion. But keep in mind that salespersons' forecasts are

FIGURE 2.78

CONTINGENCY PLANS		
Key Contingent Events (What is the event?)	**Trigger Points** (When the event occurs)	**Contingency Plans** (What we will do when the event occurs)
10.0 Neither Impro's Nor Moltec's Salespersons interested in job with Micron	10.0 Definite turn down by all desirable salespersons at Impro and Moltec	10.0 Hire headhunter
11.0 Sales fall below projections	11.0 Firm orders for less than six units by 6/1	11.0 See if Corporate is willing to accept a lower CTC. If not 11.1 Postpone hotline until Year 2 11.2 Cap advertising expenditures at 60 K.

usually excessively optimistic or pessimistic. As a rule of thumb, an "old" sales force will generally come in with projections that are too low, a "new" sales force with projections that are too high.

Besides forecasting your total sales, you'll probably want to make sales forecasts for different key customers, territories, and salespeople, or for a combination of the above. Here again, you'll also want to get your sales force involved in forecasting.

Make sure that you use appropriate time periods. For example, if your company has a large number of customers who make frequent purchases (such as a supermarket), you might find it sensible to forecast daily sales. On the other hand, it would not be practical for you to forecast daily sales if your firm has only several key accounts who purchase on a monthly basis. The sample worksheet in Figure 2.79 is set up by total sales, gross profit, and by salespersons.

What happens if your revised forecast should not meet performance goals, as you previously thought it would? The answer is to straighten it out now. Perhaps you can make shifts in your marketing plan at this point so that you can reach your performance goals. Or, in a worst-case scenario, you may find that you will have to scrap the original plan.

Step 8.8. Budget Expenditures

Since budgeting timetables and formats are usually "set" within most companies, detailed methods of budgeting will not be covered here (in case you are interested in learning more about budgeting, we've included several excellent sources at the end of this step).

Two points on budgeting, however, should be stressed. First, operational plans create the framework for budgets. Programs should determine budgets. In other words, previous-years' budgets should not be automatically raised by a certain percent (possibly to compensate for inflation). Nor should there be across-the-board budget cuts for economy reasons. Instead, you should first justify the needs for funds. Programs must contribute to your strategic and annual plans.

Second, you should allow flexibility in your budgeting process. You can do this through variable budgeting, a procedure which is described below.[1]

FIGURE 2.79

Total Sales (in $1,000) in 1992 $

Date	Planned Sales $	Actual Sales $	Planned GP	Actual GP
1st Qtr	1,000	—	565	—
2nd Qtr	600	—	339	—
3rd Qtr	200	—	113	—
4th Qtr	1,000	—	565	—
Total	2,800	—	1582	—

Existing Salesperson

Date	Planned Sales $	Actual Sales $	Planned GP	Actual GP
1st Qtr	600	—	339	—
2nd Qtr	200	—	113	—
3rd Qtr	200	—	113	—
4th Qtr	400	—	226	—
TOTAL	1,400	—	791	—

New Salesperson

Date	Planned Sales $	Actual Sales $	Planned GP	Actual GP
1st Qtr	—	—	—	—
2nd Qtr	200	—	113	—
3rd Qtr	—	—	—	—
4th Qtr	400	—	226	—
TOTAL	600	—	339	—

Marketing Manager

Date	Planned Sales $	Actual Sales $	Planned GP	Actual GP
1st Qtr	400	—	226	—
2nd Qtr	200	—	113	—
3rd Qtr	—	—	—	—
4th Qtr	200	—	113	—
TOTAL	800	—	452	—

Determine Expense Structure. Divide costs into those that are variable, fixed-bedrock, and fixed-discretionary. For example:

- Variable costs are directly affected by sales, such as commissions and bonuses or co-op advertising.
- Fixed-bedrock costs are those that are essentially unchangeable during the planning period, such as salaries for key people or leases on branch offices.
- Fixed-discretionary costs are those that can be cut back within the planning period without having an immediate impact on sales, such as recruiting, training, advertising, the use of outside agencies (market research, consultants), expense accounts, and/or staff reductions.

Consolidate Costs. Arrive at total costs according to variable, fixed-bedrock, and fixed-discretionary costs.

Prepare Measures of Profitability at Various Levels of Sales. If you only market one product/service to one target market, these measures will not be difficult to determine. But you probably have a number of products/services-target markets, each having different cost structures, both direct and allocated. Consequently, to really do it right, you would need to calculate profits for different levels of sales for all of your products/services-target markets.

That will be reasonably difficult to do, however, unless your planning system is highly computerized. If not, why not do the next best thing: figure your profitability for an across-the-board sales decrease. (You could also make such calculations for a sales increase, but for simplicity we've stayed with a sales decrease).

Determine Actions to Be Taken in the Event of a Sales Slowdown. Suppose that sales turn out to be 10 percent lower than forecasted. Further, suppose that the slump would call for a reduction–or postponement–of $50,000 in fixed-discretionary expenses in order to meet profit projections.

In determining the expense structure, you singled out these particular discretionary expenses. Although they may be postponed without having serious short-term effects, the long-range effects may range from minor inconvenience to disaster. Since long-range effects vary, fixed-discretionary expenses selected should be those whose effects, as much as possible, would involve only minor inconveniences.

The basic idea is similar to Emerson Electric Company's ongoing ABC system of budgeting. Budget A is the base plan, Budget B is for a 10 percent drop in sales, and Budget C is for a 20 percent decline. Managers are serious about the development of the plan since up to 40 percent of their salaries is based on meeting their commitments.[2]

If you'd like excellent, easy-to-get sources of budgeting, check the following:

Glen A. Welsch, Ronald W. Hilton, and Paul N. Gordon, *Budgeting, Planning and Control*, 8th Edition, (Engelwood Cliffs, N.J.: Prentice-Hall, Inc., 1988). A classic primer on budgeting.

Robert G. Finney, *Powerful Budgeting for Better Planning and Management*, (New York: AMACOM, 1993). Transform your budget from a routine task into a useful planning and management tool. Using a ficticious company, the author vividly illustrates common budgeting problems and their solutions. He pinpoints techniques and processes for developing sound budgets, and shows how to establish the context and select the format, deal with uncertainty, and develop the content and encourage excellence. This book not only presents a proper process flow and describes how to organize the details, but it also helps you make the transition from what you're doing now to the rewards of powerful budgeting.

Charles J. Woelfel, *Accounting, Budgeting and Finance: A Reference for Managers*, (New York: AMACOM, 1990). This convenient reference delivers exactly that level of information you need, when you need it. Some 475 alphabetical entries–not mere definitions–explain the full range of topics in accounting, finance, management, economics, foreign operations, and business ethics. Cross-references and "entries within entries" shed further light on key concepts. And for those who want to explore any topic in greater depth, most entries contain short bibliographies that highlight primary and secondary sources.

Allen Sweeny and John N. Wisner, Jr., *Budgeting Fundamentals for Nonfinancial Executives*, (New York: AMACOM, 1975). An easy-to-read primer on budgeting. Explains what budgets are, how they work, and how to prepare and present them.

Reginald L. Jones and H. George Trentin, *Budgeting: Key to Planning and Control.* (New York: AMACOM, 1971). A more-detailed explanation of the fundamentals. Including steps and variable budgeting. Deviation analysis. Examples, tables, evaluations, and forms.

Step 8.9. Forecast Profitability

Once you have finalized your sales forecasts and budgets, finalize your forecast of profit. If all goes well, you will be able to meet your profit performance goals. If not, perhaps you can make some adjustments in your plan to take up the slack (your variable budget may give you some ideas). But again, face the fact that it may require plan revisions.

It's obvious that the nature of planning necessitates "the capacity to dangle." You can't decide on your strategy unless it enables you to meet your performance expectations in the short range. But of course, you can't forecast this until you have developed your annual plan. And, you can't develop your annual plan until you've developed your strategy. For this reason, it's recommended that you follow a mini-midi-maxi process in going through Steps 8.1-8.9.

First, go through the steps with a "broad brush." Then, if everything seems all right, go through the steps in greater detail. If the plan still seems satisfactory, then put the finishing touches on it.

Step 8.10. Consider Factoring in Next Year's Inflation

Most firms work with current dollars in determining the next year's annual plan. Yet, if you believe that the rate of inflation will be significant, use projected inflated dollars. If there is an appreciable change in inflation rate, and if you don't adjust your earnings accordingly, you'll be getting a distorted picture of your results.

Assume that you will be adjusting your annual plan for inflation. Some things may not be affected, such as multiyear leases on equipment. But many other expenditures and revenues, perhaps most, will have to be adjusted. While forecasting the environment for next year, you probably came up with some projection of inflation rate. If you didn't, do so now. It may be that for your business you'll need to project quarterly–or perhaps even the monthly–rates of inflation as well as the annual rate.

Of course, other functional areas within your company will have to use the same inflation rate while developing their plans. And, to do this it will also take considerable judgment on their part. For example, production will have to estimate how the inflation rate will affect, among other things, the costs of materials, transportation, and utilities. Personnel will have to judge the increase in wage rates and salaries. And finance will have to determine how the projected inflation rate will affect the cost and availability of money.

DEPARTMENTAL PLANNING

Have your subordinates develop their own plans for those tasks assigned to them. While you will certainly review these plans and make final approvals, you will find that managers will be far more committed to plans that they have developed themselves. After all, as we have pointed out, it is comparatively easy to fail at tasks that are imposed upon us. Failing our own plans involves a much more painful and personal defeat.

The total quality approach should operate at the departmental level just as it did at the business unit level. Intradepartmental teams will create more departmental involvement and commitment to the plan. Why limit the benefits of total quality planning to the business level?

Here's how to go about it. Assume that you're the director of marketing. Furthermore, assume that marketing is divided into two departments, sales and advertising, and that each department is responsible for plan development and execution.

You have been working with these department managers while preparing the marketing plan. Furthermore, your managers have already committed themselves to tentative plans and budgets that mesh with those of marketing. Now it's time for these managers to flesh out and document their department plans and budgets.

Call a meeting. Supply each department manager with a detailed description of the marketing plan and highlight tasks assigned to them (Step 8.3). Ask them to prepare their formal plans and budgets using the same procedure and forms that you used. Again, there is no use in complicating things by having several sets of procedures and forms.

Allow them about two weeks. (Two weeks is probably adequate since they have, in general, already done much of the work). After giving everyone a chance to review the formalized plans, you and your department heads should get together to critique them.

Closely examine the logic of each plan. Do sales forecasts seem reasonable given projected economic conditions and the past history of key customers? Or are they hockey-stick projections? If sales to a key customer are to increase by 20 percent within the next year, just how will this be done? What was the increase last year? If it was only 5 percent, what will your sales department be doing to encourage this customer to buy more? How are your salespeople planning to entice this customer to buy less from your competitors? And how will these competitors react to your intrusion?

Then, do schedules seem realistic? Is there enough time allocated? Is there enough person power or have they fallen into the trap of overcommitment? What about product/service availability?

Besides checking each plan, you'll have to analyze carefully the mesh of the departmental plans. Suppose you plan to open new territories. Will your sales department have the trained personnel available at the required time? Does advertising's support seem realistic and on time for this territoritoral expansion?

Particular attention should also be paid to making sure departmental "outputs" mesh with the marketing plan. Considering the most basic (and important) aspect, does the sales manager's forecast match the sales forecast of the marketing plan?

What happens if a department's plan should fail the test of logic and/or be incompatible? Get it straightened out now. If it's something the department manager can do, give him or her a chance to do it. But if the department manager can't do it, and the problem area is critical to the success of the marketing plan, it will probably require the work of a marketing department task force. You can, of course, impose your will on your subordinates. But when you do, you're forcing them to accept reporting dates and/or numbers they believe are unrealistic. Your staff may go along with you–while hoping for miracles and, perhaps, while circulating their resumes. But at the end of the year you'll just have another bunch of missed projections.

If all goes well, none of this will require changes in the marketing plan. But, once again, you should face the fact that it may. If you find that changes must be made, let management know about it as soon as possible.

FORMATTING THE PLAN

Your next task is the simplest–and the easiest. It's to put together what you've already decided upon (or assembled)–key facts, activity schedules, forecasts, and budgets–so that they're easy to communicate to others and so that your plan is laid out in such a way that it will serve as a working document; one you can refer to daily to see if you're on course. And, if you need to change your plan (which you probably will have to do), it will be easy to do so.

Figure 2.80 outlines formats for two separate situations: (1) planning for a single product/service-single target market, and (2) planning for multiple products/services-target markets.

Single Product/Service-Single Target Market Plan Format

Column (A) contains an outline of a format for a single product/service-single target market plan. Figure 2.81 is a sample format with explanations. Forms for this type of plan can be found in Appendix D.

Plan Format to Consolidate More than One Product/Service-Target Market Plan

If you have to develop more than one product/service-target market plan, then in addition to these product/service-target market

FIGURE 2.80

(A)	(B)
Single Product/Service-Single Target Market	Multiple Products/Services-Multiple Target Markets or Single Product/Service-Multiple Target Markets or Multiple Products/Services-Single Target Market
SWOTs analysis	Summary Plan
Strategy	Overall Strategy
Sales and profit objectives	Consolidated sales and profit objectives
Action plans	Product/service-target market strategies and sales and profit objectives
Contingency plans	
Detailed sales and profit forecasts	General program action plans
Budget	General program budget
	Consolidated budget
	Product/Service-Target Market Plans
	SWOTs analysis
	Strategy
	Sales and profit objectives
	Action plans
	Contingency plans
	Detailed sales and profit forecasts
	Budget

plans you will also need a summary plan. This summary plan will make it easier for you to monitor total sales, profits, and expenses. It will help you coordinate with other functional areas, such as production/operations, human resources, and finance. It also will give you a better sense of overall operations. And finally, management also will want to see a summary plan so they, too, can get the big picture.

Although there are many variations, here's the best way to handle such planning situations. Look again at Figure 2.80. Note that the format outline for the product/service-target market plans under column B is identical to the format outline for single product/service-single target market in column A.

To use this format:

- First, develop marketing plans for each product/service-target market using the format for a single product/service-single target market plan format (Figure 2.81).
- Next, develop a summary marketing plan to provide the necessary overview. Figure 2.82 is a sample format (and explanations) for a summary marketing plan.

Forms for the summary plan can be found in Appendix E.

ADAPTING FORMATS TO MEET MANAGEMENT'S NEEDS

If you'll have to present your plan to management, you may need to modify the formats we've just talked about. But note: first–and we emphasize *first*–develop your marketing plan as we've prescribed. Then adapt your finished plan for presentation.

Consider Your Purpose

The formats presented here are suitable for planning, implementation, and control. But, in some instances you may need a document to explain, only in general terms, your objectives, marketing strategy, supporting programs, and required resources. Again, we emphasize that you should *first* develop your marketing plan as we prescribe in this book. Then modify for presentation.

FIGURE 2.81

PRODUCT/SERVICE-TARGET MARKET PLAN

Product/Service _____

Target Market _____

Key Buying... Key Success Factors

Cover Sheet: Information from Fact Book

i

TABLE OF CONTENTS

ii

STRENGTHS/WEAKNESSES/OPPORTUNITIES/THREATS

STRATEGY

The Present 19___   The Future 19___

Major Problems (Negatives)   Major Problems (Negatives)

Strategy:
Copy directly from Fact Book, p. 18.

SALES AND PROFIT OBJECTIVES

Month	Sales			Profit		
	Planned	Actual	Variance	Planned	Actual	Variance
Jan						
Feb						
Mar						
Apr						
May						
Jun						
Jul						
Aug						
Sep						
Oct						
Nov						

Sales and Profit Objectives: Used here is gross profit. You may wish to use some other criterion, such as net merchandising profit.

2

Major Opportunities (Positives)

Forecast of Target Market Demand

19 _____
19 _____

Inflation Adjustments

1

Curr

Copy "The Present" directly from Fact Book.
For "The Present," directly from Fact Book, consider one of three variations:
1. Copy directly from Fact Book.
2. Change Strategy" on your company's part.
3. Just show "The Future," reflecting future conditions under your proposed strategy.
Which variation to use would be company situational.

Show "The Future," "The Present," under a "No-

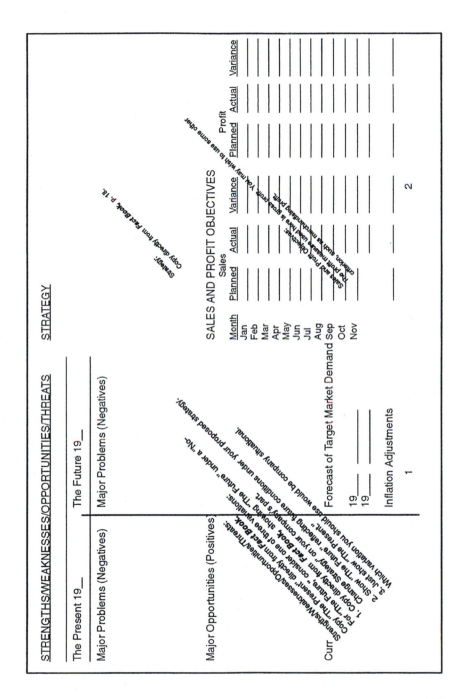

FIGURE 2.81 (continued)

ACTION PLANS

ACTION PLAN when	Responsibility	Budget (in $1,000)	Start Date	Completion Date	Formal Review

Action plans: Describe each major step program. Specify what steps need to be carried out, the persons responsible. Use as many pages as necessary. Then, fill out the timetables. See text, Step 8.

CONTINGENCY PLANS

Key Contingent Events (What is the event?)	Trigger Points (When the event occurs)	Contingency Plans (What we will do when the event occurs)

Contingency Plans. Get from Fact Book, p. 21. Also see text, Step 8.

3

6

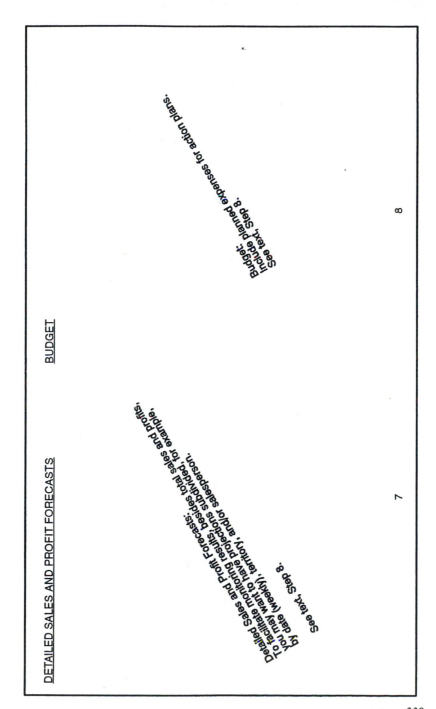

DETAILED SALES AND PROFIT FORECASTS   BUDGET

7   8

Detailed Sales and Profit Forecasts:
You may want to have monitoring prior and
by date (weekly) plan, and project results,
subdivision.
besides total for, sales and profits,
by subdivisions; territory,
for example,
and profits,
See text, Step 8.

Budget:
Include planned expenses for action plans.
See text, Step 8.

FIGURE 2.82

SUMMARY MARKETING PLAN

TABLE OF CONTENTS

i

OVERALL STRATEGY

Overall strategy: _____

Because the production of the product/service is very important to the various
to a single resource using a matrix of increased/decreased/continued. To various the
presentation, consider Step 7. Appendix (market plan).
strategic, consider Step 7. (In comparison
services, consider the text.
one in the

CONSOLIDATED SALES AND PROFIT OBJECTIVES

Month	Sales			Profit		
	Planned	Actual	Variance	Planned	Actual	Variance
Jan						
Feb						
Mar						
Apr						
May						
Jun						
Jul						
Aug						
Sep						
Oct						
Nov						
Dec						

Consolidated Sales and Profit Objectives:
Figures will be totals of individual product/service
target market plans. Copy from product/service
target market plans. p. 2.

1

ACTION PLAN	Responsi-bility	Budget (in $1,000)	Start Date	Comple-tion Date	Formal Review

General Program Action Plans:

General Program: Perform to any of the plans, such as sales/advertising/service/research in blending each of these major steps. Identify what and the marketing program. Use as many steps as necessary. List and sequence each of the initiatory steps. For each, designate the person responsible. Use as many persons as necessary. See text, Step 8.

You may need to add some programs such as product/service-research or meet the following product/market advertising which are not related to market. Also, it may apply to more than one plan. Apply to more.

4

PRODUCT/SERVICE-TARGET MARKET PLAN

Product/Service _____

Target Market _____

Strategy _____

Sales and Profit Objectives

Month	Sales			Profit		
	Planned	Actual	Variance	Planned	Actual	Variance
Jan						
Feb						
Mar						
Apr						
May						
Jun						
Jul						
Aug						
Sep						
Oct						
Nov						

For each Product/Service-Target Market Plan:
— Description of Product/Service
— Copy (Major) Objectives
Strategy from Profit objectives
Copy and appropriate
Sales from
Copy

2

FIGURE 2.82 (continued)

CONSOLIDATED BUDGET

Consolidated Budget.
Summary of the general program budget and budgets for each product/service-target market plan.

8

GENERAL PROGRAM BUDGET

General Program Budget.
Include planned expenses from general program. Also, any planned overhead costs not included in individual product/ service-target market plans.
See text, Step 8.

7

For example, a vice president for a stock exchange was charged with developing a marketing plan to increase the visibility of the exchange. This plan was to be presented to the board of directors. They needed to understand the benefits of sharpening visibility, the objectives of her proposed program, and her strategy. Her plan was formatted accordingly. Since the board of directors had little interest or involvement with implementation and control, these details were briefly summarized. The marketing plan, in this case, was strategic in nature.

For this type of marketing plan, the sole purpose of which is explanation, the first section should be an executive summary. This summary should give an overview of objectives, of the current and future marketing situation, the marketing strategy, action plans, and required resources. In some instances, such as a marketing plan presented to a bank as documentation for a loan, the executive summary should be preceded by a short company history.

The next part, the detailed plan, should contain background data on the current marketing situation, including information as to present competition and appropriate macroenvironmental factors (such as governmental regulatory bodies and the national and international situation). Future projections should also be included. This information would be more detailed here than it would be in a plan used solely for purposes of implementation and control, but it would still be synthesized, with greater detail kept separately in a fact book. The detail of action plans and required resources should be customized according to the reader's background and interests, but in general, it should be briefer than in a plan for implementation and control.

Consider Management's Familiarity

Management's familiarity with your proposed plan will also determine the right format. In the Micron case, the president was the person who reviewed the annual marketing plan. He was very familiar with the sales objectives, the overall marketing strategy, and to a certain extent, with the marketing activities necessary to carry out these strategies. Consequently, all he wanted to see is whether the vice president of marketing had a well-thought-out plan for the next year. The president wanted to know the timing for the plan, the resources (budget) required, and monitoring points. Given this situation, the format used by Micron was satisfactory.

However, if your management has little prior knowledge of your marketing plan, then you'd better consider, for example, including an executive summary (similar to that described above) and greater detail of the SWOTs analysis.

Consider Logical Order

The plan format should be such that it will lead the reader/user from one step to the next in a logical sequence. What might be a logical order again depends on what management is accustomed to. For example, if management is used to seeing sales and profit objectives first, then that's the way it should be presented.

Consider Present Company Formats

If your company has a required planning format, of course the marketing plan you submit to management will follow that format.

But what if this format is not suitable for developing the type of marketing plan that you know needs to be developed? Again, *first* develop your marketing plan as we prescribe in this book. Then adapt the finished plan for presentation. Use the original plan for implementation and control.

Consider Company Jargon

Adapt. Save yourself time and trouble.

Time Considerations

A good format will help you organize your data in useful ways; it's the planning itself that's time-consuming. If you have to plan for a number of products/services for different target markets, you probably won't have time to fully develop plans for every situation. You'll have to make compromises and decide which situations merit "maxi" plans. For your various products/services-target markets, decision criteria would include: (1) major products/services and/or target markets; (2) those situations offering the greatest opportunity; and/or (3) those situations that are critical–for example, those which show rapid loss of market share or those which show severe profit and/or cash-flow drains.

But what about those products/services that do not merit maxi plans? Follow the eight steps presented in this book. Instead of going through each step in a thorough manner, speed up the planning process by going through the steps in a more cursory way. For example, use executive judgment instead of secondary data and field research. The resulting marketing plans, of course, could consist of less-detailed action plans.

We urge you to keep a fact book for every product/service-target market. Following the A-B-C-D Rule, spend a few minutes every week keeping it up to date. Then, when it comes time to put together a plan, your job will be greatly simplified.

A word of caution. Recognize that any short-cut procedure is less than optimum. Plans developed in such a manner, when implemented, are less-likely to produce the results you desire. If you're operating from a false base, again it's like "building a house on a foundation of sand."

POINTS LEARNED

1. Fleshing out, documenting, and formatting the annual marketing plan is, in many ways, the easiest part of the planning process. Yet, it's often given short-shrift because it's dog work. But neglect this step and you can count on your marketing plans going awry.
2. Continue to involve others while completing your total quality marketing plan. This includes other functional area managers as well as marketing department personnel.
3. Follow these ten steps while fleshing out and documenting your marketing plan:

   Step 8.1. Fully Describe Each Major Activity
   Step 8.2. Develop Action Plans for Each Major Activity
   Step 8.3. Assign Tasks
   Step 8.4. Set Up Action-Plan Timetables

Step 8.5. Number Major Activities and Action Plans
Step 8.6. Consider Contingency Planning
Step 8.7. Forecast Sales
Step 8.8. Budget Expenditures
Step 8.9. Forecast Profitability
Step 8.10. Consider Factoring in Next Year's Inflation

4. Let your subordinates develop their own plans for those tasks assigned to them. The total quality approach should operate at the departmental level just as it did at the business unit level.
5. If you have to develop more than one product/service-target market plan:
   - Use the same forms that you would use for a single product/service-target market.
   - Develop a summary plan to tie them all together.
   - Plan presentation may require you to modify the formats we've suggested. If so, of course make the changes. But note: first–and we emphasize *first*–develop your marketing plan as we've prescribed. Then adapt your finished plan.

SECTION III:

RETROSPECT AND EXPECTATION

A Look Back and a Look Ahead

A LOOK BACK

A typical reader's reaction to the approach presented in this book is: "It's common sense." And that's right.

Let's look first at the three key elements of a total quality environment. Starting with total quality planning, answer the questions, "Who are our customers?" "What do our customers value?" "What are we offering to them?" and "Is there a gap between what our customers value and what we have to offer?" Then, develop product/service features that respond to targeted customers' needs and develop processes able to produce the features.

The second key element is quality control: evaluating actual product/service performance; comparing actual performance to product/service goals; and acting on the difference.

The third key element of a total quality environment is constant improvement.

Central to these three key segments is employee involvement. And empowerment. And, to make sure that they have the right "tools," employee training. A total quality environment is common sense. And almost intuitive.

As for the eight steps in the planning process, they're also almost intuitive: we consider our strengths, weaknesses, opportunities, and threats; we decide what it is we wish to accomplish; then we develop strategic and operational plans; and, finally, we think about what we'll do when things go wrong.

The major benefit of this book and the accompanying formats is that they show us how to formalize what we do instinctively. The value of the formal approach is, certainly by now, readily apparent.

When you've put into practice each of the eight steps, you'll have gained a lot.

- You'll have developed performance profiles of the marketplace and of your internal operations, and you will have prepared a critical summary. You'll have put into proper perspective the major opportunities and threats that you face.

- You'll have formulated a strategy based on precision target marketing that has a proper competitive focus.
- You'll have set yearly marketing goals in specific terms, such as sales, profits, market-share points, and number of distribution outlets.
- You'll have designed a work plan that converts marketing objectives and strategies into detailed action steps. A careful review on each of these action steps will better enable you to judge the plan's feasibility. After all, remember that a plan is a rehearsal for action.
- You'll have established marketing controls that enable you to compare actual versus planned performance and that force corrective actions when goals are not being met. And how important this is! After all, the purpose of planning is not to produce a plan. The purpose of planning is to produce results.

While doing this, you will have gotten people involved. And it's tempting to say that this may be the most important benefit of all. Even if you have not been operating in a total quality environment– but if you've put into practice the principles in this book–you've probably made converts. Perhaps some of the newly converted are ready to work with you toward developing a total quality environment. At the very least, the other functional groups within the company have a better understanding of the marketing plan. And of course, you have a better understanding of their strengths and limitations.

The process is simple. Yet, it's not easy. Data has to be accumulated, organized, and synthesized. And this takes time. It's necessary that you recognize that you'll never have all of the data, money, staff, and time to do as thorough an analysis as you'd like to do. As Drucker put it, you'll usually have less to work with than you would like to have. So do the obvious first. Success is usually a matter of drive and common sense.

But now let's take a look ahead.

A LOOK AHEAD

Marketing planning in a total quality environment demands that you adapt to your customers' changing needs. If your market planning process is a once-a-year effort–and that's it–it will never work. Although you must update your plan officially once a year, you must also reevaluate your marketing plan periodically throughout the year–say quarterly. Consider the practice of one company. Besides formal annual and quarterly updates, the business unit's planning team holds meetings every two weeks. If someone feels the need to modify the plan, he/she can make his/her case.

When making changes, or the second time around, you'll find developing the annual marketing plan much easier–and quicker–to do. Particularly if you've developed a consensus on total quality. Other members of your planning group will appreciate that the annual marketing plan (as well as their own plans) are products of continuous information gathering, planning, quality control, and quality improvement.

You should now have rather complete fact books. All they will require is updating. Furthermore, you, and others within your firm, will be familiar with the process. You'll be able to make certain adjustments (company-situational) which will make the process even easier and more effective.

As you prepare future marketing plans, be sure to continue to monitor the external environment. Because of rapid advances in manufacturing, transportation, data processing, and communications, to name a few areas, the world of tomorrow will be different. The marketing battles, like those of the military, will not be fought on the same battlefields.

Let's look at some historic examples from the military battlefields of yesteryear. The massive guns of Manila, for instance, could have blown the Japanese Imperial Navy out of the water in 1941. Enemies had always attacked Manila from the sea. But the Japanese approached from inland, a direction in which the guns could not fire.

United States involvement in Vietnam offers a more painful example. The American army operated with the same strategy that had proved successful in World War II and the Korean War. Moreover, it was aided by extraordinary advances in the technology of warfare. But conventional strategy failed anyway, for at least three major reasons: A large element of South Vietnam's population remained indifferent to the outcome; the tropical terrain was less hospitable than the forests and fields of Europe, or the bare hills of South Korea; and South Vietnam's extensive borders proved impossible to defend against guerilla infiltration.

Company after company has failed for a similar reason–clinging to the past and failing to innovate. Take the Baldwin Locomotive Works. When the diesel engine was introduced, Baldwin chose to make improvements in their steam engines–such as reducing the descaling time. As a result, they produced the finest steam engine in the world; but at that moment in time, no improvements could make the steam engine competitive with the diesel. The company folded.

It's hard to shake methods that have worked. But always ask yourself whether these methods will be successful in the environments of tomorrow.

*   *   *

Your countless daily fires will prevent you from finding time to plan. *You will have to make time*. When your continual crises seem to raise the cost of planning, keep in mind this question: "What are the costs of *not* doing formalized, annual marketing planning in a total quality environment?"

SECTION IV:

APPENDIXES

Appendix A

SECTION 1:
FORECASTING TECHNIQUES

Following are the most commonly used forecasting techniques. The ones which you are most likely to use are explained in detail, and with examples. Others, those that are relatively sophisticated (and that require greater computational effort), are only briefly described. In case you're interested in examining any of these techniques in greater detail, two excellent sources are listed at the end of this section.

There are two basic types of forecasting techniques: qualitative and quantitative.

Qualitative Techniques

In general, these are better suited for forecasting situations when the past is not a good indicator of future sales. However, these techniques are often subject to two major types of bias:

Law of Overriding Negativism: Negative factors are usually given excessive weight.
Law of Current Situations: Projections are unduly influenced by conditions of the present.

Five major qualitative techniques are mentioned here:

Executive Opinion
Expert Opinion
Sales Force Composite
Survey of Buyers' Intentions (Industrial)
Survey of Buyers' Intentions (Consumers)

Executive Opinion

Executive opinion refers to the forecasts of one or more of the firm's executives. Usually views of executives from diverse functional areas such as sales, purchasing, finance, and production/operations will be solicited to broaden the judgment base of the forecast.

These opinions may be gathered in a number of ways. For example, (1) one person gathering executive opinions through casual encounters and then consolidating them for consideration; (2) a group of executives arriving at a forecast consensus during a meeting; and (3) selected executives submitting forecasts and supporting reasons for their opinions, then as a group examining the data and arriving at a final forecast.

Advantages

- It is quick.
- Management is often extremely knowledgeable.
- Because management is involved, forecasts are more likely to be used.
- This may be the only feasible method for a small company.
- This system works equally well with start-up situations, where there is no history from which to extract data.

Limitations

- It is purely subjective.
- Management may not be knowledgeable (the longer an executive has been away from the firing line, the less dependable will be his/her forecasting accuracy).
- Inbred thinking is most likely to prevail with this system.
- Forecasts are usually based on the current situation.
- There is a tendency to average different opinions.
- This type of assessment may be biased by bandwagon effects.

Expert Opinion

This is similar to executive opinion, except that in this case the forecasts are made by one or more well-informed experts outside the company. These experts may consist of, among others, industry consultants, suppliers, and friendly competitors (those located outside of your market area).

Advantages

- It is quick (sometimes).
- It is inexpensive (sometimes).
- Nonbiased opinions; i.e., avoidance of inbred beliefs and boss-pleasing projections (sometimes).
- A number of viewpoints can be evaluated.
- Good for "history-less" situations.

Limitations

- The results may be purely subjective.
- Sometimes the expert doesn't understand your *specific* industry, product/services, target markets, and competitors.
- Good forecasts and bad forecasts may be given equal weight.

Sales Force Composite

This method combines the views of all the salespersons to create a forecast of company–or industry–sales. To accomplish this, each salesperson forecasts sales for his or her territory. These forecasts are then combined for a total forecast.

Here's an example. A sales manager asked each salesperson to forecast the most-probable, the most-pessimistic, and the most-optimistic sales for each product/service-target market for his/her entire geographic territory.

The sales manager then compared each of these forecasts with last year's sales. In case of any seemingly unreasonable forecasts, he discussed the specific cases with the salespersons responsible. During the discussion they then arrived at mutually agreed upon forecasts.

Finally, the sales manager assigned probabilities to each forecast, multiplied each forecast by its probability figure, and then aggregated these forecasts. This gave the sales manager most-probable, most-pessimistic, and most-optimistic sales forecasts for each sales-person, for each product/service-target market, and for total company sales.

It should be noted that most companies make some adjustments to salespersons' forecasts.

Advantages

- Salespeople have intimate knowledge of customers, of uses of a product/service, and of direct and indirect competitors.
- This method is good for history-less situations. It's likely to pick up changes in technology, new competition, etc.
- Results of these forecasts can be measured by product, territory, customer, and salesperson.
- If forecasts are to be used for quotas, salespersons are more likely to accept the quotas since they have been involved in their creation.

Limitations

- These results can be either overly optimistic or pessimistic.
- Salespersons may be unaware of general economic trends or of company plans.
- This method increases paperwork for salespersons.

In addition to forecasting sales, salespersons are often used to predict industry changes, such as new technologies, competition, and so forth.

Survey of Buyers' Intentions (Industrial)

This method surveys a representative sample of users to determine their expectations of future purchases. In cases where the market is small a census can be taken. In some cases, buyers also may be used to help predict industry changes, such as new product/service development, competitive delivery dates, and pricing levels.

Here's an example of industry buyers being used to forecast company sales. In order to determine the demand for its product, a firm surveyed a representative sample of present and potential users of its particular product. This target market was asked to indicate how much of the product was needed for the upcoming year, and also how much of the product they would buy from the company in question. In order to get a range of expectations, each respondent was asked to give answers to both questions using a probability factor.

For example see Figure A-1. By multiplying the quantity forecasts for each probability category, the firm was able to estimate the expected sales in units-per-customer. In customer A's case, this would be 15,800 units–all to be purchased from the firm (as indicated by the X in the 100% column).

$$\frac{.25 \times 10,000 + .5 \times 20,000 + .75 \times 15,000}{1.5} = 15,800 \text{ units (rounded)}$$

After aggregating the responses from all present and potential users, then a projection of the firm's sales for the next year could be made.

Advantages

- There is direct contact with the purchaser.
- Users of this method will have early recognition of customers' changes in purchasing intentions and preferences.
- It is good for predicting short-range demand.
- If the number of buyers is few, the cost of reaching them may be minimal.

Limitations

- Buyers may be reluctant to state their purchasing forecasts.
- Purchasing forecasts are based on predictions (of the general economy, their own sales forecasts, etc.) which may be in error.
- Buyers may not plan their purchases.
- Buyers may not have firm purchasing intentions.

Syndicated services, such as Predicasts of Cleveland, Ohio give forecasts by Standard Industrial Classification and may prove useful in attempting to predict buyers' intentions.

Figure A-1

Customer A				
	Probabilities			
	25%	50%	75%	100%
Expected quantity needed (in units)	10,000	20,000	15,000	
% to be purchased from the firm				X

For an extensive listing (approximately 13,000) of syndicated market research reports, studies, and surveys, check *Findex,* (Telephone number 1-800-843-7751).

Survey of Buyers' Intentions (Consumers)

Basically, this method of evaluation is quite similar to the survey of industrial buyers already discussed. In general, the same strengths and weaknesses apply to surveys of consumers' buying intentions and surveys of industrial buyers' intentions. However, two points need to be emphasized.

- Buyers of convenience goods such as soap, mouthwash, and toothpaste, seldom think of their annual use. Or, if they use more than one brand, they seldom have a clear idea about how they divide their purchases.
- Consumers are better at predicting their purchases of durable products than of consumables. However, they usually base these estimates on future economic conditions–and consumers (like experts!) have not shown much expertise in such forecasts.

As with industrial buyers' intentions, there are syndicated services such as the University of Michigan's Surveys of Consumers. A description of its services follows.

The University of Michigan's Surveys of Consumers are conducted each month, and are based on nationally representative samples of U.S. households. Initiated in 1946, these periodic surveys provide regular assessments of consumer attitudes and expectations, and are used to evaluate economic trends and prospects. The surveys are designed to explore why changes in consumer attitudes and expectations occur, and how these changes influence consumer spending and saving decisions.

Each monthly survey contains 40 core questions which probe different aspects of consumer sentiment. The core questions cover three broad areas, including personal finances, business-cycle developments, and buying conditions. Assessments of past and expected changes in personal finances are supplemented by measures of expected income and price changes in the coming year. Consumers' expectations for business conditions and the general economy are measured by a series of questions about inflation, unemployment, and interest rates. Attitudes toward buying conditions are measured by probing the respondent's appraisal of present buying conditions for large household durables, houses, and vehicles. These attitudes about buying conditions are supplemented by the respondents' reasons for their opinions. In addition to the standard economic measures, each survey contains questions which are pertinent to current economic conditions. These questions measure reactions to issues such as proposals to change tax laws and international trade policies.

For additional information, call (313) 763-5224, or write to:

> The University of Michigan
> Surveys of Consumers
> P.O. Box 1248
> Ann Arbor, MI 48106-1248

Quantitative Techniques

Now, let's take a look at three major classifications of quantitative techniques.

> Time-series analysis
> Multiple regression analysis
> Econometric modeling

Each of these techniques uses history as a basis for projections.

Descriptions are provided here along with brief explanations (for most) on how to do them. But with the exception of time-series analysis (in its simplest form), it doesn't make sense for you to use these techniques without the aid of a computer. Packaged personal computer programs can be very helpful and several are listed at the end of this section.

Seasonal Adjustments

Regardless of which of the above quantitative techniques you may use, seasonality in the raw data may make your forecasting efforts more difficult and even misleading. Therefore, make deseasonalizing the data your first step.

Seasonal variations are those rhythmic changes in sales that occur within the year, and are consistent from year to year. For example, year in and year out, soup sales go up in the winter and down in the summer. This holds true whether it is a good year or a bad year for soup sales.

Figure A-2 shows a hypothetical example of a sales curve with seasonal data. Notice that while there is a rhythmic variation consistent between years, there is also an upward trend in the data.

While there are a variety of ways to deseasonalize data and many computerized techniques incorporate deseasonalization into their analyses, the method shown here is a simple, effective way to accomplish this task.

Figure A-3 shows three years of hypothetical sales data (shown graphically in Figure A-2). The data in the table as created by actually taking a simple time series with a constant trend and then adding a seasonal factor to the trend data.

The "real seasonal indices" are shown in Figure A-3 as well. Of course, in an actual situation the planner does not know the real seasonal indices, since that is the purpose of deseasonalizing. We show them here only to compare them to the calculated values.

If there was no seasonal effect or trend, you would expect exactly one-twelfth (8.33 percent) of the year's sales to occur in each month. Therefore, a seasonal index would be the actual percentage of a year's sales within a month divided by the expected percentage (8.33 percent) if *no* seasonality were present, multiplied by 100.

Using this method with sample data, the seasonal indices are calculated for each year separately (see Figure A-4). Compare these to the "real seasonal indices" in Figure A-3 (remember, the real indices are known only because they were built into the sample

FIGURE A-2

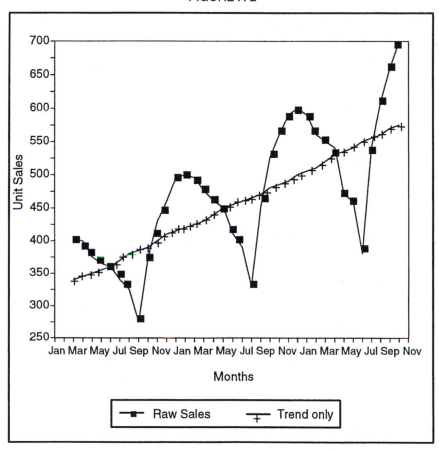

data). Notice that the calculated values slightly underestimate the real values in the beginning of the year and overestimate the values at the end of the year. Also, notice that they do this for all three years.

The over- and underestimation is due to the trend in the data. The end of the year will always have higher sales than the beginning of the year because of sales growth. Therefore, the deseasonalizing should be done on detrended data.

In the sample data, we used simple linear regression on the raw data to calculate the trend. The regression equation indicated that

FIGURE A-3

Month	Real Seasonal Indices	Unit Sales		
		Year I	Year II	Year III
Jan	120	408	502	602
Feb	116	396	493	590
Mar	110	383	475	568
Apr	105	373	461	549
May	100	362	446	530
Jun	90	332	408	483
Jul	85	320	391	462
Aug	70	268	327	386
Sep	95	371	430	530
Oct	108	429	519	610
Nov	115	465	561	658
Dec	120	493	594	695

the intercept was 340 units and a slope of 6.955. We then calculated the projected data with only trend and used the ratio of the raw data to the trend-only data (see Figure A-5).

Finally, we took the average of the three years for the final estimates of seasonal effects (Figure A-6). Note that with the trend removed, you no longer have the bias toward higher end-of-year indices and the calculated index conforms rather closely with the "real seasonal indices."

To review: If the raw data has a possible trend, remove the trend using regression analysis (or similar techniques). Calculate the "trend-only" time series using the regression coefficients and the intercept. Finally, use the average of the ratio of the raw data to the calculated "trend-only" data as the seasonal indices.

All the remaining analysis should be done on deseasonalized time series or data sets, but be sure to seasonalize the data after the deseasonalized forecasts are made.

Time-Series Analysis

Forecasts from this technique are derived solely by extrapolations of past sales. The underlying rationale is that past patterns will

FIGURE A-4

Month	Year I Seasonal Index	Year II Seasonal Index	Year III Seasonal Index
Jan	106	107	108
Feb	103	105	106
Mar	100	101	102
Apr	97	98	99
May	94	95	95
Jun	87	87	87
Jul	83	83	83
Aug	70	70	69
Sep	97	96	95
Oct	112	111	110
Nov	121	120	118
Dec	129	127	125

reoccur in the future. In some cases, the past may be a good predictor, for instance, when the industry environmental conditions (supplier relationships, products demanded, and so forth) are stable. Be aware, however, that the validity of this method is questionable under conditions of environmental change.

The advantages and disadvantages of these techniques, as a group, are as follows.

Advantages

- They are very accurate in projecting future sales if future relationships (demand, competition, etc.) follow past patterns.
- They are relatively easy to use and require little time.

Limitation

- Forecasts may be in error if the industry environment is undergoing change, for example, if there are new competitive products and pricing policies, major shifts in governmental restrictions, and/or new substitute products.

Time-Series Techniques

Simple Trend Line Extrapolation (Linear)

This technique is the easiest of all to use. All you have to do is plot past sales, establish a trend line, and then project future sales on basis of the trend line.

Here's an example. Suppose sales for the past five years were as follows (in 1,000 units with T –0 being the current year, T –1 being the previous year, etc.).

(T – 0)	110
(T – 1)	105
(T – 2)	95
(T – 3)	90
(T – 4)	95

To develop a trend line, two basic techniques can be used, graphical and mathematical.

Graphical. Plot the sales/data on graph paper. Put unit sales on the vertical axis and years on the horizontal. Next, draw a line

FIGURE A-5

	Trend Only Time Series		
Month	Year I	Year II	Year III
Jan	347	431	514
Feb	354	438	521
Mar	361	445	528
Apr	368	452	535
May	375	459	542
Jun	382	466	549
Jul	389	473	556
Aug	396	480	563
Sep	403	487	570
Oct	410	493	577
Nov	417	500	584
Dec	424	507	591

FIGURE A-6

Month	Calculated Index	Real Index
Jan	117	120
Feb	113	116
Mar	107	110
Apr	102	105
May	97	100
Jun	88	90
Jul	83	85
Aug	68	70
Sep	93	95
Oct	105	108
Nov	112	115
Dec	117	120

which represents a visual average of past sales. Extend this line into the future. In this example, projected sales for one year in the future (T + 1) are 113 units, for five years in the future (T + 5), 133 units (see Figure A-7).

Mathematical (Least Squares). If you're going to use this technique, use a software package. Consult one of the sources recommended at the end of this section.

Moving Average

This method consists of averaging past sales. Averages can be computed for any useful period of time, but for this example, let's use monthly sales. As the most recent month's sales figures become available, they are added and the sales figures from the most-distant month dropped. This makes the average "move" through time.

There are two basic methods for forecasting with the moving average approach: unadjusted and weighted.

Unadjusted Moving Average. To forecast next period's sales, total the previous periods' sales and divide by the number of previous periods.

FIGURE A-7

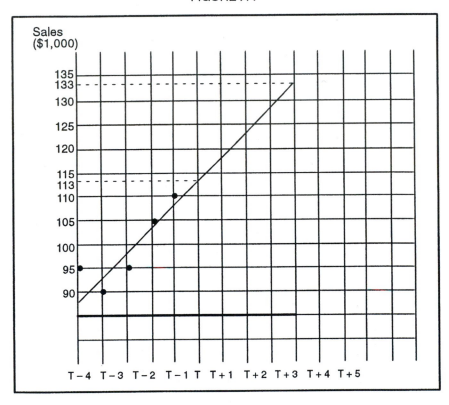

Assume that we have the following data, and we're using just the past five months' sales for our forecast (notice the sixth month was dropped).

Month	Sales
T – 5	103
T – 4	100
T – 3	98
T – 2	95
T – 1	98
T – 0	95

$$\text{Sales Forecast T} + 1 = \frac{100 + 98 + 95 + 98 + 95}{5} = 97.2$$

Weighted Moving Average. This technique is a better choice when sales data are not following a clearly defined trend. For example, assume that you believe that the more recent periods should receive the greater weight. For example, the most recent month's sales would have five times the weight of the most distant, the next most recent month would have four times the weight of the most distant, and so on.

To arrive at a forecast using the above assumptions, first determine the sum of the months using the formula $\frac{n(n + 1)}{2}$, where n = the number of months. The sum of the months = 15.

(1) Month	(2) Sales (Y)	(3) Weights	(4) = (2) × (3) Weighted Sales
T − 4	100	1/15 = .0667	6.7
T − 3	98	2/15 = .1333	13.1
T − 2	95	3/15 = .20	19.0
T − 1	98	4/15 = .2667	26.1
T − 0	95	5/15 = .3333	31.7
T + 1			96.6

The sales forecast for T + 1 is the sum of the weighted sales, or 96.6.

The weighted average technique gives you more flexibility in determining which periods should receive the greater weight. However, unless you have a rationale for adjusting the weights, use the unadjusted method.

Exponential Smoothing

This forecasting approach, as with other time-series methods, uses past sales to forecast future sales. It's a more-complex weighted moving-average method. In fact, exponential smoothing is a special case of a moving-average where the "weights" can be represented by a more complex algorithm. Many of the computerized algorithms have an automatic adjustment for seasonal effects.

The generic equation is $F_{t+1} = F_t + W (D_t - F_t)$.

F_t is the forecast of demand for the current period, made from $t - 1$

F_{t+1} is the forecast of demand for $t + 1$

D_t is the observed demand (sales)

W   is a weight between $0 < W < 1$, sometimes called the smoothing constant. A weight closer to 1 gives less influence to the immediate past for prediction.

Exponential smoothing is most useful when you need to make frequent forecasts for a large number of products/services for short periods of time.

Specific advantages of the exponential smoothing approach are:

- Once the model is set up, you need to carry forward only a very limited amount of data (the weighting constant and exponent).
- Calculations are quick and simple.
- Only the exponent value needs to be specified rather than a long string of weights.

Each of the approaches (unadjusted moving average, weighted moving average, and exponential smoothing) assumes that sales were not subject to trends or to seasonal or cyclical patterns during the forecast period. Through decomposition analysis, long-term trends and cyclical and seasonal fluctuations can be detected. These pattern fluctuations can be incorporated into future projections.

Simple Regression Analysis

The trend-line extrapolation example of the least squares was a simple regression analysis. Past sales (the independent variable) was used to predict future sales (the dependent variable).

However, there are cases where you have a better independent variable. Take the producer of building insulation. Sales of insulation are dependent on housing starts. Using past data of housing starts, you can calculate how insulation sales are effected by housing starts. Then, you can use estimates of government housing starts to predict insulation sales.

The key to regression analysis is understanding how your sales are related to some other variable.

Multiple Regression Analysis

Most marketing forecasts require more than a single independent variable. For example, if a marketing manager wants to forecast next year's sales, he/she might consider not only past industry sales but also such independent variables as industry promotional expenditures, industry price level, and GDP.

Multiple regression analysis is similar to simple regression analysis, except that you're dealing with more variables and the mathematics are more complex. To set up a regression model, you'll have to experiment with a number of different independent variables which you believe have been significant in predicting sales in the past (e.g., industry promotional expenditures, industry price levels, and GDP). Stepwise regression analysis will give you the predictive values of each of the independent variables. The coefficient of determination (R^2) will also give you the predictive value of the model.

Rather than go into the mathematics here, we recommend that you examine one of the software packages listed at the end of this section. But considering some of the advantages and disadvantages of multiple regression may help you decide if this technique is worth your further investigation.

Advantages

- The forecast is more than a rearview-mirror approach. You are forecasting the value of independent variables which create sales for your product.
- Regression analysis is extremely useful when lead-lag relationships can be established between the independent variables and sales, such as (possibly) between the independent variables of housing starts and GDP, and the dependent variable of carpet sales.
- A number of values for the variables and their coefficients can be used to determine how sensitive the forecast is to possible errors in the forecasted values and the coefficients of the variables.

- Since variables must be identified and quantified, usually it is a good learning experience to go through this exercise. It forces you to think–concretely–about what creates demand for your product/service.

Limitations

- You still have to rely on the past to determine independent variables and their coefficients, so this is still partially a rear-view-mirror approach.
- Cause and effect must go only one way–from causal factors (independent variables) to sales (dependent variables). In other words, sales must not affect the causal factors. For example, in some industries the amount that companies spend on advertising and sales promotion is determined by past sales–or on the sales forecast. In such an industry, the industry's projected advertising and sales budgets could not be used as independent variables.
- It may be as difficult to forecast the independent variables as it is to determine the dependent variable. There is the old saw about how to determine the exact weight of a pig when you don't have a scale: Get a beam–suspend it over a fence. Put a basket on each end. Put the pig in one basket and fill the other basket with stones. When the beam balances, guess the weight of the stones. Then you will know the exact weight of the pig.
- Independent variables must not be interrelated.

Econometric Modeling

You will find it impractical to do econometric forecasting in-house unless you have one or more resident economists on staff. There are, however, syndicated econometric services available–you may want to look into hiring one of these services.

Strictly speaking, regression analysis (just discussed) is the primary tool of econometrics. However, econometrics usually implies economic theories represented by sets of regression equations. Thus, an econometric model includes a number of equations to be solved simultaneously.

The major advantage of econometric models is that the variables' interrelationships in any single equation can be included in other equations and their values determined. This tends to take into consideration the complex interrelationships among variables. On the other hand, in regression analysis values for each independent variable must be specified by the forecaster.

But the complexity of econometrics runs up the cost. Thus, such models are only used for highly aggregated data, such as national, industry, or for very large company forecasts.

However, if you or anyone in your company has the expertise, time, and inclination to do econometric modeling, you might wish to contact Data Resources, Inc. Supported by computer-accessible business and economic data, the DRI professional staff works with clients to solve their business and policy problems. DRI's data services are combined with local user-supplied information for manipulation, analysis, and reporting. To meet individual requirements, customized applications are developed using a range of software tools. DRI/McGraw-Hill, Inc., 24 Hartwell Avenue, Lexington, MA 02173. Telephone: (617) 863-5100/FAX: (617) 860-6416.

If you'd like more information concerning forecasting techniques, you might consult the following:

David M. Georgoff and Robert G. Murdick, "Managers Guide to Forecasting," *Harvard Business Review,* (1986), Vol. 64, pp. 110-120. This is a practical guide to help determine which forecasting techniques to use and how to get the best results from forecasts. It also discusses 20 of the most common forecasting techniques in relation to (1) time and resource requirements, (2) data input required, and (3) forecast outputs received. In addition, the authors highlight important considerations involved in utilizing forecasting, such as time horizon, technical sophistication, variability and consistency of data, and they offer suggested ways to improve the forecasting process, such as combining forecasts, simulating a range of input assumptions, and selectively applying judgment.

Charles W. Gross and Robin T. Peterson, *Business Forecasting* (Boston: Houghton Mifflin Company 1976). This is an excellent basic primer on forecasting techniques. It includes an introduction to forecasting, a review of judgmental methods, trend analysis, and discussions of regression and correlation, time-series analysis, forecasting by surveys and test markets, model building and simulation, indirect methods, and assessment and implementation.

Recommended Software Packages for Time-Series and Multiple Regression

Two easy-to-use (if your data is on Lotus 1-2-3) software packages for the above techniques, are:

SmartForecasts™ Version 3. SmartForecasts' automatic forecasting feature automatically projects sales, budgets, and product demand, as well as handling statistics. Its EYEBALL utility allows you to incorporate business knowledge into the forecasting process. SmartForecasts works with latest releases of Lotus 1-2-3 and Excel, in addition to ASCII and DIF files downloaded from company databases. Prices vary according to product features, starting at $595. Smart Software, Inc., 4 Hill Road, Belmont, MA 02178. Telephone: (800) 762-7899/FAX: (617) 489-2748.

Forecast!™ Designed for novices and experts alike, Forecast! includes a wide variety of time-series models, such as trend analysis (linear, exponential, hyperbolic, and S-curve), moving averages, exponential smoothing, decomposition analysis and seasonal adjusted forecasts. Forecast! also offers multiple regression models and a statistical analysis module, including histograms. Up to 300 observations and up to 10 variables may be entered simultaneously; the program will forecast up to 52 periods into the future. Data may be easily loaded from an existing worksheet, or from the Windows clipboard. Price $165. Intex Solutions, 35 Highland Circle, Needham, MA 02194. Telephone: (617) 449-6222/FAX: (617) 444-2318.

Appendix A

Here are a number of "do's" and "don'ts" which practitioners generally agree are good guidelines for forecasting.

Avoid Falling Victim to the Law of the Instrument

The Law of the Instrument states: "Give a small boy a hammer and everything he encounters needs pounding." Some forecasters seem to suffer from familiarity with a specialized forecasting technique. They seem to use the same technique on every occasion.

Recognize that there is no such thing as the ideal forecasting technique. Ask yourself: What is the purpose of the forecast? To determine market potential? To determine company sales forecast?

What is the forecasting horizon?

What is the accuracy required–the acceptable range–of the forecast? Does it have to be exact because the firm has to make a number of costly, fixed decisions based on the forecast? Or, does the firm have a number of built-in escape hatches, in case your forecast is in error?

How much time you have to prepare the forecast? Do you have time to complete a survey of buyers' intentions? Or, will you have to settle for secondary data that's readily available? What about the personnel doing the survey? What is their level of expertise and how much time do they have to spend on the forecast?

What kind of budget are you working with? For example, can you hire outside experts?

What kind of data is available? In some industries, such as housing, a number of syndicated services provide information suitable for use in a regression analysis. In other industries, especially "new" ones, there may be little historical data, and you may find that qualitative techniques are the only viable ones in these cases.

What are management's inclinations? Do they want a highly scientific forecast? If so, and if other conditions are right, you may wish to subscribe to the syndicated service of a firm such as Data Resources, Inc, or utilize relatively sophisticated techniques, such as regression analysis. On the other hand, if management is suspicious of such tools, you may wish to use simpler methods, such as trend-line analysis and sales-force composite.

Also, remember that the techniques you use will depend upon whether you're in industrial or consumer marketing. There are differences.

- Industrial markets are usually highly concentrated geographically (only a few customers make up the bulk of the demand), and their purchases are planned. A survey of this market is more feasible than a survey of the consumer market.
- Since industrial demand is a derived demand, it's more volatile than consumer demand. Because of this, industrial forecasting is more concerned with general economic and business conditions than is consumer forecasting.
- Group buying is more prevalent in industrial than in consumer markets.
- Industrial market forecasts are mainly concerned with market size and potential estimation. Unlike consumer marketing, there is little attention given to psychological market segmentation.
- The industrial marketing manager has less money and time to spend on each product category. Thus, he/she typically does not use consultants and has to rely more heavily upon secondary data, executive opinion, and sales force composite.

Use Multiple Methods

Use a collage of techniques, some quantitative and some qualitative. This approach helps the forecast to stand the test of common sense. Too often forecasters get so enamored of a technique they accept the results without question. This danger is perhaps especially prevalent when using esoteric quantitative techniques.

But one technique you should always use–even though you may not incorporate its results in your findings–is a trend line. Do this because others in your company will always make a forecast from the trend line (even though it may be a very crude trend line). If your forecast should deviate from the trend line, you'll want to make sure that you know by how much and why. Following this approach also helps your forecast stand the test of common sense. For example, one CEO had this to say about an MBA he had hired, "He [the MBA] came up with a very precise forecast using regression analysis. The forecast was considerably different from the industry trend. His explanation of why the forecasts differed was very weak. I asked him if he had drawn a trend line, and he replied that he hadn't." The MBA no longer works for this company.

Be Wary of Transition Periods

Are there structural changes taking place within your industry? Such as when the product/service is changing from one stage to another, for example, from introduction to growth? If you use quantitative techniques during these periods, make sure that you adjust the formula with qualitative judgments.

Search for Causal Relationships

There is the story about an Indian lying down with his ear pressed to the ground. A cowboy rode up, saw the Indian and asked, "What is it?" The Indian replied, "Half hour from here. Wagon. Four wheels. Pulled by two horses. One beige. One roan. Drive by white man in black suit. Black hat. Woman riding next –"

The cowboy cut him off. "Why that's tremendous. To be able to hear all that."

The Indian replied, "I didn't hear, I saw. Wagon ran over me one-half hour ago!"

Sometimes things aren't what they seem. Make sure you understand the correct causal relationships. If you haven't done so, consider putting together a demand formula (multiple regression) for your industry. You may not have all the data necessary to "run" the formula, but the mere effort to formulate will help you better understand the causal relationships within your industry.

Consider Potential Competitive Actions

Too many forecasts just do not take into account potential competitive actions. Such forecasts usually are based on the assumption that competitors will be benign, that they will continue to do the same thing they have done in the past. Short shrift is given to the prospect that competitors may design their product better. Or come out with new models. Or improve their productivity. Or, in an effort to increase their market share, lower their prices.

Get Management Involvement

The market forecast is the basis for all company activity. Consequently, management must believe in the forecast if it is to be used. But, depending on the point of view of the functional managers, forecasts will always be more or less acceptable. For example:

- Manufacturing, to keep production costs low, wants a narrow product line and long production runs. It also tends to want to keep raw-materials inventory at maximum so it doesn't run out of materials which would, later on, cause overtime. On the other hand, in order to keep down inventory carrying costs, it wants to keep finished-goods inventory at a minimum.
- Marketing tends to want a large variety of products to provide customers with choice, and it wants a large finished goods inventory so it can provide quick delivery.
- Finance tends to want to keep all inventories at a minimum in order to reduce cash requirements.

Less acceptable forecasts will usually be more questionable. The forecast will be especially suspect if it is not "surprise-free," that is, if it differs from what management expects to happen—"conventional wisdom."

Forecast believability will be highly questionable if the forecast differs from the past trend, or if the firm is operating in a high-change environment where structural stability is under stress. Thus, the less the forecast is surprise-free, the greater the need for involvement.

Don't minimize the importance of involvement, especially in high-change environments. One staff executive, in setting up long-range forecasting methodology for his company, visited a number of firms. Of one company's procedure he said, "I was convinced that their process was likely to end up in failure because of the way the planning department allocated its time. They spent 80 percent of their time developing their scenarios, and 20 percent involving and influencing top management. I thought this was the wrong mix; that it should be the other way around." He went on to say that this company had difficulties trying to gain acceptance for its forecasts after the fact. In his words, "That's the wrong time to do it. You should be trying to gain acceptance as you go along." (Techniques for involving management were discussed in Step 4.)

Of course, there are costs involved in managerial involvement. It's time consuming. (Make sure that the procedure you use for involving management is considered productive.) Then, too, you must make certain that management is informed of general economic and industry trends prior to direct involvement. A group of uninformed executives assisting in developing the forecast will not improve its quality. The Two Heads Fallacy states "two heads are *only* better than one if the probability is better than 50 percent that both heads would arrive at the correct decision independently."

Avoid the Dowser-Rod Syndrome

Some people claim that people who "witch" for water are using the dowser rod as an excuse for drilling a well in a location where they would like the well to be. In forecasting, make sure that you do not seek out a forecasting methodology likely to give you the results you'd like to see. Avoid the temptation to prepare a forecast that will give you an excuse for doing what you want to do.

Remember, nobody sees the world as it actually exists; everyone sees a somewhat distorted picture of that world. People utilize an unconscious process of selective perception in order to sort and discard information taken in. Studies show that a person tends to perceive selectively (intake) the environment that supports his/her beliefs in order to keep these beliefs free from attack.

One of the best ways to minimize selective perception is to consciously gather information which does not conform to your present beliefs. To do this, the forecast section of the plan should have a sheet of paper titled "Disquieting Information." Here, record those concepts and ideas about future market conditions that do not conform to commonly held beliefs. Study them carefully. Refer back to them on occasion. You may find yourself revising your forecast as a result of this list.

Be Careful of Intuition

Often, people know industries so thoroughly that they think they have intuitive abilities. But what they're doing, in reality, is making subconscious evaluations. Subconsciously they create trend lines and adjust them for seasonal and competitive behavior, for example. And many times these people will be quite accurate. When they are apt to fail will be in cases of overconfidence because of perceived psychic abilities.

For instance, a very successful travel agent had established his business from scratch. He was proud of his accomplishment. And rightfully so. While basking in his success, however, a client offered him what he thought was a great business deal. The client had planned to set up a retail shop selling African art, jewelry, and floor coverings, but the client's partner backed out at the last minute. The client then offered to sell the travel agent his inventory at a "considerable bargain." The travel agent, believing his retailing experience to be universal, snapped up the deal. He found a location. Two months later he opened the store. Two months after that, the store was closed, a dismal failure.

One might say, of course, that that could happen to a small businessperson, but in a large corporation, preventive checks and balances exist. A closer look, however, reveals that bad business decisions occur at all levels.

A number of years ago, for example, a director of marketing for a billion-dollar bank hired a consultant to do a market research study. The goal was to determine if there was any future for a medical/dental billing service that the bank had been offering for over four years. Projections were that it would take over 800 accounts for the bank to break even, and currently they had only 14 accounts on line. Was the low (nil) market penetration due to poor marketing or was the service itself not a viable product? A quick market survey revealed that the service was not one the medical profession wanted.

How did the bank happen to offer this service? It seems that an executive vice president (who had been most successful in commercial lending) was sitting in a dental chair one morning and the idea came to him. After the appointment he rushed to his bank to explain this great idea. "And one doesn't question his ideas," the director of marketing lamely added.

You might say that such an error in judgment could happen with a product/service line, but it wouldn't happen with major investments, such as acquisitions. Don't be too sure.

The CEO of one company related the cautionary tale of his firm–which he had started in a booth of a restaurant. His new business had been extremely successful. Its sales had reached over $150 million, the business had practically no debt and its ROI (return on investment) exceeded 10 percent after tax. He, along with his management team, decided they should diversify. Within two years, the firm was almost bankrupt.

As you might expect, this caused the CEO to do a lot of soul-searching. As he did this, he realized where he and his management team had failed. Because they had been so successful in their basic business, they believed the reason for their success was simply that they were good managers, and consequently, that they could manage anything.

"But," as he explained, "that was not the reason for our success. We had grown up in our industry. We knew it inside and out. We were continually making adjustments, subconsciously, for competition, buyer demands, production capabilities, inventory levels, and so forth. Although those actions were never formalized or put into writing, each action was based on a keen sense of the industry.

"However, when we moved into different industries, we had no background. It was as if we understood German IV and now we had moved into Chinese IV, without having taken Chinese, I, II, and III," the CEO said.

Be careful of intuition.

Seek Out–but Scrutinize–Secondary Data

Often the information you need is in published sources. Unfortunately, it's hard to find. Although there are any number of sources which will prove useful to your planning efforts, here are some of the major ones you shouldn't overlook:

- Your industry association. It may be that your trade association has a library. Why not keep in constant contact with the librarian? Also, make sure that you are on good terms with the other association staff, and that they're aware of the type of information you need.
- Libraries. Make several librarians aware of your information needs.
- Syndicated data sources, such as Mead Nexus. Get a better picture of available services by spending some time meeting with sales representatives of syndicated sources.

Make sure, however, that you check the authenticity of the secondary data. First, determine its timeliness. Even if you are using the most recent available data, it still may be woefully out-of-date. For example, if in early 1988 you were using the *Census of Manufacturers,* Bureau of the Census data, the most recent report would have been published in 1982.

Second, did the person/agency who conducted the research have a vested interest in its outcome? It's so easy to distort results. Disraeli is attributed with saying, "There are three kinds of lies: lies, damned lies, and statistics."

In addition, if the data were based on a survey, examine these three levels:

Level 1.   Did the survey investigate the right universe?
Level 2.   Was the sample representative from that universe?
Level 3.   What about the survey instrument and execution itself? Did they seem appropriate? Or were they likely to create bias?

Watch Out for Target Fixation

One of the dangers of low-level fighter strafing is that pilots tend to become so involved in destroying a truck, tank, and so on that they lose their senses of closure. "That truck, I've hit it a number of times. Why doesn't it blow up? Just a few more shots and I'll have it," the pilot thinks. But, unfortunately, that same pilot gets so wrapped up that he gets too close to the ground. By the time he "comes to his senses," he has crashed.

Sometimes you'll get so involved in trying to find a certain bit of information on a particular customer that, before you realize it, you will have a highly disproportionate amount of time invested in the search.

You can avoid target fixation by planning and budgeting the time involved in your forecasting process. Obviously, this is just common managerial sense. But that doesn't mean this caution can be lightly dismissed. In planning your time, you should understand (or determine):

- The accuracy required. What is the magnitude of the decision resting on this forecast? What is the acceptable range of the forecast accuracy in terms of dollars and/or units?
- When must the forecast be completed?
- What kind of budget do you have to work with in terms of personnel, time, and money?

Then, lay out the steps that you will have to complete in order to finish the forecast. Why not use an arrow diagram to help organize your thinking? On each activity, specify the time and resources required. This will help you to avoid spending excessive time on noncritical areas.

If you've delegated the forecasting task, make sure that person knows, in specific terms, what you want accomplished (see above). Avoid such loose terms as "determine potential." Rather, let him/her know the degree of accuracy required, how his/her tasks fit into the forecasting process, and what actions will be taken as a result of the forecast. Suggest that he/she lay out the planned procedure on an arrow diagram.

Don't Wait for All the Facts

Follow the advice of Lee Iacocca.

If I had to sum up in one word the qualities that make a good manager, I'd say that it all comes down to decisiveness. You can use the fanciest computers in the world and you can gather all the charts and numbers, but in the end you have to bring all your information together, set up a timetable, and act.[1]

Appendix B

HOW TO ADJUST FINANCIAL STATEMENTS FOR INFLATION

If you decide to adjust your financial statements for inflation, perhaps you can neutralize inflationary effects on sales by using units sold instead of dollars. However, this measurement often isn't practical. The number of types of products sold may be many. Furthermore, the mix may be constantly changing. Such would probably be the case with a wholesaling company. Even if you're selling only one product/service, changes in product/service features could make units of sale not comparable from year to year. Then, too, by using just units sold, how would you measure the effects of inflation on expenses and profits?

Of the firms that adjust sales for inflation, most use one or several price indices. Many firms have found the Consumer Price Index-All Urban Consumers (CPI-U), All Items, to be satisfactory.

Below (Figure B-1) are relevant figures from the index and a formula showing how to make the adjustment.

In 1988, the CPI-U, All Items, was rebased, using the year 1982-84 = 100. Starting with the release of data for January 1988, the standard reference period is 1982-84 = 100. The new index does not affect the period-to-period rate-of-change measurement–just the basing period. The previous index, using 1967 as a base period, was getting out of hand (1987 = 345.7). The new index is shown in Figure B-2. However, as a convenience to users, the Bureau will also continue to compile and publish CPI-U, All Items, inflation statistics using the former base of 1967 = 100.

Concerning profit, using a price index to adjust nominal dollars to constant dollars has limitations if your company has extensive fixed assets. If this is the case, consider using the current-cost method. In this system, you will adjust inventories, plant, and

385

FIGURE B-1

U.S. Department of Labor Bureau of Labor Statistics Washington, DC 20212	Procedure to adjust sales, profits, etc. for inflation. To adjust more distant year to most recent year:

Consumer Price Index–
All Urban Consumers
(CPI-U), All Items

Price Index	Adjustment
(more recent year) =	figure
Price Index	(to be multiplied
(more distant year)	by the more dis-
	tant year figure)

YEAR	PRICE INDEX DECEMBER 31
1967	101.6*
1968	106.4
1969	112.9
1970	119.1
1971	123.1
1972	127.3
1973	138.5
1974	155.4
1975	166.3
1976	174.3
1977	198.1
1978	202.6
1979	229.9
1980	258.5
1981	281.5
1982	292.4
1083	303.5
1984	315.5
1985	327.4
1986	331.1
1987	345.7
1988	360.9
1989	377.6
1990	400.9
1991	413.0
1992	425.2
1993	436.7

Example:
More-distant-year sales figure, 1987 = 10,000

Problem: To adjust 1987 sales dollars to 1992 dollars (more recent year).

$$\frac{425.2}{345.7} = 1.23$$

$$1.23 \times 10,000 = 12,300$$

*The average index for 1967=100. The year-end index was used to facilitate year-to-year comparisons.

FIGURE B-2

Consumer Price Index–All Urban Consumers (CPI-U, All Items)	
YEAR	PRICE INDEX DECEMBER 31
1982	97.6
1983	101.3
1984	105.3
1985	109.3
1986	110.5
1987	115.4
1988	120.5
1989	126.0
1990	133.7
1991	137.8
1992	141.9
1993	145.7

equipment to reflect current replacement costs. This profit calculation will give you an idea of whether your firm has covered the replacement of your present fixed assets and whether you are making a profit after inflation.

At any rate, before adjusting sales, expenses, and profit for inflation, check with your finance department. Get its input as to the index (or indexes) that should be used. Make it a joint project. Don't, and you'll have real adversaries when you make your presentation. The people from finance will have dozens of reasons why you've done it wrong. Or accounting will even argue why there shouldn't be adjustments made for inflation.

Practice involvement. That's the way to get things done. As the former manager of the New York Mets, Casey Stengel, used to say, "The problem isn't getting ball players. The problem is getting ball players who will play together."

Appendix C

FACT BOOK

Business Unit Information

CONTENTS

Pertinent Business Unit Information Analysis
   (such as P&Ls, Cash Flow)
Product/Service Analysis
Product/Service-Target Market Analysis

(The Fact Book is in two sections. This section is on *Business Unit Information*. Pertinent Business Unit Information such as P & Ls and cash flow are company situational, so no forms are provided for these statements.

The second section of the Fact Book is on *Product/Service-Target Market Information*. It starts on page 392.)

SALES AND PROFITABILITY	19 ___		19 ___		19 ___		19 ___		19 ___		% Change	
PRODUCT/SERVICE	$ Volume	% Total	$ Volume	% Total	$ Volume	% Total	$ Volume	% Total	$ Volume	% Total	$ Volume	% Total
PRODUCT/SERVICE (___)												
SALES	— —	— —	— —	— —	— —	— —	— —	— —	— —	— —	— —	— —
PROFIT	— —	— —	— —	— —	— —	— —	— —	— —	— —	— —	— —	— —
PRODUCT/SERVICE (___)												
SALES	— —	— —	— —	— —	— —	— —	— —	— —	— —	— —	— —	— —
PROFIT	— —	— —	— —	— —	— —	— —	— —	— —	— —	— —	— —	— —
PRODUCT/SERVICE (___)												
SALES	— —	— —	— —	— —	— —	— —	— —	— —	— —	— —	— —	— —
PROFIT	— —	— —	— —	— —	— —	— —	— —	— —	— —	— —	— —	— —
PRODUCT/SERVICE (___)												
SALES	— —	— —	— —	— —	— —	— —	— —	— —	— —	— —	— —	— —
PROFIT	— —	— —	— —	— —	— —	— —	— —	— —	— —	— —	— —	— —
PRODUCT/SERVICE (___)												
SALES	— —	— —	— —	— —	— —	— —	— —	— —	— —	— —	— —	— —
PROFIT	— —	— —	— —	— —	— —	— —	— —	— —	— —	— —	— —	— —

	19___		19___		19___		19___		% Change	
PRODUCT/SERVICE TARGET MARKET	$ Volume	% Total	$ Volume	% Total	$ Volume	% Total	$ Volume	% Total	$ Volume	% Total
PRODUCT/SERVICE										
TARGET MARKET ( )										
SALES	— —	— —	— —	— —	— —	— —	— —	— —	— —	— —
PROFIT	— —	— —	— —	— —	— —	— —	— —	— —	— —	— —
PRODUCT/SERVICE										
TARGET MARKET ( )										
SALES	—	—	—	—	—	—	—	—	—	—
PROFIT	— —	— —	— —	— —	— —	— —	— —	— —	— —
PRODUCT/SERVICE										
TARGET MARKET ( )										
SALES	—	—	—	—	—	—	—	—	—	—
PROFIT	— —	— —	— —	— —	— —	— —	— —	— —	— —
PRODUCT/SERVICE										
TARGET MARKET ( )										
SALES	—	—	—	—	—	—	—	—	—	—
PROFIT	— —	— —	— —	— —	— —	— —	— —	— —	— —

FACT BOOK

Product/Service-Target Market Information

Product/Service _____

_____

Target Market _____

_____

CONTENTS

Performance Profiles
    Performance Profile: The Marketplace
    1. Target Market
    2. Distribution Channels
    3. Direct Competition
    4. Other External Forces
    Performance Profile: Internal
    Sales and Profit Forecast
    Performance Profile: Critical Summary

Gap Analysis (Under a No-Change Strategy)

Strategy Development
    Strategy Description
    Assessment of Competitors' Reaction to Proposed
        Strategy
    Assessment of Internal Capabilities
    Contingency Plans
    Strategic Plan Worksheet: Timetable of Major Activities
    Strategic Plan Worksheet: Funding Requirements

PERFORMANCE PROFILE: The Marketplace

1. Target Market

Category	The Present	The Future 19____
1.1. Target Market (description)		
1.2. Key Buying Motives		
1.3. Other Factors		
1.4. Target Market Demand	Trend to Date (describe) and Volume (if available)	Forecast: 19__ _____ 19__ _____ Inflation Adjustments

PERFORMANCE PROFILE: The Marketplace (continued)

Target Market (Other Factors)

Characteristics of Target Market	Trend to Date	The Present	The Future 19____
Position of Product/ Service on Life-Cycle Curve			
Cyclical Factors	Same/Changing	_____	_____
Seasonal Factors	Same/Changing	_____	_____
Geographical Location	Same/Changing	_____	_____
Size of Target Market Firms	Larger/Same/ Smaller	_____	_____
Concentration of "Key Accounts" in Industry	Increasing/Same/ Decreasing	_____	_____
Backward Integration	Extensive/Some/ Nonexistent	_____	_____
Bargaining Power	Greater/Same/ Less	_____	_____
Rate of Growth of New Customers in Target Market	Increasing/Same/ Decreasing	_____	_____
Number of Customers in Target Market	Increasing/Same/ Decreasing	_____	_____
Purchasing Influencers	Nonexistent/ Same/Changing	_____	_____
Other Characteristics (Specify)			

PERFORMANCE PROFILE: The Marketplace (continued)

2. Distribution Channels (other than direct sales force)

Category	The Present			The Future 19___		
Sales, by Distribution Channels	% of Market	Trend ↑ − or ↓	Your Market Share	% of Market	Trend ↑ − or ↓	Your Market Share
_____	___	___	___	___	___	___
_____	___	___	___	___	___	___
_____	___	___	___	___	___	___

Distributor Channel Analysis (Channel _____)

Key Buying Motives
_____   _____
_____   _____
_____   _____
_____   _____

Other Factors

Distributor Channel Analysis (Channel _____)

Key Buying Motives
_____   _____
_____   _____
_____   _____
_____   _____

Other Factors

PERFORMANCE PROFILE: The Marketplace (continued)

Distribution Channel (Other Factors)

Distribution Channel _____

Characteristics of Channel	Trend to Date	The Present	The Future 19____
Size of Middleman	Larger/Same/Smaller	_____	_____
Sophistication	Same/Greater	_____	_____
Backward Integration	Extensive/Some/ Nonexistent	_____	_____
Forward Integration	Extensive/Some/ Nonexistent	_____	_____
Bargaining Power	Less/Same/Greater	_____	_____
Frequency of Purchases	More Concentrated/ Same/Less	_____	_____
Inventories Carried	Larger/Same/Smaller	_____	_____
Financial Strength	Stronger/Same/ Weaker	_____	_____
Purchasing Influencers	Nonexistent/Same/ Changing	_____	_____
Other Characteristics (Specify)			

PERFORMANCE PROFILE: The Marketplace (continued)

3. Direct Competition (The Present)

	Your Firm	Competitor	Competitor	Competitor
Key Success Factors	(Ratings of Comparative Key Success Factor Strengths: High = 3; Average = 2; Low = 1 and Trend by ↑; – ; or ↓)			
1.				
2.				
3.				
4.				
5.				
	(List Key Success Factors)			
Management's Current *Major* Emphasis				
	(%, and Trend ↑; – ; or ↓)			
Market Share				
	(Superior, Above Average, Average, Below Average, Inferior)			
Target Market's Rating of Augmented Product/Services				
	(Very Strong = 3; Average = 2; Weak = 1 and Trend ↑; – ; or ↓)			
Relative Financial Strength				
	(Aggressive = 3; Holding = 2; Divestment = 1)			
Company Commitment				

Other Factors

PERFORMANCE PROFILE: The Marketplace (continued)

Direct Competition (The Present)

Buying Motives			Competitive Ratings 10 = high 1 = low			
Primary	Secondary	Tertiary				

PERFORMANCE PROFILE: The Marketplace (continued)

3.1. Direct Competition (The Future)

	Your Firm	Competitor	Competitor	Competitor
Key Success Factors	(Ratings of Comparative Key Success Factor Strengths: High = 3; Average = 2; Low = 1 and Trend by ↑; – ; or ↓)			
1.				
2.				
3.				
4.				
5.				
Management's Current *Major* **Emphasis**	(List Key Success Factors)			
Market Share	(%, and Trend ↑; – ; or ↓)			
Target Market's Rating of Augmented Product/Services	(Superior, Above Average, Average, Below Average, Inferior)			
Relative Financial Strength	(Very Strong = 3; Average = 2; Weak = 1 and Trend ↑; – ; or ↓)			
Company Commitment	(Aggressive = 3; Holding = 2; Divestment = 1)			

Other Factors

PERFORMANCE PROFILE: The Marketplace (continued)

Direct Competition (Other Factors)

Characteristics of Channel	Trend to Date	The Present	The Future 19___
Number of Competitors	More/Same/ Fewer	_____	_____
Structure (size)	Larger/Same/ Smaller	_____	_____
Management Sophistication	Same/More	_____	_____
Product/Service Offerings	More/Same/ Fewer	_____	_____
Channels of Distribution Used	Same/Changing	_____	_____
Marketing Practices	Same/Changing	_____	_____
Research and Development	Same/Changing	_____	_____
Other Characteristics (Specify)			

PERFORMANCE PROFILE: The Marketplace (continued)

Direct Competition (Summary Sheet)

Category	The Present		The Future 19____	
Key Success Factors	_____		_____	
	_____		_____	
	_____		_____	
	_____		_____	
	_____		_____	
Direct Competitors	Market Share	Augmented Product/Service	Market Share	Augmented Product/Service
Your Firm _____	____	_____	____	_____
_____	____	_____	____	_____
_____	____	_____	____	_____
_____	____	_____	____	_____
Comments (emphasis, financial strength, and/ or commitment)				
Comments on General Trends				

PERFORMANCE PROFILE: The Marketplace (continued)

3. Direct Competition/Distribution Channel _____ (The Present)

	Your Firm	Competitor	Competitor	Competitor
Key Success Factors	(Ratings of Comparative Key Success Factor Strengths: High = 3; Average = 2; Low = 1 and Trend by ↑; − ; or ↓)			
1.				
2.				
3.				
4.				
5.				
Management's Current *Major* Emphasis	(List Key Success Factors)			
Market Share	(%, and Trend ↑; − ; or ↓)			
Distribution Channel's Perception of Company/Competitors	(Superior, Above Average, Average, Below Average, Inferior)			
Relative Financial Strength	(Very Strong = 3; Average = 2; Weak = 1 and Trend ↑; − ; or ↓)			
Company Commitment	(Aggressive = 3; Holding = 2; Divestment = 1)			

Other Factors

PERFORMANCE PROFILE: The Marketplace (continued)

Direct Competition/Distribution Channel _____ (The Future)

	Your Firm	Competitor	Competitor	Competitor
Key Success Factors	(Ratings of Comparative Key Success Factor Strengths: High = 3; Average = 2; Low = 1 and Trend by ↑; – ; or ↓)			
1.				
2.				
3.				
4.				
5.				
Management's Current *Major* **Emphasis**	(List Key Success Factors)			
Market Share	(%, and Trend ↑; – ; or ↓)			
Distribution Channel's Perception of Company/Competitors	(Superior, Above Average, Average, Below Average, Inferior)			
Relative Financial Strength	(Very Strong = 3; Average = 2; Weak = 1 and Trend ↑; – ; or ↓)			
Company Commitment	(Aggressive = 3; Holding = 2; Divestment = 1)			

Other Factors

PERFORMANCE PROFILE: The Marketplace (continued)

Direct Competition/Distribution Channel _____ (Summary Sheet)

Category	The Present		The Future 19___	
Key Success Factors	_____		_____	
	_____		_____	
	_____		_____	
	_____		_____	
	_____		_____	
Direct Competitors	Market Share	Channel's Perception	Market Share	Channel's Perception
Your Firm _____	____	_____	____	_____
_____	____	_____	____	_____
_____	____	_____	____	_____
_____	____	_____	____	_____
Comments (emphasis, financial strength, and/ or commitment)				
3.4. Comments on General Trends				

PERFORMANCE PROFILE: The Marketplace (continued)

4. Other External Forces

Category	The Present	The Future 19___
4.1. Indirect Competition		
4.2. Technological		
4.3. Economic:		
4.4. Governmental:		
4.5. Other Forces: (major)		

PERFORMANCE PROFILE: Internal

Category	The Present

SALES AND PROFIT FORECASTS

(Assuming You Continue Your Present Strategy, but Your Operating Environment Changes.)

Forecast	19___ Annual Forecast	19___ Most-Distant Forecast
Sales Forecast		
Profitability Forecast (Contribution to Corporate)		

Methodology:

Sales Forecast

Profit Forecast

PERFORMANCE PROFILE: Critical Summary

The Present 19____	The Future 19____
Major Problems (Negatives)	Major Problems (Negatives)
Major Opportunities (Positives)	Major Opportunities (Positives)
Current Target Market Demand	Forecast of Target Market Demand 19____ _____ 19____ _____ Inflation Adjustments

GAP ANALYSIS (UNDER A NO-CHANGE STRATEGY)
(in $1,000, 19   dollars)

	19_____	19_____
Sales Planning Target		
Projected Sales		
Projected Gap		
Contribution to Corporate Planning Targets		
Projected Contribution to Corporate		
Projected Gap		

STRATEGY DESCRIPTION

Product/Service _____

_____

Target Market _____

_____

Key Buying Motives _____

_____

Key Success Factors _____

_____

Competitive Focus _____

_____

_____

_____

Major Elements of the Marketing Mix

Product/Service _____

_____

Changes _____

_____

Promotion _____

_____

Price _____

_____

Place _____

_____

Other _____

_____

ASSESSMENT OF COMPETITORS' REACTION TO PROPOSED STRATEGY

Reaction to Specific Competitors (or groups)		
Competitor	Competitor	Indirect Competition
Reaction to Strategy	Reaction to Strategy	Reaction to Strategy

ASSESSMENT OF INTERNAL CAPABILITIES

Proposed Strategy _____

Functional Area	Key Success Requirements	Evaluation of Current Abilities	Corrective Action Required
Marketing			
Design & Engineering			
Manufacturing			
Finance			

Feasibility Assessment

CONTINGENCY PLANS

Key Contingent Events (What is the event?)	Trigger Points (When the event occurs)	Contingency Plans (What we will do when the event occurs)

STRATEGIC PLAN WORKSHEET

TIMETABLE OF MAJOR ACTIVITIES

Functional Area	Year 1	Year 2	Year 3	Year 4	Year 5

STRATEGIC PLAN WORKSHEET

FUNDING REQUIREMENTS

Functional Area	Year 1		Year 2		Year 3		Year 4		Year 5	
	Expense	Capital	Expense	Capital	Expense	Capital	Expense	Capital	Expense	Capital

Appendix D

PRODUCT/SERVICE-TARGET MARKET PLAN

Product/Service _____

_____

Target Market _____

_____

Key Buying Motives	Key Success Factors
_____	_____
_____	_____
_____	_____
_____	_____
_____	_____
_____	_____

CONTENTS

Strengths/Weaknesses/Opportunities/Threats
Strategy
Sales and Profit Objectives
Action Plans
Contingency Plans
Detailed Sales and Profit Forecasts
Budget

STRENGTHS/WEAKNESSES/OPPORTUNITIES/THREATS

The Present 19____	The Future 19____
Major Problems (Negatives)	Major Problems (Negatives)

Major Opportunities (Positives)   Major Opportunities (Positives)

Current Target Market Demand   Forecast of Target Market Demand

19____   _____

19____   _____

Inflation Adjustments

STRATEGY

SALES AND PROFIT OBJECTIVES

Month	Sales			Gross Profit		
	Planned	Actual	Variance	Planned	Actual	Variance
Jan	_____	_____	_____	_____	_____	_____
Feb	_____	_____	_____	_____	_____	_____
Mar	_____	_____	_____	_____	_____	_____
Apr	_____	_____	_____	_____	_____	_____
May	_____	_____	_____	_____	_____	_____
Jun	_____	_____	_____	_____	_____	_____
Jul	_____	_____	_____	_____	_____	_____
Aug	_____	_____	_____	_____	_____	_____
Sep	_____	_____	_____	_____	_____	_____
Oct	_____	_____	_____	_____	_____	_____
Nov	_____	_____	_____	_____	_____	_____
Dec	_____	_____	_____	_____	_____	_____
TOTAL	_____	_____	_____	_____	_____	_____

ACTION PLANS

ACTION PLAN	Responsi-bility	Budget (in $1,000)	Start Date	Comple-tion Date	Formal Review

ACTION PLANS (Continued)

ACTION PLAN	Responsi-bility	Budget (in $1,000)	Start Date	Comple-tion Date	Formal Review

ACTION PLANS (Continued)

ACTION PLAN	Responsi-bility	Budget (in $1,000)	Start Date	Comple-tion Date	Formal Review

CONTINGENCY PLANS

Key Contingent Events (what is the event?)	Trigger Points (when the event occurs)	Contingency Plans (what we will do when the event occurs)

DETAILED SALES AND PROFIT FORECASTS

Appendix E

SUMMARY MARKETING PLAN

CONTENTS

Overall Strategy
Consolidated Sales and Profit Objectives
Product/Service-Target Market Strategies and Sales
    and Profit Objectives
General Program/Action Plans
General Program Budget
Consolidated Budget

OVERALL STRATEGY

CONSOLIDATED SALES AND PROFIT OBJECTIVES

	Sales				Gross Profit		
Month	Planned	Actual	Variance		Planned	Actual	Variance
Jan	_____	_____	_____		_____	_____	_____
Feb	_____	_____	_____		_____	_____	_____
Mar	_____	_____	_____		_____	_____	_____
Apr	_____	_____	_____		_____	_____	_____
May	_____	_____	_____		_____	_____	_____
Jun	_____	_____	_____		_____	_____	_____
Jul	_____	_____	_____		_____	_____	_____
Aug	_____	_____	_____		_____	_____	_____
Sep	_____	_____	_____		_____	_____	_____
Oct	_____	_____	_____		_____	_____	_____
Nov	_____	_____	_____		_____	_____	_____
Dec	_____	_____	_____		_____	_____	_____
TOTAL	_____	_____	_____		_____	_____	_____

PRODUCT/SERVICE-TARGET MARKET PLAN

Product/Service _____

_____

Target Market _____

_____

Strategy

Sales and Profit Objectives

	Sales				Gross Profit		
Month	Planned	Actual	Variance		Planned	Actual	Variance
Jan	_____	_____	_____		_____	_____	_____
Feb	_____	_____	_____		_____	_____	_____
Mar	_____	_____	_____		_____	_____	_____
Apr	_____	_____	_____		_____	_____	_____
May	_____	_____	_____		_____	_____	_____
Jun	_____	_____	_____		_____	_____	_____
Jul	_____	_____	_____		_____	_____	_____
Aug	_____	_____	_____		_____	_____	_____
Sep	_____	_____	_____		_____	_____	_____
Oct	_____	_____	_____		_____	_____	_____
Nov	_____	_____	_____		_____	_____	_____
Dec	_____	_____	_____		_____	_____	_____
TOTAL	_____	_____	_____		_____	_____	_____

PRODUCT/SERVICE-TARGET MARKET PLAN

Product/Service _____

_____

Target Market _____

_____

Strategy

Sales and Profit Objectives

	Sales				Gross Profit		
Month	Planned	Actual	Variance		Planned	Actual	Variance
Jan	_____	_____	_____		_____	_____	_____
Feb	_____	_____	_____		_____	_____	_____
Mar	_____	_____	_____		_____	_____	_____
Apr	_____	_____	_____		_____	_____	_____
May	_____	_____	_____		_____	_____	_____
Jun	_____	_____	_____		_____	_____	_____
Jul	_____	_____	_____		_____	_____	_____
Aug	_____	_____	_____		_____	_____	_____
Sep	_____	_____	_____		_____	_____	_____
Oct	_____	_____	_____		_____	_____	_____
Nov	_____	_____	_____		_____	_____	_____
Dec	_____	_____	_____		_____	_____	_____
TOTAL	_____	_____	_____		_____	_____	_____

GENERAL PROGRAM/ACTION PLANS

ACTION PLAN	Responsi-bility	Budget (in $1,000)	Start Date	Comple-tion Date	Formal Review

GENERAL PROGRAM/ACTION PLANS (Continued)

ACTION PLAN	Responsi-bility	Budget (in $1,000)	Start Date	Comple-tion Date	Formal Review

GENERAL PROGRAM/ACTION PLANS (Continued)

ACTION PLAN	Responsi-bility	Budget (in $1,000)	Start Date	Comple-tion Date	Formal Review

GENERAL PROGRAM BUDGET

BUDGET

Notes

SECTION I:
INTRODUCTION

1. Philip B. Crosby, *Quality is Free* (New York: New American Library, 1979), p. 13.

2. Peter F. Drucker, *Innovation and Entrepreneurship, Practice and Principles* (New York: Harper & Row, 1985), p. 228.

3. David A. Garvin, "Competing on the Eight Dimensions of Quality," *Harvard Business Review*, Vol. 65, Nov.-Dec., 1987, pp. 101-109.

4. J.M. Juran, *Juran on Leadership for Quality* (New York: The Free Press, 1989), p. 22.

5. Thomas A. Stewart, "Reengineering: The Hot New Managing Tool," *Fortune*, Aug. 23, 1993, pp. 40-48.

6. Otis Port, "Back to Basics," *Business Week*, Special Issue, "Innovation in America," 1989, p. 18.

7. Peter Nulty, "The Soul of an Old Machine," *Fortune*, May 7, 1990, pp. 52-60.

8. As you move toward mass customization, continuous improvement will not be enough. You'll need to think in terms of an organization consisting of a dynamic network of relatively autonomous operating units. See B. Joseph Pine II, Bart Victor, and Andrew Boynton, "Making Mass Customization Work," *Harvard Business Review*, Vol. 71, Sept.-Oct. 1993, pp. 108-119.

9. Peter F. Drucker, *Adventures of a Bystander* (New York: Harper & Row, 1978), pp. 268-269.

10. Drucker, *Innovation and Entrepreneurship*, p. 189.

11. *Ibid.*, pp. 225-230.

12. Howard Sutton, *The Marketing Plan in the 1990s* (New York: The Conference Board, 1990), p. 7.

13. Adapted from Derek F. Abell and John S. Hammond, *Strategic Market Planning* (Englewood Cliffs, NJ: Prentice-Hall, 1979), pp. 27-29.

14. Bruce D. Henderson, *Henderson on Corporate Strategy* (Cambridge, MA: Abt Books, 1979), p. 38.

15. William Giles, "Marketing Planning for Maximum Growth," *Marketing Intelligence and Planning*, Vol. 3, No. 3 (1985), p. 81.

SECTION II:
THE EIGHT PLANNING STEPS

Step 1

1. Charles T. Horngren, Walter T. Harrison, and Michael A. Robinson, *Principles of Financial Management Accounting* (Englewood Cliffs, NJ: Prentice-Hall, 1993), ch. 23.

2. Victor P. Buell, *Marketing Management: A Strategic Approach* (New York: McGraw-Hill, 1984), p. 240.

Step 2

1. Henderson, *Corporate Strategy*, p. 38.

Step 3

1. Bernard A. Rausch, *Strategic Marketing Planning* (New York: American Management Association), pp. 32-33.

2. For a case history on how conjoint analysis helped an offshore drilling company rank its buyers' buying motives, see Gabriel M. Gelb, "Conjoint Analysis Helps Explain the Bid Process," *Marketing News*, Mar. 14, 1988, pp. 1, 31.

3. Gerald Myers, "Trade Buyers Are Influential, But Unresearched," *Marketing News*, Feb. 1, 1988, p. 12.

4. William C. Johnson, "Sales Promotion: It's Come Down to 'Push Marketing,'" *Marketing News*, Feb. 29, 1988, p. 8.

5. This approach is adapted from J.M. Juran, *Juran on Planning for Quality* (New York: The Free Press, 1988), pp. 38-42.

6. A.C. Cooper and D. Schendel, "Strategic Responses to Technological Threats," *Business Horizons*, Feb. 1964, p. 61.

7. Richard N. Foster, *Innovation: The Attacker's Advantage* (New York: Summit Books, 1986), pp. 162, 182.

8. Adapted from pioneering works of Robert S. Weinberg, former manager, marketing research, IBM.

9. "Soup Research Defends Ad Claims by Citing Federal Data," *Marketing News*, Feb. 2, 1984, p. 3.

10. Michael E. Porter, *Competitive Strategy: Techniques for Analyzing Industries and Competitors* (New York: The Free Press, 1980), p. 371.

Step 4

1. David S. Hopkins, *The Marketing Plan* (New York: The Conference Board, 1981), p. 10.

2. Stella M. Eisele, "A Ban on Radar Detectors in Big Trucks Is Considered," *Philadelphia Inquirer*, Nov. 14, 1993, p. E11.

3. Henderson, *Corporate Strategy*, p. 73.

4. Buell, *Marketing Management*, p. 213.

5. Excerpt (adapted) from Robert E. Linneman and Harold E. Klein, "Scenarios: A Tool for Assessing High-Change Environments for Strategic Decision Making," *Business Horizons*, Jan.-Feb. 1985, pp. 67-68. Reprinted with permission.

Step 5

1. Rochelle O'Connor, *Corporate Guides to Long-Range Planning* (New York: The Conference Board, 1976), p. 67.

2. Peter Finch, "Roger Penske, Running on 16 Cylinders," *Business Week*, June 1, 1987, p. 74.

3. Frederick R. Kappel, *Vitality in a Business Enterprise* (New York: McGraw-Hill, 1960), pp. 37-38.

4. For a more complete discussion on "Must" and "Want" goals, see Charles H. Kepner and Benjamin B. Tregoe, *The Rational Manager* (New York: McGraw-Hill, 1965), pp. 183-190.

5. John D. Kennell, "Strategic Objectives: The Challenge of Top Management," unpublished manuscript, 1988, p. 4.

Step 6

1. Charles H. Travel, *The Third Industrial Age, Strategy for Business Survival.*Translated by Donald C. Caldwell (Homewood, IL: Dow Jones-Irwin, Inc., 1975), p. 1.

2. William E. Rothschild, *Strategic Alternatives: Selection, Development and Implementation* (New York: AMACOM, 1979), pp. vii-viii.

3. Bruce Steinberg, "The Mass Market Is Splitting Apart," *Fortune*, Nov. 28, 1983, pp. 76-82.

4. John Koten and Bill Richards, "The Shattered Middle Class," *The Wall Street Journal*, Mar. 9, 1987, p. 23.

5. Christine Dugas, Mark N. Vamos, Jonathine B. Levine, and Matt Rothman, "Marketing's New Look," *Business Week*, Jan. 26, 1987, p. 68.

6. Mark D. Fefer, "How to Win in a Land of Losers," *Fortune*, Aug. 23, 1993, p. 80.

7. Dugas et al. "Marketing's New Look," pp. 64-69.

8. Thomas E. Ricks, "Branching Out," *The Wall Street Journal*, Apr. 3, 1987, p. 1.

9. Carol Hymowitz and Francine Schwadel, "In Specialty Clothing, A Sameness Syndrome Threatens a Shakeout," *The Wall Street Journal*, Oct. 7, 1987, p. 1.

10. Russell Mitchell, "GM's New Luxury Cars: Why They're Not Selling," *Business Week*, Jan. 1, 1987, pp. 94, 98.

11. Al Haas, "It's Not the Same Old Olds – Change Is in the Wind," *The Philadelphia Inquirer*, July 28, 1991, p. 1F.

12. David E. Sanger, "Taking in the Tokyo Auto Show," *The New York Times*, Oct. 24, 1991, p. C1.

13. James C. Abegglen and George Stalk, Jr., *Kaisha: The Japanese Corporation* (New York: Basic Books, 1985) pp. 69. "Lean production" is another name for flexible production. For an informative, interesting explanation, see James P. Womack, Daniel T. Jones, and Daniel Roos, *The Machine that Changed the World (The Story of Lean Production)* (New York: Harper Perennial), 1991.

14. Abegglen and Stalk, *Kaisha*, p. 97.

15. *Ibid.*, pp. 91-92.

16. Arch G. Woodside, Victor J. Cook, Jr., and William A. Mindak, "Profiling the Heavy Traveler Segment," *Journal of Travel Research*, Vol. 15, Spring 1987, pp. 9-14.

17. Gary J. Coles and James D. Culley, "Not All Prospects Are Created Equal," *Business Marketing*, Vol. 71, May 1986, pp. 52-58.

18. "Business Bulletin," *The Wall Street Journal*, February 16, 1989, p. A1.

19. Joe G. Thomas and J.M. Koonce, "Differentiating a Commodity: Lessons from Tyson Foods," *Planning Review*, Sept.-Oct. 1989, pp. 24-29.

20. Coles and Culley, "Not All Prospects" pp. 52-58.

21. Cheryl Russell, "25 Particle Markets." ©*American Demographics* (Ithaca, NY: 1990). Reprinted with permission.

22. Philip Kotler, *Marketing Management: Analysis, Planning and Control*, 5th Edition (Engelwood Cliffs, NJ: Prentice-Hall, 1984), p. 271.

23. Philip Kotler and Gary Armstrong, *Principles of Marketing*, 6th Edition (Englewood Cliffs, NJ: Prentice-Hall, 1994), p. 377.

24. Christine Donahue, "The Customer Is Always Right. Campbell Returns to Basics in Bid for Share," *Adweek's Marketing Week*, Sept. 28, 1987, pp. 1, 4.

25. The discussion on value chains was adapted from Michael E. Porter, *Competitive Advantage: Creating and Sustaining Superior Performance* (New York: The Free Press, 1985), chs. 2-4.

26. Alexander Stuart, "Meat Packers in Stampede," *Fortune*, June 29, 1981, pp. 67-71.

27. Porter, *Competitive Advantage*, p. 43.

28. *Ibid.*, p. 51.

29. Al Ries and Jack Trout, *Marketing Warfare* (New York: McGraw-Hill, 1986), pp. 3-4. Readers who would like a more complete–and very entertaining–coverage of marketing warfare are urged to read this book.

30. *Ibid.*, pp. 26-29.

31. *Ibid.*, pp. 61-63.

32. *Ibid.*, pp. 158-159.

33. For a comprehensive treatment on attacking the leader, see Porter, *Competitive Advantage*, pp. 513-536. Most of the methods discussed here came from this section.

34. Abegglen and Stalk, *Kaisha,* pp. 48-51.

35. Barry J. James, "Deterrence–Strategy that Pays," *Business Horizons,* Nov./Dec. 1985, pp. 60-64.

36. Porter, *Competitive Advantage,* pp. 489-492.

37. "Japanese Put the Heat on the Watch Industry," *Business Week,* May 5, 1980, pp. 92-103.

38. For an excellent reference on signaling, see Porter, *Competitive Strategy,* ch. 4.

39. Ries and Trout, *Marketing Warfare,* pp. 26, 102.

40. *Ibid.,* p. 83.

41. Kotler, *Marketing Management,* 8th edition, 1994, p. 400.

42. Kotler, *Marketing Management,* 5th edition, 1984, p. 378.

Step 7

1. Alix Freedman, "National Firms Find That Selling to Local Tastes Is Costly, Complex," *The Wall Street Journal,* Feb. 9, 1987, p. 21.

2. *Ibid.*

3. *Ibid.*

4. Max Gunther, *The Luck Factor* (New York: Macmillan, 1977), pp. 168-181.

5. Alan Murray, "Passing a Test: Fed's New Chairman Wins a Lot of Praise on Handling the Crash," *The Wall Street Journal,* Nov. 25, 1987, p. 1.

6. Henderson, *Corporate Strategy,* p. 73.

7. "Warrent Buffet: How I Goofed," *Fortune,* Apr. 19, 1990, pp. 95-96.

8. For a more complete description, see Michael E. Porter, *Competitive Strategy: Techniques for Analyzing Industries and Competitors* (New York: The Free Press, 1980), pp. 3-29.

9. Drucker, *Innovation and Entrepreneurship,* p. 137.

Step 8

1. Dennis Cooper-Jones, *Business Planning and Forecasting* (New York-Toronto: John Wiley & Sons, Halsted Press, 1974). Chapter 5, "Contigency Planning," contains a more detailed–and

slightly different–explanation on how to implement variable budgeting.

2. "Emerson Electric's Rise as a Low-Cost Producer," *Business Week*, Nov. 1, 1976, pp. 47-48.

SECTION IV:
APPENDIXES

Appendix A

1. Lee Iacocca and William Novack, *Iacocca* (New York: Bantam Books, 1984), p. 50.

Index